"This book is a tho[rough?]... scholars, and policym[akers?]... exploration of the creative economy. From cultural economics and market dynamics to creative ecosystems and equitable development, it covers the spectrum of issues crucial to understanding and working in the creative economy. The chapters offer comprehensive insights and practical examples, making it a valuable guide for navigating the complex landscape of the creative sector. Whether you're an arts professional or simply interested in the intricacies of the creative economy, this book is a tremendous accomplishment and a great addition to the field."

Sarah Conley Odenkirk, *Partner, Cowan DeBaets Abrahms & Sheppard, LLP; Co-Head of the Art Law Practice Group*

"*The Creative Economy* provides a fresh look at the people, places, and policies behind this ever-evolving field. The book gets under the hood of the creative economy to provide an invaluable learning resource for students, scholars, and practitioners alike."

Carl Grodach, *Foundation Professor of Urban Planning and Design, Monash University, Australia*

"Whether you are new to the field or a seasoned practitioner keeping up with the times, *The Creative Economy: Arts, Cultural Value and Society in Practice* is an excellent guide to understanding the ways in which the creative economy affects physical and social infrastructure to shape human life. This book is a heartening must-read for planners, artists, and researchers alike."

Jessica Wallen, *Arts and Culture Research Fellow, American Planning Association, New York*

The Creative Economy

The creative economy permeates our everyday lives, shaping where we live, what we buy, and how we interact with others. Looking at dimensions of people, place, policy, and market forces, the book offers a comprehensive perspective on arts and culture, in both economic and social life.

The book explores the multifaceted components that make up this complex field. Underlying this journey is the throughline of diversity, equity, and inclusion as watchwords of today's global paradigm. Capital, gentrification, pay disparities, and the hegemonic confines of cultural production are a few of the key issues analyzed. Using case studies and stories of artists and creatives from the worlds of fashion, design, music, and the media arts, the book also delves into gastronomy, literature, architecture, and theatre—presenting a nuanced look at the ways in which the creative sector impacts the world today. Readers will benefit from features such as key takeaways, discussion questions, and activities, throughout the chapters.

Students, scholars, policymakers, and the general public will find this a valuable resource. This book offers the reader a chance not only to understand the cultural and creative industries, but to internalize its elements and embrace the creative spirit that imbues the sector.

Amanda J. Ashley is Professor of Urban Studies and Community Development and the Director of the School of the Arts at Boise State University, USA.

Carolyn G. Loh is Professor of Urban Studies and Planning at Wayne State University, USA.

Matilda Rose Bubb is the City of Boise's Cultural Planner, a Public Policy and Administration Ph.D. candidate at Boise State University, USA, and a visual artist.

Shoshanah B.D. Goldberg-Miller is Associate Professor in the Department of Arts Administration, Education, and Policy and Affiliate Associate Professor of City and Regional Planning at The Ohio State University, USA.

Discovering the Creative Industries

Series Editor: Ruth Rentschler

The creative and cultural industries account for a significant share of the global economy. Gaining and maintaining employment and work in this sector is a challenge and chances of success are enhanced by ongoing professional development.

This series provides a range of relatively short, student-centred books which blend industry and educational expertise with cultural sector practice. Books in the series provide applied introductions to the core elements of the creative industries. In sum, the series provides essential reading for those studying to enter the creative industries as well as those seeking to enhance their career via executive education.

Orchestra Management in Practice
Salvino A. Salvaggio

Cultural Leadership in Practice
Beyond Arts Management and Cultural Policy
Edited by Steven Hadley

Understanding Cultural Policy
Government and the Arts and Culture in the United States
Carole Rosenstein

Legal Issues for Arts Organizations
A Practical Guide
Kristi W. Arth

The Creative Economy
Arts, Cultural Value and Society in Practice
Amanda J. Ashley, Carolyn G. Loh, Matilda Rose Bubb and Shoshanah B.D. Goldberg-Miller

For more information about this series, please visit: www.routledge.com/Discovering-the-Creative-Industries/book-series/DCI

The Creative Economy

Arts, Cultural Value and Society in Practice

Amanda J. Ashley, Carolyn G. Loh, Matilda Rose Bubb and Shoshanah B.D. Goldberg-Miller

LONDON AND NEW YORK

Designed cover image: benedek

First published 2024
by Routledge
4 Park Square, Milton Park, Abingdon, Oxon OX14 4RN

and by Routledge
605 Third Avenue, New York, NY 10158

Routledge is an imprint of the Taylor & Francis Group, an informa business

© 2024 Amanda J. Ashley, Carolyn G. Loh, Matilda Rose Bubb and Shoshanah B.D. Goldberg-Miller

The right of Amanda J. Ashley, Carolyn G. Loh, Matilda Rose Bubb and Shoshanah B.D. Goldberg-Miller to be identified as authors of this work has been asserted in accordance with sections 77 and 78 of the Copyright, Designs and Patents Act 1988.

All rights reserved. No part of this book may be reprinted or reproduced or utilised in any form or by any electronic, mechanical, or other means, now known or hereafter invented, including photocopying and recording, or in any information storage or retrieval system, without permission in writing from the publishers.

Trademark notice: Product or corporate names may be trademarks or registered trademarks, and are used only for identification and explanation without intent to infringe.

British Library Cataloguing-in-Publication Data
A catalogue record for this book is available from the British Library

Library of Congress Cataloging-in-Publication Data
Names: Ashley, Amanda J., author. | Loh, Carolyn G., author. | Bubb, Matilda Rose, author.
Title: The creative economy : arts, cultural value and society in practice / Amanda J. Ashley, Carolyn G. Loh, Matilda Rose Bubb, Shoshanah B.D. Goldberg-Miller.
Description: 1 Edition. | New York, NY: Routledge, 2024. | Series: Discovering the creative industries | Includes bibliographical references and index.
Identifiers: LCCN 2023050301 | ISBN 9780367707262 (hardback) | ISBN 9780367707231 (paperback) | ISBN 9781003147688 (ebook)
Subjects: LCSH: Creative ability—Economic aspects. | Cultural industries—Economic aspects. | Culture—Economic aspects. | Creation (Literary, artistic, etc.)—Economic aspects. | Intellectual capital.
Classification: LCC HC79.E5 A845 2024 | DDC 338.9/27—dc23/eng/20231030
LC record available at https://lccn.loc.gov/2023050301

ISBN: 978-0-367-70726-2 (hbk)
ISBN: 978-0-367-70723-1 (pbk)
ISBN: 978-1-003-14768-8 (ebk)

DOI: 10.4324/9781003147688

Typeset in Calvert
by Apex CoVantage, LLC

Amanda J. Ashley: To Seth, William, and Benjamin, the creative forces of joy in my life.

Carolyn G. Loh: To my parents, who taught me to love the arts and our city.

Matilda Rose Bubb: To my professors, colleagues, and co-conspirators who inspire and guide me in new ways to apply my passionate love of art and community.

Shoshanah B.D. Goldberg-Miller: To Scott J. Morgan, my muse and my anchor; and in memory of my mother, Grace Safeer Goldberg, who taught me the truth about beauty.

Contents

Acknowledgments   x

1. Welcome to the creative economy   1
2. Cultural economics and the creative sector   10
3. Creative economy fundamentals   36
4. Place and the creative economy   81
5. Creative economy ecosystems   113
6. Centering artists and creatives   153
7. Policy and the creative economy   197
8. Champions of the creative economy   233
9. Examples of equitable creative economic development   269
10. Moving forward in the creative economy   301

Index   312

Acknowledgments

Amanda J. Ashley: Thank you to Leslie Durham, Dean of the College of Arts & Sciences, the School of Public Service Research Committee, and the National Endowment for the Arts for supporting aspects of research areas that are covered in this book project. Thank you to Aaron Williams, our public policy and public administration graduate research assistant, who helped collect data for our team. I am grateful to my Boise Foothills running partners, Jen Stevens and Emily Wakild, and to my Boise family, Lori Hausegger and Jaci Kettler, who cheered me on during the writing process and helped me through methodological roadblocks. I'm grateful to Carolyn G. Loh, for our wonderful work collaboration and friendship that has been so much fun. I'm grateful to the Lady Council (Ioana Barza, Jenny Bilenker, Anna Dubrovsky, Sasha Emmons, Elisa Karp, Michelle Militello, and Jennifer Reed Perez) for their encouragement on this project. I'm deeply thankful to Seth for his love and backrubs that have sustained me during my marathon writing sessions. Thank you to William and Benjamin for helping me remember to laugh at silly jokes, take breaks at Elm Grove Park, play Uno after dinner, and dance to silly songs to refresh myself during this book process. Thank you to my parents who gave me every opportunity, and who are always there for me and my family. Finally, I'm grateful to our Routledge team and my co-authors for undertaking this rewarding project and for valuing meaningful collaboration.

Carolyn G. Loh: I would like to thank Stefani Haas at the Toledo Lucas County Public Library and Aaron Williams of Boise State University for their help with research for this book. Jonathan Jae-an Crisman and Ken McAllister at the University of Arizona, Maya Berry and Scott Fin at CAST, Ted Ligibel at Eastern Michigan University, and Mark Snyder and the East Toledo Historical Society all made connections or shared photos that appear in this book. Rachel Richardson of Art Corner Toledo shared her family's experiences to help illuminate the chapter on artists. I'm grateful for the wonderful research partnerships I've been fortunate to have over the past few years, convened and sustained by Amanda J. Ashley. I appreciate my co-authors, Tilley Bubb and Shoshanah B.D. Goldberg-Miller, for welcoming me into this project mid-stream. My parents, Ted and Patty Gillespie, made countless trips to the Toledo Art Museum and the Peristyle, so I could take art classes and see and play in concerts. They were also very connected to the city and its institutions, and made sure I was too. Toledo, Ohio, had and still has an incredible arts ecosystem, which should get much more national attention than it does. Finally, thank you to my husband, Brian, and kids, David, Andrew, and Emily, for always asking good questions and making my life full and interesting.

Matilda Rose Bubb: Thank you to the generous cultural professionals who took the time to participate in interviews with me, offering their heartfelt observations and experiences. This book would not be what it is without their contributions. Enormous gratitude to Dr. Amanda J. Ashley for her guidance, encouragement, and leadership throughout the book research and writing process and for her mentorship throughout my Ph.D. program at Boise State University. Thank you to fellow-collaborators Dr. Carolyn G. Loh and Dr. Shoshanah B.D. Goldberg-Miller for sharing their expertise and insights. Thank you to my late husband, Robert Engbers, for inspiring me to go back to school and participating in the process with me. And lastly, I extend much gratitude to my family, birth and chosen, and dear circle of friends for their unconditional support for my creative and professional endeavors.

Shoshanah B.D. Goldberg-Miller: I wish to thank my co-authors on this book, Amanda J. Ashley, Matilda Rose Bubb, and Carolyn G. Loh, and especially acknowledge Dr. Ashley for her leadership. I am grateful to my sister, Toby Ellen Goldberg, my brother-in-law, George Leong, and my nephew, Jacob Leong for their love and support. My canine companions, Remy and Ella Gracie have been by my side steadfastly throughout this process. I would like to also thank Jane Akiba, Tabitha Buess, Lynn Darkow, Lynn Halper Rosen, Katherine Lesse, Sheri Taub, and Alla Tsitsior for being my dear friends and compatriots.

My deepest appreciation goes to Scott J. Morgan, whose love, encouragement, and inspiration make my world a brighter place. Finally, I want to acknowledge my parents, Ted and Grace Goldberg, of blessed memory, who gifted me with the intellectual curiosity I so value.

Welcome to the creative economy

Chapter 1

Welcome to the creative economy—a multi-dimensional field that includes topics such as the creative class, cultural policy, and arts economics. The creative economy "consists of economic activity that depends on individuals and organizations using their creativity to drive jobs, revenue, community resources, and cultural engagement" (Americans for the Arts, 2023). It includes artists, entrepreneurs, knowledge workers, and government employees. The creative economy encompasses a wide variety of people, businesses, and cultural entities. It permeates everyday life and shapes where we live, what we buy, and how we interact with others.

This book helps identify how the creative economy works in a variety of contexts and become familiar with the broad scope of cultural and creative industries. Here, you will have the chance not only to understand cultural and creative industries, but to internalize elements from the industries and embrace the creative spirit that imbues the sector. The journey will be accomplished through a variety of means, specifically by pulling the curtain aside to understand the multifaceted components that make up this burgeoning area of study.

We cover the nuances of cultural economics, explore the intricacies of policy and place in shaping the creative sector, and investigate the shifting roles that society affords creatives and their outputs. While the field is ever changing and growing rapidly, this book presents the pillars that underlie the cultural

DOI: 10.4324/9781003147688-1

and creative industries and those involved in production and consumption—providing an anchor with which to observe and evaluate its progress from the inside out.

Issues of diversity, equity, and inclusion inform the thematic content of each of the book's elements. We delve into issues such as the role of the arts in fostering sustainable and resilient communities, how the creative economy contributes to the health and wellbeing of individuals, and the importance of maintaining authenticity in city and regional interventions. This book provides the opportunity to see your world through the lens of the cultural and creative economy, specifically including the perspective of social and economic equity.

The examples sprinkled throughout the book, highlighting the stories of creative people and entities, serve to illustrate concepts and bring them to life. By weaving in stories of creative individuals, including artists, musicians, designers, and arts administrators, we present a more nuanced and richly developed story of the ways in which this sector impacts our world today. We have also covered how the arts and creative economy help communities solve challenges, the importance of multiple perspectives, and the centering of artists in the creative economy. Finally, we offer some smart practice options, for practitioners and academics alike, to move toward a more nuanced and equitable approach to creative economy interventions.

OVERVIEW AND THEMATIC STRUCTURE

The main themes of this book are as follows: (1) economics of the cultural and creative industries; (2) how place plays a role in shaping a variety of aspects of the creative economy; (3) leveraging cultural policy tools in numerous contexts; and (4) ever-changing perceptions of creatives and their outputs in society. We employ several key theoretical frameworks throughout the book to ground this substantive discussion. These can be understood in three categorical components: (1) planning and place; (2) cultural economics; and (3) social construction of the creative economy.

While there is significant depth, the book provides an orientation with which to understand the broad scope of the sector. Here, we delve into the various fields and actors that are included in the broad concept of creative and cultural economies. This provides a framework that allows you to understand those involved in the field—such as independent artists as well as large and small businesses—and anchor cultural institutions. We explore the fundamental characteristics of areas such as: workforce delineation; sector boundaries; local, regional, national, and international definitions and scales; and global market forces. Through this book, we seek to make creative industries and the players in them visible; show how they are connected through interdependent networks; explore how players move in and out of the public and nonprofit and for-profit sectors; and demonstrate how their work is valuable both intrinsically and in ways that contribute to local, regional, and national economies.

Economics of the cultural and creative industries

We look at major business models that creatives choose to leverage their goals. The decisions about establishing each kind of entity are something that you can keep in mind, including considerations of purpose, market, and financial structure. Arts entrepreneurship, the gig economy, and the challenges of shifting demographics together play a role in the success and challenges of people, places, and organizations.

Topics such as consumer choice, market forces, public good, and positive externalities may seem to be quite distant from any student or practitioner experience; but they do have a profound impact on a wide variety of artists and entities. Buying and consuming creative outputs and understanding the wide range of consumer take-up of creative economy goods and services—including the contrast between local consumption and virtual consumption—all have a role to play on a global scale. The rise of internet purchasing of creative products, digital music platform options, and the importance of social media as an option for consumption are key areas to keep in mind as the book unfolds.

How place plays a role in shaping a variety of aspects of the creative economy

Why are certain creative industries located in particular regions and cities worldwide? We cover topics such as the ways that the presence of cultural and creative industries and those who work in them can shape the physical urban environment and contribute to its success, or alternatively, can pose challenges. We frame the ways that a variety of actors influence the landscape of the creative sector, especially in the urban context. This includes municipal stakeholders, the private sector development community, and the role of public entities as well as the polis in effecting the take-up of arts and cultural interventions. The repurposing of city-owned land and buildings, tax incentives for developers, interventions that target educational options for the creative class, the fostering of Creative City reports, and cultural plans are tools that policymakers employ toward developing the Creative City.

Leveraging cultural policy tools in numerous contexts

How do government actors decide which industries and sectors to support, which rules and regulations to adopt, and how to spend money? How do governments see the value of the creative economy and choose to support it or not? The choices about rules and resources are policy decisions, and they strongly affect the capabilities and limits of the creative economy. Compared to many other sectors, creative industries rely more on public funding sources and incentives to thrive. We examine policies that affect the creative economy, such as support for nonprofit arts tourism; but we also broaden the coverage to include new arts disciplines, for-profit industrial and occupational sectors, and considerations on how to brand and market their artistic strengths to attract and retain knowledge workers. For example, in the last couple of decades, state and local governments have increasingly adopted policies around film and television tax incentives, artist-friendly property development, and incubation of new or hidden industries like music.

Ever-changing perceptions of creatives and their outputs in society

This book delves into the complex web of issues that underlie the creative and cultural industries and their role in society. We discuss the intrinsic value of arts and culture and frame this, looking at aspects of the human experience. Key concepts imbued in the book include the social value of the arts, the establishment of norms and trends, the role of cultural identity and heritage, instrumentalism, and the importance of the creative sector in facilitating self-expression.

STRUCTURE OF THE BOOK

Following the introduction, Chapter 2, "Cultural economics and the creative sector," introduces key economic principles, providing a foundation and context for understanding the creative economy. Concepts such as efficiency, equity, perfect markets, and market equilibrium frame ways to consider how resources are allocated for culture. Market failures, market-based solutions, and government failure give shape to broader system dynamics that impact cultural arenas. Welfare state economics and various government points of view weigh equity and social value against capitalist valuation standards, giving us different approaches to think about the mechanisms at work in the creative economy.

Chapter 3, "Creative economy fundamentals," delivers a creative economy framework that grounds you in its characteristics—including its actors; workforce delineation; sector boundaries; local, regional, national, and international definitions; and global market forces. It offers various definitions and valuations for the cultural and creative economy, industries, and occupations. Practical examples and insights from practitioners and primary sources illuminate the field, so that you can apply the framework to help define what creative economy means to them in their communities. The chapter concludes with suggestions on how to move forward with evaluating assets, with techniques such as community mapping and the collection of input from residents.

Moving from frameworks to place, Chapter 4, "Place and the creative economy," reviews place-centered strategies such as public art programs, economic development projects, and creative placemaking concepts such as festival marketplaces. Some critiques and pitfall examples are offered in counterpoint, including gentrification, cultural displacement, and loss of authentic-place identity. Lastly, the chapter offers tools and strategies for approaching place-based creative economic development.

In Chapter 5, "Creative economy ecosystems," we discuss the dynamic actors and organizations networked within these complex adaptive systems. The concepts of policy and arts entrepreneurs are reviewed, along with the organizational models these leaders create, to leverage their interests. The factors that go into deciding whether to establish a nonprofit or for-profit entity are shared, including considerations of purpose, market, and financial structure. Related topics—such as the government's role in the creative ecosystem, the gig economy, and the opportunities and challenges of shifting demographics—provide you with a comprehensive look at this area of the creative economy.

In Chapter 6, "Centering artists and creatives," we center individual artists and creatives in the community clusters and global networks of the creative economy. We explore the role of artists and creatives in economic development, by overturning detrimental myths about artists and creatives; and we provide examples of institutions, artistic spaces, and artistic experiences that are designed to advance careers and creative ambitions, which are highlighted through stories and illustrations. We highlight the ways they work as entrepreneurs, community organizers, and economic developers. We identify some of the primary challenges in centering artists in the creative economy; and we explain how these are policy and planning issues. As a whole, this chapter presents a nuanced and richly developed story of the ways in which this sector impacts our world today.

In Chapter 7, "Policy and the creative economy," we frame out the variety of ways actors influence the context and landscape of the creative sector through policy. This includes municipal stakeholders, the private sector development community, and the role of public entities as well as the polis in affecting the adoption of cultural interventions. We use the multiple streams framework to explore creative economy policy processes.
A range of creative economy tools are discussed, including tax incentives, creative clusters and districts, education and training, and the fostering of "Creative City" branding efforts through reports and cultural plans.

Who is studying, presenting, and measuring the creative sector? Chapter 8, "Champions of the creative economy," discusses the global interest in this field, including how UNESCO decides which cities are creative, and the organizations that have been formed to coalesce around the burgeoning interest in cultural and creative industries. Here, we discuss the role of policy boosters in municipalities that use the Creative City paradigm to foster interest in their urban centers for tourism, commerce, and residents as well as use policy transfer and diffusion theories to illustrate how ideas move from one place to another.

Chapter 9, "Examples of equitable creative economic development," introduces real-world examples of place-based creative economic development strategies, including alternative funding approaches, arts districts, placemaking, artist live-work spaces, pro-arts zoning, and building code changes. These examples can be used as models of what to do, or, in some cases, what not to do. The potential successes and unintended consequences exhibited in these stories illustrate how various cities manifest similar concepts to meet different ends. You will learn about: how unforeseen events can drive policy change; what it takes to be an arts entrepreneur; the role planning can play in developing arts and place-based development strategies; and the role of artists in gentrification. These practical takeaways will leave you with ideas applicable to their communities and cities.

The book concludes with Chapter 10, "Moving forward in the creative economy," which provides a summary of some of the overarching themes of the book as well as thoughts for moving ahead subsequent to the topics covered here. This offers you the chance to understand how to implement these ideas in everyday life, so that you can identify and explain any creative economy examples you see. We provide nine overarching themes that cut across chapters and that should be at the forefront of how you embed the book in your practice and civic life moving forward. Successful interventions such as cultural mapping, public participation opportunities, and financial literacy for creatives are areas that can be explored going forward. A focus on integrating these and other tools within existing systems, both at the local level and beyond, will add a sense of breadth to this aspect of the discussion. While tremendous variations and changes will always be found in the creative and cultural industries, the core concepts on which this book is built will not change. Topics such as geography, policy, technology, and the social value of the creative sector are pillars that will remain important in the future. Finally, we encourage you to be mindful of sustainability, shifts in demand, and the intrinsic value of creative outputs and activities.

HOW TO APPROACH THIS BOOK

We deliberately assembled contributors for this book who bring different backgrounds and experiences to our work. We are scholars, urban planners, arts and cultural planners, community and economic development practitioners, artists, arts and cultural organization leaders, music industry veterans, and experts in policy, arts administration, land use, and economic development; we wear several hats. In our many roles, we have seen how arts, culture, and creativity transform people, places, and communities in ways that are personal as well as collective and qualitative as well as quantitative—for the fulfillment of a particular outcome. We believe strongly in the "artful life" that National Endowment for the Arts Chairperson Maria Rosario Jackson champions in the organization's work (NEA, 2023). In this book, we explore this artful life from an economic and community development lens, studying the creative economy.

We hope this book reflects the enthusiasm we have for the ways arts and culture, and how the creative economy clearly enriches our lives. We hope you will be able to relate the concepts in this book—some of which are admittedly dense—to what you see happening around you, both where you live and online.

To that end, in each chapter, we've provided opportunities to reflect on the topics covered through three important tools. First, we offer takeaways of the key concepts presented. Second, we provide discussion questions that can spark interesting conversations in the classroom, the boardroom, or the office. Third, each chapter presents an opportunity for reflection in ways that allow you to integrate the ideas, examples, and theories into your own life and work.

We are thrilled that you are beginning or advancing your knowledge about the creative economy. This book is a step in that direction, and we encourage you to add to this foundation in ways that are authentic and aligned with your goals, organizational mission, and community needs.

Get ready to take an exciting journey into the world of the creative economy—and remember to enjoy the ride!

REFERENCES

Americans for the Arts. (2023). *Creative Economy.* www.americansforthearts.org/by-topic/creative-economy

National Endowment for the Arts. (2023). In Celebration of Artful Lives. *American Artscape.* No. 1. https://www.arts.gov/stories/magazine/2023/1/celebration-artful-lives

Cultural economics and the creative sector

Chapter 2

INTRODUCTION

This chapter provides insights into the broader world of economics, offering a context through which to understand the segment of the field known as cultural or arts economics. Grounding this analysis is an overview of economics, including topics such as consumer choice, market forces, public goods, and positive externalities. The complex landscape of the creative economy includes two key aspects of the field: those who create the products or services and those who consume them. Cultural economics plays a role in analyzing and understanding the broad scope of the creative sector.

Consumer take-up of creative economy goods and services varies widely; for example, consider the contrast between local consumption versus virtual consumption. Interestingly, global trends such as the rise of internet purchasing of creative products, digital music platform options, and the importance of social media offer alternatives to in-person experiences for the

DOI: 10.4324/9781003147688-2

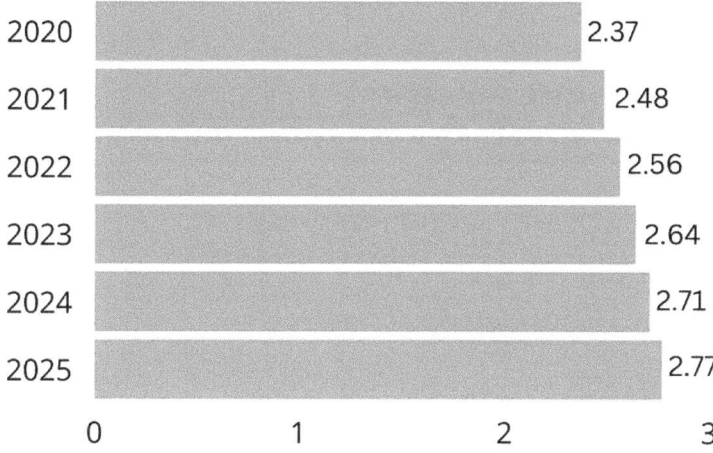

Figure 2.1 Number of online shoppers worldwide.
Source: Adapted from eMarketer.

consumption of cultural goods and services (see Figure 2.1). In addition, individual social relationships affect the production and valuation of culture through collaboration, gatekeeping, and taste-making.

There are numerous actors involved in analyzing the cultural economy. These include scholars, policymakers, corporate entities, and individual artists. Many cultural economists have looked at how arts and culture generate financial means, contribute to economic development, and translate goods and services into money. A key recent shift in cultural economics includes issues such as the importance of symbolic value, the power of trends, the way early adopters can spark interest, and the role of influencers, especially in the social media sphere where content creators have become ubiquitous (see Figure 2.2).

ECONOMICS AS A LENS INTO THE CREATIVE ECONOMY

In modern society, economists posit that all individuals wish to maximize the happiness they can gain through the consumption of goods or services, which is known as utility (Steinemann, 2005). Although this is usually regarded as the satisfaction

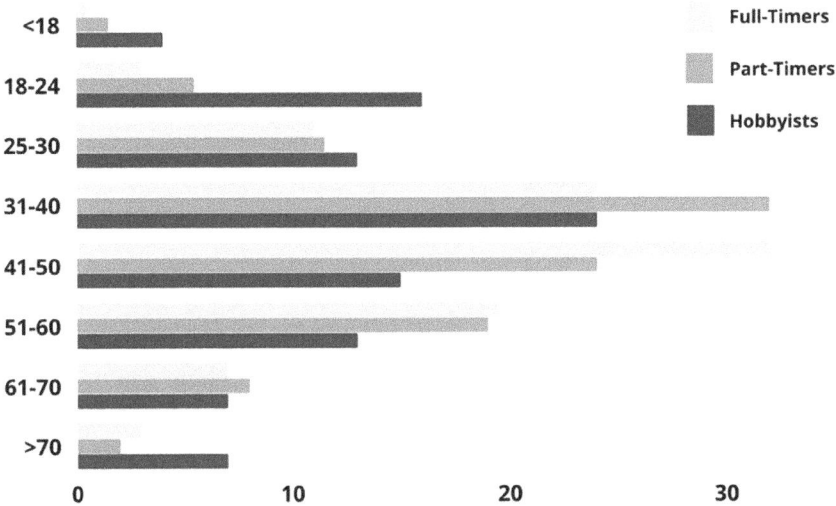

Figure 2.2 Age distribution of content creators.
Source: Adapted from ConvertKit

individuals garner from consumption, there may be instances where utility is maximized from saving rather than spending. Additionally, Steinemann notes that individuals may derive utility from donating to charity, giving nonprofits a role in social utility. Difficult and challenging to measure, the concept of utility is not always something that can be compared or that stays constant among all members of a society. Many individuals in today's world are members of complex societies and they function both according to the goals and ideas of the government and the norms and behavior of the market. Also, the consumer choice to consume cultural or creative goods is even more complex, since goods or services fostered by the creative class may not have any utilitarian function, and can be considered experience goods.

Government structures and consumer behavior

Individuals in a society are affected by government constraints or incentives for change or behavior modification. So, it is important to examine different kinds of government structures and norms. There are a number of models for support of the creative sector within the welfare state spectrum (in which governments protect and promote the economic and social wellbeing of their citizens to varying extents) and various ways these different forms of government view their roles, rights, and responsibilities toward their members, regarding arts and culture options.

Efficiency is a concept that begins with the goal of spending the least money to achieve an objective or realizing the best results with a given input (Stone, 2001). It can be seen as a ratio between costs and benefits, input and output, or coming up with the best way to use limited resources, given consumer preferences (Barr, 2000). In a situation with an efficient market, the role of the state would be negligible. However, finding and measuring the economic impacts and outcomes of state-funded interventions targeting the creative economy, such as the proliferation of cultural districts, has proven to be challenging (see Figure 2.3).

A *Pareto improvement* is something the state does that makes one member of society better off without making anyone else worse off, thereby increasing efficiency (Barr, 2000). A near-Pareto improvement would make a small group worse off, while making a large group better off. Pareto efficiency is the point at which the only way to make someone better off is to make another worse off. Imperfect information, a kind of market

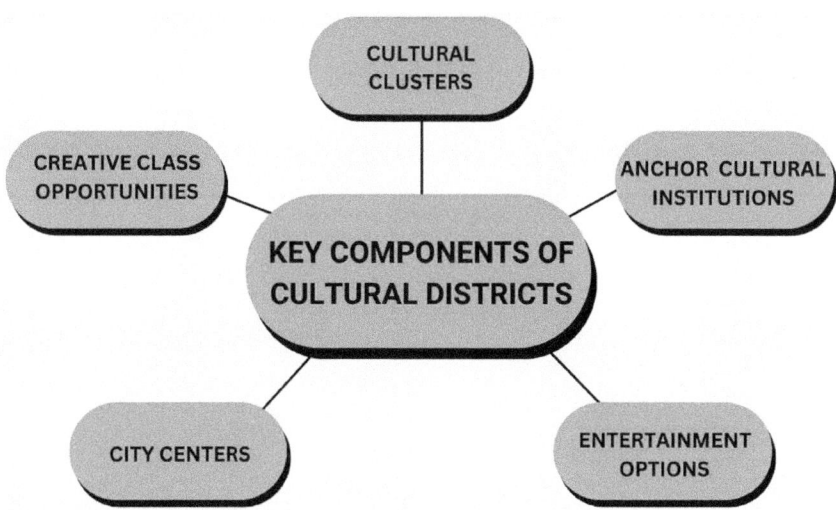

Figure 2.3 Key components of cultural districts.
Source: Adapted from Americans for the Arts

failure, is non-Pareto efficient (Stiglitz, 1998a). Stiglitz found that, during his time in the federal government, it was difficult to generate policies that provided Pareto improvements due to the opposition of special interest groups and their worry about the future, which led to an inability to make decisions.

Equity can be understood as the way society distributes resources (Stone, 2001). The concept of equity often depends on the society's idea of values, including justice, fairness, and who it is that ought to receive certain benefits and resources, as well as issues regarding access to arts and culture amenities (see Figure 2.4).

What is the fair share? This is the question raised in the understanding of equity and its role in society. Various schools of economists and kinds of governments value and define equity in different ways. Rawlsian philosophy on equity, according to Stone, places the process of deciding what is fair on center stage and sees key values as those created by members of a society where primary goods will be disbursed in a universal way.

We see Rawls' view as promoting the equal distribution of societal goods, such as cultural experiences, civil rights, income, liberties, opportunity, and even wealth. Social conservatives, such as libertarians, take a stance that advocates giving equal shares of a resource directly to the recipient—without judgments as to who may deserve more or less. The concepts of

Figure 2.4 *Harpan Concert Hall*, Iceland: An ADA compliant theater.
Source: ©2023 Google Earth

acquisition of property, opportunity, or benefits should be fairly won according to this point of view. Agreement on the terms and conditions of equity faces many challenges.

Among these are the definition and boundaries of property, how to understand and agree upon fairness, and exactly who will prove what is equitable. Problems with equity can range from ageism in hiring and discrimination toward customers with disabilities in a store to the number of males in the nursing profession or the low number of Black or Hispanic applicants among the students applying to Parsons School of Design.

Examining and weighing the tradeoffs between equity and efficiency begins with the point of view of the government under which the analysis is being made. In a system with labor in a strong position, those without significant monetary assets feel that they have someone to represent them, providing a possible reconciliation between equity and efficiency (Stone, 2001). In a society where equity is more important, the polis or public may feel empowered to work for the personal satisfaction they receive, feeling supported by the state in meeting their needs. However, some posit that with a greater amount of equity, there is low productivity and motivation to achieve, as well as the efficiency problems created by the high costs associated with a large state system of benefits administration. This is known as the "leaky bucket," and the interference of the government in this regard can be viewed as wasteful and unproductive (Blank, 2002).

THE MARKET AND THE CREATIVE ECONOMY

To understand market-based solutions in the creative economy, it is important to examine the market mechanism and discuss its breakdown. The *perfect market* is a concept that forms the basis of any discussion of market-based solutions. Perfect market conditions must exist to ensure a balance between supply and demand, which is known as market equilibrium, in any market. These include the following: the lack of any barrier to enter into or exit from the marketplace; perfect competition; perfect information; and no externalities or market distortions. In the instance of a perfect market, the welfare state would not have a great deal of involvement (Barr, 2000).

What are known as "market failures" include monopoly, externalities, public goods, and information asymmetry. These are ways to understand that a "perfect" market does not exist in these cases, as the supply and demand do not have the chance to achieve a natural balance. *Monopoly* is a market failure, because there is only one producer of a good or service, such as the MTA in Boston, Con Edison in New York City, or Indigo Books in Toronto. The problem of only one buyer for a good or service is called monopsony and is exemplified by the US government being the only purchaser of fighter jets. *Externalities* are actions outside of a market mechanism and can be positive or negative. Negative externalities include pollution, a fare hike on the MTA, or the noise one hears when a new building is being constructed nearby. Positive externalities would be walking through a public park undisturbed by jostling crowds, an education provided by the state at no cost to the student, and public art available to be seen by anyone who cares to enjoy it.

An important concept in the discussion of externalities is that of Coasian bargaining. In this context, a negative externality refers to the negotiating done among the affected parties, by themselves and outside of any government intervention, where those involved have the chance to establish ongoing relationships (Singleton, 2007). This is useful when the number of parties involved is small and the cost of bargaining is not prohibitive (Rosen & Gayer, 2008). In cases where the Coase Theorem would not apply, state intervention may be needed to correct for this type of inefficiency. Environmental issues often fall under the category of negative externalities and require government intervention, either through sanctions or inducements (Stone, 2001).

A third kind of market failure is known as *public good*, which can be viewed as a kind of positive externality (Rosen & Gayer, 2008); it is something that is non-rival and non-excludable, such as public radio, public art, the internet in a public library, research available online at no charge, public schools, and the museums in Washington, DC (see Figure 2.5). These examples illustrate the characteristics of public goods as non-rival and non-exclusive. Non-rival means that the good can be consumed without taking anything away from the ability of another to

Figure 2.5 Public art as a public good is demonstrated by this bicycle tour of art in the neighborhoods of Boise, Idaho.

Source: Mural by Sector Seventeen and photo by Matilda Rose Bubb

consume the good. And non-exclusive means that there are no barriers to an individual being able to consume or benefit from consuming that good (Steinemann, 2005).

The concept called public goods, as discussed in modern times, has its roots in the teachings of Plato, who posited that an individual could benefit from actions that would also serve the people (Mansbridge, 1998). Mansbridge argues that economist Adam Smith felt that the opposite was true; the individual's actions would enhance the welfare of the polity, through the "invisible hand" of the market. This shift in thinking about the role of the individual in the context of the greater community led the way toward understanding how economic development is fueled by the desires of a single people in the aggregate context of a community or nation. The balance between the wishes and desires of someone acting in their own self-interest and those of people working together to enhance a collective colaboration is one that is acted out in the social sphere (see Figure 2.6).

Figure 2.6 *Las Etnias* (The Ethnicities), by Brazilian street artist Eduardo Kobra in Rio de Janeiro, painted before the Rio 2016 Olympics, showing the Indigenous peoples of the world.

Source: MVmath20, CC BY-SA 4.0 <https://creativecommons.org/licenses/by-sa/4.0>, via Wikimedia Commons

There often are conflicts in the area of public goods, since what is considered beautiful or pleasing by an individual is not always agreed upon by a neighborhood, an epistemic community, or even a country as a whole (Zukin, 1995). The conversation about public goods includes many notions of who is served by this idea, including understanding specifically who is included in the "public" for whom the benefits are being provided, and what exactly would comprise the "good" for that constituency. Calhoun (1998) points out that, in the United States, the notion of the polis has evolved and now includes a wide range of diverse groups of citizens, each of whom may have differing ideas of what would serve them best.

Another type of market failure is *information asymmetry*, or imperfect information. In this case, either buyers or sellers do not have enough information available to make the kind of decision they would make under perfect conditions. Buyers may not know enough about used cars or generic drugs; conversely, there may be too much information, as in the case of insider trading. Examples of sellers with imperfect information are insurance companies who may not have complete data on a patient and security companies who may need to do extensive background checks before hiring an employee; and even then, they may not have full and accurate information.

MARKET-BASED SOLUTIONS: PRIVATIZATION, VOUCHERS, AND CONTRACTING OUT

In instances of market failure, the government may step in to create a missing market or to do the job of a market. Examples of this are regulations on monopolies, sanctions on companies that pollute, the provision of public education, transportation and mail delivery systems, mandatory labeling on food and cigarettes, and regulation of the financial industry. Through the threat of sanctions, the offering of incentives, and the investment in the development of human capital, the state attempts to balance the key components of efficiency, by trying to make up for an inefficient market, and of equity, by attempting to even the playing field (Vocino, 2003).

An important issue, and one that may be the underlying factor in the skepticism about and hostility toward the government in America is what is called *government failure*. This has two aspects, both of which may influence the public's attitude toward trusting the state. The first aspect is that of possible self-interest, by the representatives within the government who are elected to create and execute public policy (Weimer & Vining, 2004). Often swayed in their decision making by special interest groups who often seek appropriations, these politicians may have inadequate monitoring by their constituencies. Although they are sensitive to media attention and public opinion, as they are elected, this may not be enough to keep policymakers away from the dangers of self-dealing and corruption.

In addition, government failure speaks to the problem in a direct democracy—that is a result of the separation between the representative aspect of the state and its administrative side. Accountability regarding the administrative functions of the US government is not comparable to that of the market, since most civil service jobs have a lack of profit motive and are part of an inflexible system. There is no market efficiency valuation of the outputs of public service workers and often no accountability, and many state agencies survive despite inefficient operation.

This structure does not allow its employees to gain through the kinds of financial incentives found in the corporate world; so, supervisors must screen potential employees to determine their intrinsic motivation to join the state system and reward them for good work with honors rather than bonuses. The public face of this decentralized, complex, and bureaucratic system often reflects the lack of cooperation within the government as well as the challenges of enforcing policies. This causes frustration and animosity in the polis. The current interest in looking at market-based solutions, as possible remedies for some of these problems, echoes the public perception that government failure has become untenable.

In its attempt to correct for the kinds of market failure discussed previously, the state turns to other resources to accomplish its goals. The government cannot play all the roles required to implement these corrections; a variety of actors and institutions take place of the state in bringing the goals of equity and efficiency to bear. The objectives of the state, which involve balancing the goals of efficiency and equity, are achieved through the methods of regulation, financing, and production (Barr, 2000). The third area, production, is where a variety of market-based solutions can play an important role. Within the rubric of privatization, vouchers and contracting out are ways the state partners with other sectors.

The concept called *privatization* can be understood as the shifting of responsibilities—for the production of goods or services or the performance of various obligations—from the state to the private sector (Kosar, 2006). In this definition, the private sector is called upon to create, distribute, and monitor a product or activity—where the state never participated, used to participate, or chooses to retain partial responsibility. The private sector may be involved as a supplier to the government, as an agent for the state, working with them for the delivery of a good or service, or as a replacement for the state provision. Privatization may be financed using public or private funds and may be produced on a public or private basis (Barr, 2000). Contracting for services, known as outsourcing, is where the state puts out bids to engage a private firm to provide a service or agency function. The US government spends billions of dollars annually on millions of contracts such as the mail functions, the construction of public buildings, the building and maintenance of roads, and airport security screening functions, which recently have been taken over by the state. Inappropriate uses of outsourcing may include government personnel checks, running prisons, military operations, or security functions for public officials.

The government has funded organizations that deal with aspects of market failure, such as the public education system, and funds them regularly. Public education is a form of contracting out, in which the state funds an entity (in this case, the school system) to correct for the market failure of providing the public good deemed important—that of a cost-free education for all American children. The school system is one in which the issue of government failure has gained public attention.

Vouchers can be a method of containing costs and funding services on a limited basis, as exemplified by the GI bill, which allows veterans to attend the college of their choice. The proposed use of a voucher system, for primary and secondary education, has encountered a great deal of controversy. The idea of the current school voucher proposal is to provide education vouchers so that parents can choose to send their children to privately owned and operated schools, without having to pay the high cost of traditional private schools. Advocates of school vouchers feel that this is a way for poor children to attend the school of their choice; this helps improve equity and increase efficiency by creating a market for education and allowing consumers to choose their preferred alternative. These proponents feel that US schools are suffering from the effects of government failure and that a market-based solution would be a viable alternative—through the provision of incentives for effective performance (Rotella, 2010).

Another kind of privatization is that of grants, given by the government to private entities to accomplish the goals of the state. The nonprofit sector is a primary recipient of this kind of contracting out. Through grants, the government charges the private sector with the responsibility of correcting for market failure (Baumol, 1997). Examples of this are the provision of public goods such as public art, museums and galleries, public music, and theater performances; there are also grants to museums for exhibition and educational programs. A danger of this kind of provision is the problem of favoritism by the state toward certain providers of art or culture, which may result in a lack of creativity (Kimmelman, 2010).

Additional examples are funds for positive externalities, such as the New York City-funded Arts in Transit, which places art in the subway, and Percent for Art, a program that funds art in all newly constructed municipal buildings. These programs correct for information asymmetry as well, by serving to educate the public about art. The tax-exempt status, given to nonprofits by the government, can be viewed as a kind of grant, as can the tax benefits to individual and corporate donors (Frey, 2000). This way, the loss of tax revenue to the state, through both policies, is an additional way the government contracts out and relies on the nonprofit sector to correct for market failure in numerous areas (Zolberg, 2000).

Many nonprofit organizations receive government grants to run social programs for the poor as well as provide access to a variety of opportunities for diverse communities. If high-income people are altruistic, as many are in the United States—with more than $300 billion given to nonprofits last year—their utility is a mixture of their own income and that of the less fortunate. In this sense, the state's role in redistributing resources through social programs increases the utility of the wealthy, thereby increasing efficiency (Rosen & Gayer, 2008). In a sense, this kind of state support can be seen as correcting for the market failure of a negative externality, with the wealthy being concerned about the poor. By contrast, in European countries, the state provides much of the support for charitable organizations, crowding out any private provision by citizens there (Alesina et al., 1999). However, the emphasis on market-based solutions can obscure the non-competitive nature of the government. If efficiency is the goal, the nonprofit sector may lose some of its merits, since the market model values efficiency above civil society values such as social justice, fairness, and equity (Eikenberry & Kluver, 2004).

GOVERNMENT STRUCTURES AND THEIR RESPONSES

The various distinctions of welfare state regimes range in the degrees of involvement in the decisions of the polis, from relatively hands off to completely involved. According to

Esping-Andersen (1994) the welfare state's role is determined by the ways they are embedded within the political and institutional structures of a nation. Seen as a state-provided system of social guarantees by Esping-Andersen, various welfare states may have very different points of view about their relationship with the market and about a wide range of policy objectives. Each kind of government thinks about its role differently and takes suitable approach to its insertion into the market and market failures. Although the varieties of state involvement in the life of the polis are many, the government can be seen as the heart of the organic entity that constitutes a modern society (Rosen & Gayer, 2008).

Welfare state economics has two fundamental theorems. The two key assumptions of the first theorem are that (1) providers and consumers act as perfect market competitors and that (2) a market exists for every commodity. The second theorem asserts that the state makes an allocation of resources suitable to the situation and then allows consumers to trade freely (Rosen & Gayer, 2008). The second theorem can be understood through the illustration of a race in which some runners are at a disadvantage, each for a different reason. In this example, the state would evaluate the disadvantage of each runner and, based upon his or her issue, would adjust their starting block accordingly and then let the race begin. This is an illustration of another key concept in understanding the role of the state—that of seeking to ensure Pareto efficiency.

The *libertarian* point of view has a proscribed role for the government and mainly sees it as the enforcer of contracts and the provider of limited public goods, namely national defense (Friedman, 1962). The government creates and maintains the military and enjoys a monopoly on the legal use of force without any constrictions (Stiglitz, 1998). The libertarian seeks to restrict the impact of the state on the rights and freedoms of the individual, especially where the market is concerned, positing that any kind of intervention or decision about equity and its largesse gives the state too much power and constricts individual goals and actions to the point where it is a moral affront to the members of a society (Barr, 2000).

Using a "hands-off" approach, libertarians favor little state correction for market failures, and think that any of the public goods provided by some governments, as well as the funding given to many nonprofits, should be freely given by the private sector exclusively. This kind of philosophy does not favor redistribution, because it may limit creativity and inhibit personal ambition. Libertarians prefer individual wealth passed to heirs and disparage high taxation. From the libertarian point of view, any market-based solution to market failures, including the provision of any public good, would be desirable. Economists, including Milton Friedman, have been proponents of the school voucher system, leading to the hypothesis that libertarians would welcome the contracting out of many of the functions of the current US government.

Utilitarian and Rawlsian points of view, both considered liberal, see the state as an arbitrator and a kind of protector. Rawls had an interesting idea, which he called the "veil of ignorance," regarding the role of redistributional equity in a society (Rosen & Gayer, 2008). He posited that if state decision-makers were distanced from personal interests, and in effect did not know to which class of a society they would belong, they would create extremely equitable outcomes, since they themselves might be the beneficiary of the state's largesse (Barr, 2000).

Both liberal points of view are concerned with the maximization of total welfare in a society through the aggregate utility of its members, which is known as social welfare. In utilitarian and Rawlsian welfare states, the state may be acting as a kind of referee for those too weak to act on their own (Stone, 2001). Rawls feels that a society cannot have total welfare unless the least well off is able to maximize his or her utility. In a utilitarian or Rawlsian society, there could be a few ways that market-based solutions might be received. Since these kinds of welfare states favor solutions that take into account equity considerations, at times at the expense of the achievement of efficiency goals, methods such as privatization, vouchers, and contracting out would not necessarily have appeal.

Marxists and *socialists* see the government as the protector of the polis and as the arbitrator for class conflicts (Foley, 1978). Viewing the state's concerns either as of the worker or of the bourgeois, Marxist philosophy points out how education plays a role in passing along the values of a government to a people. This form of government posits that those who receive education have the chance to try for better jobs and the continuation of class divisions. Marxists advocate for the working class to have control over the power in government; they see, within the state's role, the regulation of the labor supply and the ability to ensure stability in the political and social arenas —to foster investment by foreign entities (see Figure 2.7).

Marxists, as well as socialists, would take the point of view that the state and the private sector are aligned and those who work for the state have the best interests of all of society in mind. The market model is not favored in this kind of government, and privatization and vouchers would not be something of which they would think highly. However, contracting out some of the functions of the state might create more jobs and spread the government's redistributive funds throughout the polis, so the government might be in favor of increased forms of this kind of market-based solution. Foley's description of the state, as protecting the ability of government to attract investment, leads to the premise that the Marxist state would wish to keep its contracts and implement corrections for market failures itself, since equity would seem to be of greater value than efficiency.

Within the varieties of capitalist states are *liberal market economies (LMEs)* and *social market economies (SMEs)* (Pontusson, 2005). SMEs favor a cooperative stance in which business, government, and labor work together to solve problems and accomplish goals; they also have a high level

Figure 2.7 *798 Arts District*, Beijing.
Source: ©2023 Google Earth

of investment in education, as a public good. Although these economies may have a great deal of contracting out for social services, they would not be in favor of vouchers or of privatization of government services. Though SMEs favor high spending on education, the idea of a competitive school alternative might be attractive to them, as it may produce higher quality opportunities.

LMEs are the sites of more conflict between labor and management, with lower social protection and market transactions as the defining relations of the economy. Also, LMEs spend lesser state funds on social welfare and use the means testing method to determine who receives benefits (Pontusson, 2005). LMEs, such as the United States, would be in favor of all three kinds of market-based solutions. Their focus on efficiency outcomes makes LMEs the kinds of social environments that would implement market-based solutions, such as contracting out and vouchers.

The current interest in privatization, in its many forms, appears to utilize the strengths and positive aspects of market forces—by allowing for consumer preferences and using the private sector as a partner in the state's correction of market failures. One of the caveats in consideration of any market-based solution is the question of building trust for the government, among members of the polis. Only through transparency of the contracting out process on the part of the state, the implementation of systems of accountability for vendors and grantees (Hanushek & Raymond, 2005), and the consistent evaluation of programs will the American government be able to overcome the current crisis of confidence and regain the respect of its people.

VALUE-BASED APPROACH

The value-based approach to the cultural economy looks beyond price, preferences, and standard transaction analysis. Instead, this way of understanding and analyzing the contribution of the cultural sector looks at values and qualities. How does this sector and its outputs contribute to the community? Does it foster aspects of national identity, social cohesion, and social justice? In this perspective, the focus is not on quantifying the factors that matter in a city, but valuing the contributions to the cultural and social qualities found therein.

If policymakers, in a Creative City, wish to take this point of view, they could put forward the kinds of values and qualities their city wants to realize. In the case of the Creative City, does this value-based approach help understand the ways that the city wants us to perceive its identity? These kinds of qualities stand in contrast to classic cultural economics, but hopefully can contribute to the kinds of data and measurement that have taken precedence in the past.

Through the adaptation of a value-based approach to the creative sector, policymakers may contribute to the practice of cultural economics by branding the identity of the city as including more than market measures. It is interesting to see if cities position the arts as a commodity or as a public good and positive externality.

CREATIVE ECONOMY EXAMPLES IN CONTEXT

The economic theories shared in this chapter are foundational to understanding the creative economy, but can be difficult to access for those who may be unfamiliar with economics. To make these concepts more accessible and relate them to the creative economy, we offer some examples that translate the economic concepts into real-world scenarios.

Examples include:

- Pareto improvement
- Near-Pareto improvement
- Pareto efficiency
- Negative externality
- Positive externality
- Concept of the polis having differing ideas on what serves them best
- Information asymmetry
- Public employee motivation
- Program seeking to achieve equitable access

Pareto improvement: An example of a *Pareto improvement* in the creative economy might be the introduction of a new music streaming platform that provided all musicians a market-rate payout and was free to all listeners. Artists benefit from the revenue from their music and fan access to the service that shares their work. Listeners benefit from the free access to their favorite music. Everybody wins.

Near-Pareto improvement: A possible example of a *near-Pareto improvement* is that there is a shift in the book publishing industry, from traditional publishers to self-publishing authors. Self-publishing authors have greater control over their work and higher royalty rates, as they don't give anything to publishers. Also, they sell their books quickly and easily. Traditional publishers may lose authors who decide to self-publish as well as their readership. Readers benefit from wider access to books and potentially lower costs for the books they want to read.

Pareto efficiency: *Pareto efficiency* could be understood from the way art sales are moving away from physical paintings to digital artwork, such as non-fungible tokens or NFTs. The digital artists benefit greatly in this scenario; as they don't need to invest in art supplies, they can reach a global audience and sell their works in an expanding market—for perhaps more than what their previous physical works fetched. The traditional painter experiences a decline in sales and, therefore, lower income.

Negative externality: The 2016 Oakland Ghost Ship fire event—where a converted warehouse space functioning as an art, performance, and living space for artists burned—resulted in several *negative externalities* for others in the do-it-yourself arts spaces, in addition to the tragic loss of life, injury, and trauma to survivors. Increased scrutiny from fire officials and building inspectors led to the shutdown of other spaces. In Denver, artists experienced a backlash from the public and officials; and the arts administrators, working with these artists, had to step in to help provide funding and assistance for them to overcome the legal, safety, and regulatory demands intended to prevent future crises. Media attention of the fire brought negative attention to underground art scenes and nontraditional spaces became more cautious about hosting public events; this reduced opportunities for emerging and marginalized artists (interview 11/21/2022).

Positive externality: Although the COVID-19 pandemic shutdown had a profoundly challenging impact on creative communities, there were some *positive externalities* that came out of it. The increased global digital engagement of patrons with artists and arts organizations extended the reach of many, resulting in audience growth. A leader in the New Orleans' creative economy commented:

> So the pandemic, as it was an economic standstill, afforded us the opportunity to utilize zoom and all of these other methods to have an opportunity to talk to more people. It allowed us to really engage more.
>
> (interview 2/27/2023)

She went on to say that visual artists, musicians, and fashion designers who had not been at their planning table before got involved virtually; and this engagement extended past the pandemic to where they are now serving on advisory councils and applying for grants.

Concept of the polis having differing ideas on what serves them best: In Minneapolis's Creative City Road Map: A 10-Year Strategic Plan for Arts, Culture, and the Creative Economy (2016), they did something unique. When gathering feedback from citizens—about topics such as how often respondents attend art offerings, ways they want to learn about arts and culture, or resources artists needed to move forward—they hired artists from the communities they served and compiled residents' answers by race and represented these responses in graphs, showing the White respondents and the respondents of color adjacent to each other. This demonstrated that these groups wanted and needed different things. For instance, White respondents were more likely to learn about arts and culture events online or in print media, while people of color relied more on social networking or personal connections. They had different ideas of what best served them. This is very unusual to see represented in a city's cultural plan; but, it reinforces Calhoun's point that the polis is not a monolithic block.

Information asymmetry: In the creative economy, an example of *information asymmetry* is how music streaming royalties are calculated and paid to musicians. The streaming platform has full access to huge amounts of data about consumer behavior, user demographics, and the geographic location of consumers. The individual artists usually don't have access to this data and, therefore, are at a disadvantage at the negotiating table when royalties are determined or if they want to strategize about how to invest in opportunities to reach new audiences and earn more money (O'Dair & Fry, 2020).

Public employee motivation: We conducted 21 interviews with those in leadership roles in city bureaucratic cultural environments, arts-related businesses, or nonprofit management; most of those we interviewed are highly educated. Areas of study include urban planning, public policy, film, marketing, theater production, anthropology, acting, voice performance, voice arts advocacy and administration, and economic development. In our interviews, we asked about their personal motivation for the work they were doing to better understand their relationship to their work.

We found individuals who expressed great passion for the work they do, sometimes originating from an earlier creative practice of their own in film, theater, or the visual arts. Others expressed that they wanted to serve their community, make communities more equitable, or give back to their hometowns. An administrator from Kansas City expressed:

> I tell people all the time, I really do feel like I kind of hit the jackpot with this job. Because as an artist, I mean, an artist is really intrinsic to who I am in my bones. I've been an actor since I was five years old. And a working actor since I was that young, and I couldn't have imagined my life in any other industry. But when I started campaigning, and when I started getting good in that world, and developing the relationships in this area that I developed . . . I started thinking, how can I put my thoughts, feelings, and understanding of the world to use for the greater good? I was in a marketing job at the time that I really didn't care for. It was just a way to pay the bills and have insurance while I pursued my art. And I said, I wanted to turn my day job into this work. And so that's when I started working for the nonprofit chamber in advocacy and public policy for the arts. And now that I get to marry the two in this work in such a special way, I feel incredibly blessed.
>
> (interview 1/27/2023)

Program seeking to achieve equitable access: In 2022, Boston launched its inaugural Cultural Space Fund to support investment in existing cultural spaces and to broaden equitable access to cultural spaces in the city of Boston. The government's goals, of equitable community access to the arts and the provision of buildings where artists could work, were met through contracts to individuals and organizations. An administrator involved with the program commented that this was a big milestone for the mayor's office and the constituents they serve (interview 1/27/2023).

TAKEAWAYS

The following are key economic principles, introduced in this chapter, that provide a foundation and context to understand the creative economy, as you move through the book:

- The creative economy is made up of *producers* who innovate and capitalize their intellectual property and *consumers* who find value in and exchange money for creative products, services, or experiences.
- *Efficiency* means to spend the least money to achieve an objective. When people talk about costs versus benefits, efforts versus results, inputs versus outputs, or how to best use limited resources, they are talking about efficiency.
- A *Pareto improvement* is something the state does to make one member of society better without making anyone else worse off. A *near-Pareto improvement* would make a small group worse off, while making a large group better off. *Pareto efficiency* is where the only way to make someone better off is to make another worse off.
- *Equity* refers to applying values, such as justice and fairness, to the distribution of resources.
- A *perfect market* is when supply and demand are balanced, forming *market equilibrium*.
- *Market failures* are when supply and demand are out of balance. These include:
    1. *Monopoly*, where there is only one producer of a good or service.

- 2 *Externalities*, which are positive or negative actions outside of a market mechanism.
- 3 *Public good*, which is something that is non-rival and non-excludable.
- 4 *Information asymmetry* or *imperfect information*, where buyers or sellers don't have enough information to make informed decisions.

• *Market-based solutions* are used when the government steps in to balance the market. Examples include:
- 1 *Privatization*, which occurs when the government shifts responsibility for the production of goods or services, from the state to the private sector, which could be in the form of a grant.
- 2 *Vouchers*, which are instruments for shifting targeted resources, from the public sector to the private sector.
- 3 *Contracting out*, which is a method used by the state to outsource services or agency functions to the private sector, through task-oriented contracts.

• *Government failure* occurs when elected or administrative government representatives act in their own self-interest, rather than in the interest of the public.

• *Welfare state economics* is when the government provides certain social or financial guarantees to citizens. Its two fundamental theorems are:
- 1 Providers and consumers act as perfect market competitors; and a market exists for every commodity.
- 2 The state makes an allocation of resources suitable to the situation and then allows consumers to trade freely.

• *Government points of view* vary depending on the dominant political perspective.
- 1 *Libertarians* see the government as the enforcer of contracts and the provider of limited goods, but restrict the impact of the state on the rights and freedoms of citizens.
- 2 *Liberals* seek to protect and maximize the welfare of citizens with equity in mind.

3 *Marxists and socialists* perceive the government as the protector of the polis and the arbitrator for class conflicts, with the working class in control of government power.

- *LMEs* have lower social protection and more conflict between labor and management. This model favors contracting out and vouchers.
- *SMEs* favor an environment where business, government, and labor work together to solve problems and accomplish goals. This model is not in favor of vouchers or the privatization of government services.
- The *value-based approach* to cultural economy looks beyond price, preferences, and standard transaction analysis; instead, it measures values and qualities that relate to social and community contributions, such as equity, identity, and social cohesion.

Discussion questions:

1. How might the creative economy contribute to Pareto improvements in both economic outcomes and cultural enrichment? And what challenges might need to be addressed to achieve a synergy of purposes?
2. How might we ensure access to and support for creative content and the development of cultural products as public goods, such as public art, while incentivizing innovation and economic sustainability in the creative economy?
3. What are examples of how libertarians, liberals, and Marxists might think differently about the creative economy?

Activities:

- **Public art as public good:** Find an example of public art in your community. How does this artwork qualify as a public good? Is it physically accessible to all? Do people understand what it means? Is anyone excluded from being able to experience it?
- **Creative economy monopolies:** As a group, identify examples of creative industries or businesses, in the creative economy arena, that have achieved monopoly status or significant market power; think music, publishing, social media, film, etc. Each participant takes one example and

researches on how they achieved this dominant status, what impact it has on the creators and consumers, and whether the monopoly affects pricing, access, or quality of content or services. Do a short presentation for your peers.

REFERENCES

Alesina, A., Baqir, R., & Easterly, W. (1999). Public Goods and Ethnic Divisions. *Working Paper 6009*. Cambridge: National Bureau of Economic Research.

Barr, N. (2000). *The Economics of the Welfare State* (4th ed.). Oxford: Oxford University Press.

Baumol, W. (1997). On the Career of a Microeconomist. In R. Towse (Ed.), *Baumol's Cost Disease: The Arts and Other Victims*. Cheltenham: Edward Elgar Publishing Ltd.

Blank, R. (2002). Can Equity and Efficiency Complement Each Other? *Working Paper 8820*. Cambridge: National Bureau of Economic Research.

Calhoun, C. (1998). The Public Good as a Social and Cultural Project. In W. Powell & E. Clemens (Eds.), *Private Action and the Public Good* (pp. 20–35). New Haven: Yale University Press.

Eikenberry, A., & Kluver, J. (2004). The Marketization of the Nonprofit Sector: Civil Society at Risk? *Public Administration Review*, *64*(2), 132–141.

Esping-Andersen, G. (1994). Welfare States and the Economy. In N. J. Smelser & R. Swedberg (Eds.), *The Handbook of Economic Sociology*. Princeton, NJ: Princeton/Russell Sage.

Foley, D. (1978). State Expenditure from a Marxist Perspective. *Journal of Public Economics*, *9*(2), 221–238.

Frey, B. (2000). *Arts & Economics: Analysis and Cultural Policy*. Berlin: Springer Verlag.

Friedman, M. (1962). Chapter 2: "The Role of Government in a Free Society". In *Capitalism & Freedom*. Chicago: University of Chicago Press.

Hanushek, E., & Raymond, M. (2005). Does School Accountability Lead to Improved Student Performance? *Journal of Policy Analysis and Management*, *24*(2), 297–327.

Kimmelman, M. (2010). In Europe, the Arts Ask for Alms. *The New York Times*. Retrieved January 21, 2010, from www.nytimes.com

Kosar, K. R. (2006). *Privatization and the Federal Government: An Introduction*. Washington, DC: Congressional Research Service.

Mansbridge, J. (1998). On the Contested Nature of the Public Good. In W. Powell & E. Clemens (Eds.), *Private Action and the Public Good* (pp. 3–19). New Haven: Yale University Press.

Minneapolis. (2016). *The Minneapolis Creative City Road Map*. https://mplsartsandculture.org/planning

O'Dair, M., & Fry, A. (2020). Beyond the Black Box in Music Streaming: The Impact of Recommendation Systems Upon Artists. *Popular Communication*, *18*(1), 65–77.

Pontusson, J. (2005). *Inequality and Prosperity: Social Europe vs. Liberal America*. Ithaca, NY: Century Foundation/Cornell University Press.

Rosen, H., & Gayer, T. (2008). *Public Finance* (8th ed.). New York: McGraw-Hill.

Rotella, C. (2010, February 1). Class Warrior. *The New Yorker*, pp. 24–29.

Singleton, S. (2007). Managing Pacific Salmon: The Role of Distributional Conflicts in Coastal Salish Fisheries. In J.-M. Baland, P. Bardhan & S. Bowles (Eds.), *Inequality, Cooperation, and Environmental Sustainability*. New York: Russell Sage Foundation.

Steinemann, A. (2005). *Microeconomics for Public Decisions*. Mason, OH: Thomson South-Western.

Stiglitz, J. (1998, Spring). The Private Uses of Public Interests. *Journal of Economic Perspectives, 12*(2), 3–22.

Stone, D. (2001). *Policy Paradox*. New York: W. W. Norton & Company.

Vocino, T. (2003). American Regulatory Policy: Factors Affecting Trends Over the Past Century. *Policy Studies Journal, 31*(3), 441.

Weimer, D., & Vining, A. (2004). *Policy Analysis: Concepts and Practice* (4th ed.). Hoboken, NJ: Prentice-Hall.

Zolberg, V. (2000). Privatization: Threat or Promise for the Arts and Humanities? *International Journal of Cultural Policy, 7*, 9–27.

Zukin, S. (1995). *The Cultures of Cities*. Cambridge, MA: Blackwell.

Creative economy fundamentals

Chapter 3

INTRODUCTION

The creative economy permeates everyday life and shapes where we live, what we buy, how we interact with others, how we connect, and how we build communities. This chapter delves into the various definitions, fields, and actors that are included in the broad concept of the creative and cultural economies. We provide frameworks that allow the reader to understand those involved in the field—such as independent artists as well as large and small businesses—and anchor cultural institutions. Here, we explore the fundamental characteristics of areas such as workforce delineation; sector boundaries; local, regional, national, and international definitions and scales; and global market forces. We provide an overview as well as references for a more in-depth discussion of these thematic areas. Real-world examples are used to bring some concepts to life, for practitioners and students. Later parts of the book provide a deeper dive into the discussed areas.

CASE: SAG-AFTRA STRIKE

It is difficult to visualize and comprehend what the creative economy is or how to understand its varied aspects. Crises often bring some of these hidden components, networks, workers, and communities into focus. We saw how hurricane Katrina decimated cultural industries and heritage sites; we witnessed the ways that the COVID-19 pandemic led to organizational and small-business failure, and how it led to temporary and permanent closing of theaters, bookstores, and music venues. As we wrote this book, we also saw this with the Screen Actors Guild and the American Federation of Television and Radio Artists (SAG-AFTRA) strike. We use the following example to show the crisis that industries and workers faced, and how that affected everyday people.

The 2023 writers and actors strike in Los Angeles had a severe impact on the economy at local and global levels. SAG-AFTRA joined the already striking Writers Guild of America (WGA) to protest against the Alliance of Motion Picture and Television Producers, who shared the financial difficulties that their studios were facing and how current conditions were unsustainable for the industry. This is a historic event, given that it's the first time these labor unions have joined together, since 1960, to protest working conditions. The WGA demands increased minimum compensation in all areas of media, residuals (compensation for reuse of work where the writer is credited), appropriate TV-series writing compensation from pre- to post-production, and contributions to pension and health plans, while strengthening professional standards and the overall protections for writers (Wilkinson, 2023). The actors want better pay, better benefits, and job security with rising inflation and the erosion of residuals. They want regulated use of generative AI and demand self-taped auditions as additional priorities (Woltmann, 2023). *The New Yorker* covered the experience of Alex O'Keefe, a writer for FX's awarding winning *The Bear*.

> During his nine weeks working in the writers' room for "The Bear," over Zoom, he was living in a tiny Brooklyn apartment with no heat; sometimes his space heater would blow the power out, and he'd bring his laptop to a public library. (He was never flown to set.) He thought that he was making a lot of money, but, after reps' fees and taxes, it didn't add up to much. "It's a very regular-degular, working-class existence," he said. "And the only future I'm seeking financially is to enter that middle class, which has always been rarified for someone who comes from poverty."
>
> (Schulman, 2023)

In a fiery widely shared speech, Fran Drescher, president of SAG-AFTRA, said that actors were being "marginalized, disrespected, and dishonored" by a business model that has been drastically changed by streaming and artificial intelligence (Reed, 2023). She further commented:

> What happens here is important because what's happening to us is happening across all fields of labor, when employers make Wall Street and greed their priority and they forget about the essential contributors that make the machine run, [she said] . . . We are the victims here. We are being victimized by a very greedy entity. I am shocked by the way the people that we have been in business with are treating us . . . I cannot believe it, quite frankly, how far apart we are on so many things. How they plead poverty, that they're losing money left and right when giving hundreds of millions of dollars to their CEOs. It is disgusting. Shame on them. They stand on the wrong side of history.
>
> (Reed, 2023)

We share this example because this strike is not about A-list actors with houses in Malibu and yachts that anchor on the Amalfi Coast. Rather, it showcases a multi-billion-dollar loss that hurts people connected to the industry, in addition to actors and writers enduring significant hardship. The film, television, and entertainment industries are sizable contributors to the regional and national economies, and this case showcases how many people are working in that space. For example, halted production affects businesses that support the industry, including catering businesses, restaurants near the studios, dry cleaners, florists, set builds, lighting designing consultants, and more. People who hold entertainment jobs and entertainment-adjacent roles account for almost 20% of the LA-area income (Liu, 2023).

This is just one example of the challenges the creative industry faces as they go through crisis flux. It is also possible that new opportunities for arts and culture emerge from economic shocks. For example, US military base closures are often catastrophic for the regional economy; but they also provide new opportunities to think about the creative economy. For example, the San Diego Naval Training Center included an arts and cultural district in their revitalization; the Naval Air Station in Alameda included temporary-use zoning for wineries and others in the artisanal beverage industry; and the Brooklyn Navy Yard transformed decommissioned space into film and television studios (Ashley & Touchton, 2016).

We urge policymakers to consider how arts and cultural industries are affected by these shocks, so they can plan, prepare, and implement strategies to offset the damage and create new opportunities. To do so, it's important to understand the fundamentals of creative economy scoping and scaling.

CONCEPTUAL BUILDING

First, we will talk about how academics and practitioners define the creative economy. Second, we will cover why these terms matter in how they are defined and conceptualized. Finally, we will provide different examples to illustrate the flexibility of these concepts, as well as the strengths and weaknesses of that flexibility.

"Creative economy" is a compelling and attractive concept that embodies arts and cultural industries, occupations, and clusters. It is also off-putting to some, because people are worried that it focuses too much on instrumental rather than intrinsic values and that it prioritizes growth over development. We believe the term is an important one to study and highlight, because it provides visibility and comprehensiveness to people, workers, organizations, sectors, and industries that have often been overlooked, misunderstood, or insufficiently resourced. We also deeply value the intrinsic value of the arts as scholars, practitioners, artists, creators, and individuals. There are many resources and reports available to learn more about this important and vital work; you can find this information on national, state, regional, and municipal arts websites, as well as the websites of arts, cultural, and creative organizations and anchor institutions. Private and civic foundations are also good places to look for artist and creator information.

In this book, we highlight the creative economy, because it speaks to an economic ecosystem shaped and built by different actors, institutions, organizations, spaces, and places—generating ideas, resources, and outputs that contribute to our economy and our communities. That creative system ultimately leads to new innovations, processes, products, organizations, or institutions. Economic developers and governments pursue different strategies, depending on their goals. For example, building a performance arts facility downtown may be designed to increase tourism as an export activity and help revitalize a decaying area. Or, using film incentives that require local workers may be a way to increase occupational expertise and make sure the incentive financing stays local.

Policymaker's focus on the creative economy stems from broader global forces. Since the late twentieth century, we have seen cities, states, and nations test new economic development strategies in response to global consolidation of industries, deregulation of traditional manufacturing, changing labor rights, and massive demographic movements of people and businesses. Many communities face an identity crisis and economic instability as massive industrial restructuring and realignment, combined with technological innovations, re-shapes the futures of cities, suburbs, and rural areas.

Business leaders and policymakers are left wondering how they are going to replace jobs, productivity, and business activity. Localized shocks provide further complications when corporate headquarters leave, neighborhoods decline, military bases close, and industry moves outward to accommodate horizontal integration. Economic developers seek new paths forward, where they no longer compete for traditional manufacturing or high-end services, but for new technologies, contemporary manufacturing industries, and creative activity.

Creative economic development is one of a handful of development strategies to create city or country winners by growing productivity. Scholars point out that all economies are creative in the sense that they continually adapt, evolve, curate, and develop new ideas, products, and systems—whether that is a lightbulb, artisanal beer, a wind turbine, an e-reader, or a semiconductor. What's new is the concept or label to explain it, narrow who and what is included, and better understand the systems that guide the flow of distribution of these ideas and goods. For example, do artisanal beer makers get their glass bottles or aluminum cans locally? Do they get their hops from local agricultural markets? Do they have local food trucks on site? And do they also work with regional farmers to provide ingredients for their restaurants that sit next to where the beer is made? Do they work with local artists on the design of their beer bottles and cans? And do they work with local graphic designers for their marketing material? Does the location of the craft brewery support their neighborhood? And is it part of a cluster of local food and beverage options that are attractive to the local workforce? The list goes on and on, in terms of how to think about the different inputs and outputs of this process and the economic development motivations that influence their decision making (see Figure 3.1).

So, what is the creative economy? It is a deeply fuzzy concept that takes on many different flavors and identities. The concept's versatility is unsurprising given its new-ness and how ideas are diffused across place and time—in ways that reflect

Figure 3.1 Visual artist Amy Westover in Germany's Derix Glassstudio, an international leader in architectural glass fabrication, where she is working with artisans to create a public artwork.

Source: Photo by Matilda Rose Bubb

different values and political and social ideologies. For example, policymakers who believe in a smaller government role may look to public-private partnerships to build arts and cultural facilities or districts. But arts and cultural planners may want to allocate more resources to new arts and creative businesses rather than established organizations—as a way to help incubate their work that may lead to new innovations and products. The blurriness also underscores the push/pull of having an authentic manifestation that's messier and harder to compare versus a singular framework that's easy to identify through comparative quantitative data, but incomplete due to the top-down nature of prescriptive efforts.

Some industries and occupations are in, and some are out. Economic developers and arts advocates deem which industries and occupations are important assets to securing a competitive and comparative advantage in a shifting economic landscape. This fuzziness is most pronounced around terminology and intended targets. Many people and places do not see a direct 1:1 alignment between arts and culture and the creative economy or between product generation and the creative economy. Coy (2000, August 27) argues that the creative economy refers specifically to "the stuff inside employees' heads." He explains, "When assets were physical things like coal mines, shareholders truly owned them. But when the vital assets are people, there can be no true ownership." Coy argues that the goal for industry is to convince these workers to stay, so they can develop ideas and help those businesses flourish. This focus on people represents the knowledge economy, where it's about educated people generally—not just educated people working in arts and culture industries. Coy also argues, like many others, that intellectual innovation is the coveted asset. Florida (2002) popularized this notion, calling it *The Rise of the Creative Class*. He argued that cities with greater concentrations of people with higher education are more likely to succeed, which became a mantra of many in economic development practice.

The Boston Redevelopment Authority's *Create Boston* program (2005) illustrates the widespread embrace of this approach. They define the creative economy as:

"Those activities which have their origin in individual creativity, skill, and talent and which have a potential for wealth and job creation. These include direct activities in which individual creativity and skills is brought to bear, and which is characterized by innovation and originality. This leads to the creation of intellectual property in the form of copyright. Also, any activity (upstream and downstream) which directly contributes to create activities such that the product would not exist in the same form without it."

This approach encapsulates many kinds of workers, industries, and has a specific focus on ownership of innovation. However, in our book, we center arts and culture, because this aligns with how many practitioners and scholars frame it at different scales of government, business, and civic life. After considering different issues, such as the worth of creativity, we focus on how to define and measure the creative economy.

DEFINING THE CREATIVE ECONOMY FROM AN ARTS AND CULTURE PERSPECTIVE

From an arts and culture angle, there is still no one-size-fits all approach for pursuing creative economic development. There is a variety of conversations in the academy around why that is and whether there should be a clearer template or pattern. Before the idea of creative economy came to fruition, there was the concept of the *cultural* economy. Typically, the cultural economy focused on nonprofit arts activity in the areas of fine arts, music arts, performance arts, and visual arts. This meant the symphony, ballet, Broadway shows, opera, orchestra, and literature—but not rock concerts, film blockbusters, poetry jams, graphic novels, commercial photography, fashion design, or tourist sites.

Culture wars in the late 1980s—1990s, where conservative forces successfully sought to deplete funding for the arts in the United States, contributed to tensions around arts support and which arts activities deserved funding (Rushton, 2015; Killacky, 2022). Polemic debates occurred around where the government should intervene and provide resources to the arts, who got to determine what was considered art, and which arts were worthy of being funded. The catalyst for this tension gained significant traction around the National Endowment for the Arts (NEA) grant program in 1989. The NEA awarded The Institute

Figure 3.2 *Fusterlandia*, a compound outside of Havana, created by Cuban outsider artist José Fuster, is a neighborhood center and tourist destination.

Source: Photo by Matilda Rose Bubb

of Contemporary Art, at the University of Pennsylvania, a grant to exhibit a retrospective of Robert Mapplethorpe's creative work, entitled *The Perfect Moment*, which showed celebrity portraits, self-portraits, interracial figure studies, floral still-life pieces, collages, and homoerotic images. Congress vehemently proclaimed the homoerotic images as "pornographic" (Killacky, 2022, n.p.). Another storm erupted when the Southeastern Center for Contemporary Arts in Winston-Salem used NEA dollars for Andres Serrano's photographic work, *Piss Christ*, where a crucifix was submerged in urine (Killacky, 2022).

NONPROFIT CULTURE TO CREATIVE ECONOMY

Around the same time, the fields of the cultural and creative economies faced off over standards of excellence, consideration for resources, and focus on programmatic areas. Nonprofit arts organizations were at the center of this conversation. Bill Ivey

(2008), former chairman of The National Endowment for the Arts, spoke about this tension in his book, as Rushton (2015, n.p.) noted:

> Because the fine arts are mostly organized as nonprofits and because the fine arts are viewed as markers of sophistication, educational accomplishment, and virtue, the sector has come to think of itself as the only significant source of quality arts programming in the United States. When arts people talk about the cultural industries the dismissive term used to characterize the for-profit arts is *commercial*, suggesting an arena in which bottom-line concerns consistently trump the demands of artistry. In contrast, the nonprofit arts are seen as "mission driven"—purveyors of "excellence." This assumed qualitative distinction, of course, does not hold up even to superficial scrutiny—many of our most highly regarded arts activities are almost exclusively organized for profit—but the notion survives as an often-invoked mark of nonprofit distinction—one that has allowed long-standing elitist prejudice to insert itself into policy. Over time the dismissive attitude of nonprofit advocates has taken on the character of a full-blown ideology—an explanation of reality that is widely shared but unexamined. Thus, the notion that a nonprofit business model invariably produces higher-quality art is a tenet of *nonprofitism*, an ideology that has encouraged a smug sense of entitlement in the arts community. In addition, nonprofitism has kept the sector isolated, preventing arts organizations and arts advocates from engaging real cultural issues like fair use, media regulation, trade in cultural goods, and the scope of intellectual property protection. Unfortunately, nonprofitism's intellectual bookends, disdain for the commercial sector combined with an obsessive concern for public and philanthropic support, have to date pretty much defined the limits of the U.S. cultural policy debate.

This pointed claim does overlook the reality that many held the view that the government should not intervene in the marketplace and support for-profit activities, because that would mean the government was competing or picking winners. This is one reason that national, state, and municipal governments overwhelmingly funded nonprofits rather than for-profit businesses in the United States (Rushton, 2015). Yet, the tie between industry and arts nonprofits remained strong, and continues to this day. Many of these arts institutions and organizations have been supported, built, and championed by boards and funders, from tycoons to industry leaders—through the industrial age, the financing age, and the technology age we see now.

The move from the nonprofit focus of the cultural economy to a more inclusive embrace of the creative economy is also marked by an embrace of neoliberalism, a political economic philosophy that re-emerged in the 1980s; it argues that economic growth is connected to greater liberty through individual choices. This conservative approach is cultivated with deregulation, open markets, and shrinking of governments through austerity and privatization. Scholars argue that neoliberalism is a primary driver for moving from cultural to creative economies. They argue that the creative economy favors wealthy workers, for-profit businesses, and trite marketing phrases that diminish where creative activity truly happens. Gentrification is the most common critique or manifestation of neoliberal policies, from their perspective.

INTRINSIC VALUE VERSUS INSTRUMENTAL OUTCOME

Given the diminished role of the state in arts funding and debates over public-good spending (like the arts), a new focus on identifying and justifying the value of arts investments has emerged. Nonprofits were trying to justify their contribution, and governments were trying to make the case for funding priorities. Multiple studies demonstrate the economic value of the arts, and that the inclusion of a commercial approach not only widens the value, but also demonstrates its weighty size. We are also seeing more studies talk about other contributions connected to health, wellbeing, and education. For example, studies have shown that music engagement, visual arts therapy, movement-based creative expression, and creative writing can contribute to improved health outcomes (Stuckey & Nobel, 2010).

In response, there are growing voices who argue that the intrinsic values of the arts are just as important as the extrinsic or instrumental outcomes (McCarthy et al., 2004). The National Endowment for the Arts Chairwoman, Maria Rosario Jackson, has a vision of an "artful life," which "is an inclusive concept containing a wide range of arts experiences, including the everyday, deeply meaningful practices and expressions within our daily lives as well as the making, doing, teaching, and learning" (American Artscape, 2023). The idea is that all people are creative and expressive in ways that feel authentic to them. The artful life includes these principles:

- All people have the capacity to be creative, imaginative, and expressive on their own terms.
- Arts and cultural activity happen in many kinds of places, not just museums and theaters, and our concept of that activity must be expansive.
- Art process can be as important as and, in some cases, even more important than art product.
- Artists, culture bearers, and designers have many kinds of relationships to the world and help us see things from different perspectives, ask questions, speak truth, and help us imagine what could be.
- The arts are intrinsically important (full stop). The arts are most impactful when they exist not in a bubble, in isolation, but in connection to other dimensions of our lives, our communities, towns, and cities—at the intersections of other areas of policy and practice like health, education, community and economic development, transportation, the environment, and more.

(American Artscape, 2023, p. 1)

These principles articulate that arts and creative works have intrinsic value and instrumental value when they are "connected" to other areas, including economic and community development. For example, Boise City's Department of Arts & History and Public Works Department commissioned multiple public artworks addressing the connections between the urban and natural environment for The WaterShed, an education center at their Water Renewal Facility (see Figure 3.3 and

Figure 3.3 Public art at *The WaterShed*, an environmental education center in Boise, Idaho.

Source: Photo by David Fish with Blu Fish Photography

3.2). The Public Works Department also developed an in-depth Public Works Public Art Master Plan to strategize future art investments, centered on environmental sustainability, which would be integrated throughout the city.

Studies have identified informal arts participation in Chicago, where "informal" refers to the "process and the context of artmaking—not, as a threshold matter, to the product of the activity, nor the characteristics of the artist's training" (Wali et al., 2002). Wallis (2011, n.p.) shares:

> The NEA Survey of Public Participation in the Arts calls them "unincorporated arts," while many refer to them as amateur, leisure-time, or community arts. Participants of case study groups described themselves as anywhere between "not ready for prime time" to "just people not professional"). The report's official definition is that the informal arts are "creative activities that fall outside traditional non-profit

and commercial arts experiences," going on to say that they usually have no permanent home, virtually no fund-raising activities or secure income, and no selective membership.

The study describes arts production as occurring on a "continuum that ranges from informal activities that occur in any ephemeral, highly spontaneous fashion in completely unstructured spaces, to the long-established, formally organized practices governed by rules for inclusion and occurring in publicly labeled 'arts' spaces" (Wali et al., 2002, n.p.). While some may not consider informal arts as creative economic development, it does help prop up the entire sector through civic vitality; and it may be the start for those exploring creative careers.

Some policymakers and staff expect program and policy evaluation for creative economy initiatives, because they want information on how public resources may or may not yield benefits to the broader community. Practitioners also point to the creative economy language to bring the arts to the core of economic development conversations, rather than being sidelined, as in the past. In other words, this is a complex discussion, when trying to define the creative economy.

With the rise of a creative economy framework, many researchers favor a more solidified conceptualization. Robust peer-reviewed research seeks to define the term, arguing that it's difficult to push for government, public-private, or private intervention without a deeper understanding of the economic landscape (Markusen et al., 2008). Howkins (2002) defined the creative economy as showing how people can make money from what is inside their head (of the ideas that they have), where he focused on how this translated into advertising, architecture, art, crafts, design, fashion, film, music, performing arts, publishing, research and development, software, toys and games, entertainment, television, radio, and video games. For example, Treefort Music Festival (TMF), which like many music festivals, has been an important creative economic generator for the city and region (see Figure 3.3). TMF was an idea that sprouted from several musicians and local arts entrepreneurs, which went from a small festival to an internationally renowned one in less than a decade.

Figure 3.4 *Treefort Music Festival* rock concert, Boise, Idaho.
Source: Photo by Conner Schumacher

OVERARCHING CREATIVE ECONOMY CONCEPTIONS

Others focus more on theoretical conceptualization to frame the creative economy. For example, Markusen et al. (2008) center the creative economy as a collection of industries revolving around a creative cluster, creative workforce, or creative community.

Some scholars look to practice to shape their conceptualizations. Ashley (2014, p. 1) notes the "century-long quest" toward the formation of this concept by looking at how practitioners tackle it. She (2014) shares a form-based approach connected to different economic modeling drivers and impulses that she labels as "arts economic development," which is symbiotic with the creative economy and emphasizes the arts and culture side. She notes a piecemeal set of seven economic development efforts, including (1) aesthetics, (2) cultural agglomeration, (3) workforce investments, (4) city building, (5) amenities and livability, (6) creative regions, and (7) community development. Callanan (2022, January 31) also observes how communities go about determining their definition and practice, by noting:

Creative economy definitions are typically tied to efforts to measure economic activity in a specific geography. A relevant set of art, culture, design, and innovation industries is determined, and the economic contribution of those industries is assessed within a region. As a result, there is no agreed upon group of industries that define the creative economy: each study determines what it means in the relevant region and builds a unique set of industries to define the local creative economy. This makes aggregation or comparisons between regions difficult.

People are also trying to understand at which geographic scale to study and support the creative economy. Some focus on the sub-city level, particularly when looking at discrete arts and cultural activities clustered in a parcel, block, district, or neighborhood. For example, scholars (Ashley, 2017; Ryberg-Webster & Ashley, 2018) study the capacity of creative economy districts to pursue their economic and community economic development ends. River North (RiNo) Arts District in Denver,

Figure 3.5 RiNo sculpture and related signage in the River North Arts District in Denver, CO.

Source: Photo by Tracy Wiel

Colorado is an organic artist-driven district that advocates for affordable artist space and art space with authentic placemaking (see Figure 3.4). The associated organization eventually became the formally recognized planning entity to represent the neighborhood (Ashley, 2014).

Many efforts also center on the city or state level, given the desire to track a comprehensive set of activities. Beyers et al. (2004) evaluates how the music industry is networked across the Seattle metropolitan region, which was one of the first industry studies to do so. In another example, the Colorado Office of Economic Development and International Trade (COEDIT, 2020) published a Colorado Creative Economy report that shares the initial impact of COVID-19 in this economic area, where the largest and fastest growing industries (music, theater, and dance) were the most severely impacted by COVID-19. Others focus on the region (Foord, 2009), given that creative workers may not live in the city where they work; they may work different jobs in different cities and may sell their products globally. Industries and businesses may buy and sell products outside their location or have their corporate headquarters elsewhere. Regions can cross cities, states, or countries. It's important to think through ideas and workflow, knowing that they may be different for different disciplines, practices, and activities.

CREATIVE ECONOMY DEFINED IN PRACTICE

In practice too, the creative economy can mean different things to different people, stakeholders, and communities. Our book is not prescriptive or normative. We don't tell you what the creative economy is or how it should be defined. We provide examples and resources. We pose a series of questions for you to consider, so that you might adopt an approach that is authentic to your community. Some of these foundational scoping questions include: What do we mean by "creative?" What industries are included? What occupations fit in this concept? Who does this work across sectors? How can we learn more about our creative economy landscape? Is data available to help with measurement or framing? And what are the strengths and weaknesses of the data? What do we do with this information? With this groundwork, practitioners can begin developing new structures, investments, and interventions in pursuit of their creative economy agendas.

As noted, organizations, neighborhoods, cities, countries, and global organizations have different ways of defining the terms. They often scope, count, or assess based on their own economic classification systems. In the following, we provide a range of examples of how the terms are defined, suggesting that it is important to have definitions that make sense for your context. To find these examples, we reviewed academic publications, popular media, community websites, and government websites and documents—drawing on the search terms of "creative economy," "Creative City," "arts economic development," and "Arts City." As expected, we found significant differences.

At the state or subnational level, we see considerable variation, which resonates with the unique attributes of these places.

The Montana Arts Council shares:

> The creative economy includes those individuals (and enterprises) who derive their income from the art, craft, and words they produce with their hands or from their minds; those firms that convert them into commercial products or ventures; those enterprises that apply art, design and creative writing to other areas of commerce. This cluster consists of all enterprises in the state whose principal competitive advantages are derived from appearance, form, or content that either distinctively define or are embedded in products or services.
>
> (2014, n.p.)

This definition depicts a broad usage of art; and it also speaks to the nature of how creators, makers, and doers may use their knowledge and abilities in a non-arts industry or organization.

We also provide an example of a municipal perspective for a city that has embedded "creative economy" into its name. The City of Philadelphia Office of Arts, Culture, and the Creative Economy is explicit in how it identifies the creative sector and inclusive in its delineation. Its scope includes the people and products that make up the for-profit and nonprofit arts-related creative industries, such as visual and performing arts, graphic design, music, fashion, public relations, and architecture. Creative workers in non-creative enterprises, non-creative workers in creative enterprises, and creative workers in creative enterprises are all included.

> Washington, DC, is one of a handful of places that also include the neighborhood scale in its city definition.
>
> Enterprises in and or which creative content drives both economic and cultural value, including businesses, individuals, and organizations engaged in every stage of the creative process—acts as a local economic driver creating a significant number of jobs, income, and revenues for the city and its residents. The creative economy also includes creative talent and creative neighborhoods that together contribute to making a community a more vital and competitive place. The District's creative base includes building arts, design, film and media, communications, performing and visual arts, museum management and culinary arts.
> (District of Columbia, 2019)

There are also regional definitions that encompass more than a singular place. The Northern Wyoming Community College District, which consists of two counties, defines the creative economy as: "The creative economy, of Sheridan and Johnson, was defined as people who earn their living from the creative content of what they produce, support, and/or sell. Sub-clusters include visual and performing arts, media and digital arts, product and environmental design, and cultural heritage and preservation" (Sheridan College, n.d.).

It's also useful to look at arts organizations to see how they approach the concept. For example, the California Otis Art Institute also has a focus on an emotional connection in addition to market impacts:

> The creative economy is defined as the market impact of businesses and individuals involved in producing cultural, artistic and design goods and services. It consists of creative professions and enterprises that take powerful, original ideas and transform them into practical and often beautiful goods or inspire us with their artistry.
> (Otis College of Art and Design, 2023)

We also looked at international organizations; we focused on the United Nations, given their connection to UNESCO and their many programs tied to the creative economy. The United Nations, as part of their sustainable development agenda, says:

> At the heart of the creative economy are the creative industries which can be defined as the cycles of creation, production and distribution of goods and services that use creativity and intellectual capital as primary inputs. UNCTAD and UNDP classify them by their roles as heritage, art, media, and functional creations . . . these industries include advertising, architecture, arts and crafts, design, fashion, film, video, photography, music, performing arts, publishing, research and development, software, computer games, electronic publishing, and TV/radio.
> (United Nations, n.d.)

As the United Nations notes, there are also entities that have different names, other than "creative economy," to talk about similar areas. Colombia defines their creative economy with an important subset called the Orange Economy. They share that it is:

> The sector whose goods and services are based on intellectual property, estimated to make up about 6 percent of the world's GDP. They refer to cultural industries within it as "The Orange Economy, for its part, comprises cultural industries divided into three categories: 1) traditional works for which there is often an artifact (books, newspapers, magazines, libraries, film, television, photography, radio), 2) other works that are based more in experience (visual and performing arts, dance, opera, fashion, design, museums, architecture, gastronomy), and 3) new works that tend to be digital or multimedia and have come about in the last half-century or so (video games, software, advertising, new media)."
> (Sonneland, 2018)

While these examples show a range, we also found regional approaches as well that did try to find a common language around the creative economy, so that they could measure and frame it easier. For example, the New England Foundation for the Arts developed a region-wide partnership in 1998 to provide a shared framework, where they emphasized the production of cultural goods and services and intellectual property: Creative Cluster, Creative Workforce, and Creative Communities, which broadly refer to businesses and organizations, places, and people (DeNatale & Wassall, 2007).

Many policymakers, economic developers, and arts advocates are trying to either leverage their Creative City assets or are trying to develop them. Civic boosters, economic developers, urban marketers, real estate developers, multi-level policymakers, and arts policy entrepreneurs often tag, market, or share how their cities are creative—whether their workers, industries, or organizations generate artistic ideas, processes, products, places, or communities. Or their creatives take their unique skill sets and translate them to other non-arts industries, occupations, and opportunities. These perspectives proclaim that this creative ecosystem is pronounced in their place. Civic boosters hope to use this proud proclamation to draw even more creative assets to a particular locale to build industries that rely on arts activities, as an amenity, to attract non-arts workers or to build arts specific industries that generate different sources of revenue or prestige.

There is a growing momentum to take this concept of the creative economy and re-name divisions, government agencies, and strategies to incorporate this focus. For example, Colorado Creative Industries Division, within the Colorado Office of Economic Development & International Trade, was formed in 2010 to better position the state to harness the potential of the creative sector to contribute to the state economy (State of Colorado: Colorado Creative Industries (CCI); Colorado Office of Economic Development and International Trade, 2023). They did so by merging the Council of the Arts and Art in Public Places, where they focus on design, film, and media, literary and publishing, performing arts, visual arts and design, and heritage. This broadening and tilting of focus connects to its mission where:

> CCI believes in the power of creativity to inspire human connections, create social change, and support economic

vibrancy throughout Colorado. We focus on strengthening the vitality of visual, performing, and literary arts through promotion, resources, and funding opportunities. Our mission is to promote, support and expand the creative industries to drive Colorado's economy, grow jobs and enhance our quality of life.

(Colorado Office of Economic Development and International Trade, n.d.)

They curated a series of interventions and incentives to support community and economic development. For example, they developed the Colorado Creative Districts program that certifies designated clusters that add to the state's economy through increasing jobs, incomes, and investments. They can draw on cash awards, technical assistance, marketing inclusion, and highway signs to note their presence, economic and workforce data to show their impacts, and other resources (Colorado Office of Economic Development and International Trade, n.d.). They also built the Space to Create Colorado program, where artists, creative enterprises, and creative organizations can access affordable live-work and commercial spaces to support rural community social and economic needs. They have a Creative Forces Program, funded by the National Endowment for the Arts, Department of Defense, and Department of Veterans Affairs, to place music therapists in recovery centers. In addition, the program provides funding for an online community called Military Arts Connection where veterans, military members, and their families can access local arts enrichment experiences to create community, develop new skills, and help nurture creativity within the participants. Colorado also has an Office of Film, Television, and Media to provide resources and incentives for consent creation that brings in economic growth.

There are also many local municipalities that have film and/or television offices in addition to traditional arts and culture offices. The Seattle Office of Film and Music offers small-business grants, film permit assistance, and other types of tools and support (see Figure 3.5).

What is important to note is that creative economy is not always an inclusive term. There are places that practice and invest in the creative economy that do not refer to it by that term. This could be because marketing costs money or because people may not be familiar with the new term yet. It may also not be palatable to those in positions of power. Others may not have the knowledge or desire to call-out or name their creative economy. In some of those cases, they may also use different terminology. It is also possible that changing their title from "cultural" to "creative" economy is not about adopting a new set of strategies; it may just be about trying to adjust to new expectations or a political landscape that is more likely to support these arts and cultural activities if it is named that way.

We now move from this conceptual work of the creative economy to focusing more on its components. We choose to highlight creative industries and creative occupations here. We cover creative places in Chapter 4 and creative entrepreneurs, institutions, and structures in Chapters 5, 6, and 8.

Figure 3.6 Seattle Office of Film and Music website, City of Seattle.

CREATIVE INDUSTRIES

The term "creative industries" gained momentum in the late 1990s. In the UK, for example, it was used to describe the cultural sector by UK New Labour in 1998; and it rapidly gained traction globally (O'Connor, 2017, n.p.). In part, this marked a shift or a "bargain" where the arts were able to access some of the resources at the "grown-ups table" if they were able to broaden how they thought about the arts from just a nonprofit, traditional arts perspective to a commercial one too (O'Connor, 2021, para. 2; Loh et al., 2022). To tally the regional economic contribution of the arts, data crunchers would total the revenue of larger arts organizations by counting the expenditures of those audiences and then demonstrating multiplier effects.

Again, this typically focused more on nonprofit tourism activity than a broader conceptualization. As the Creative Industries Policy and Evidence Centre notes, "creative industries are a diverse and complex sector made up of a variety of sub-sectors, from performing arts to computer games, and graphic ensign to advertising" (Beckett, 2022, para. 1). In 2001, the Creative Industries were defined by the Department for Digital, Culture, Media, and Sport (DCMS) as those industries "which have their origin in individual creativity, skill, and talent and which have a potential for wealth and job creation through the generation and exploitation of intellectual property" (Creative Industries Policy and Evidence Centre, 2022). They list the following subsectors: advertising and marketing; architecture; crafts; design and designer fashion; IT, software, and computer services; publishing; museums; galleries and libraries; music; and performing and visual arts.

It is important to note that not all creative occupations are encompassed in the concept of the creative industries. For example, you could be a visual artist who works as an art teacher for a primary school; that does not often get counted in occupational analyses. Or, you could be an events planner who works for publishing; this is not a creative occupation, but is in a creative industry. Not all international organizations, nations, states, cities, or sub-city units include the same industries either.

A good starting point is to consider the following creative industries, knowing that they may not all be appropriate:

- Cultural/heritage sites
- Traditional crafts and artisanal work
- Performing arts (music, theater, dance, opera, and circus puppetry)
- Film, television, radio, and broadcasting
- Visual arts (paintings, sculpture, photography, printmaking, drawing, metal work, ceramics, and glass)
- Publishing and printed media (books and press)
- New media (gaming, animation, and content creation for web)
- Design (graphic, interior, fashion, jewelry, architecture, and landscape architecture)
- Commercial music

Figure 3.6 shows deeper examples of these industries. What is important to note is that not all industrial classifications capture these; it is difficult to do so, given the ways the systems are set up. In addition, some information may be protected, if it is possible to identify people or businesses through them. It is also useful to remember that this is not a one-size-fits all approach, and it can be adapted to your context and place.

The businesses themselves, within the creative industry, also have unique characteristics compared to other industries and largely center around small-to-medium-sized business (Creative Industries Council, 2018). They tend to be "small, young, and growing" (Beckett, 2022, n.p.). According to a 2018 report from the Creative Industries Council, 65% of creative businesses have 2–5 employees, and the 65% were also set up in the last five years (Beckett, 2022, n.p.; Creative Industries Council, 2018). Only 14% of creative businesses have been trading for more than 15 years, compared to 46% of small-and-medium-sized enterprises (SMEs) in the rest of the economy (Beckett, 2022), which shows that it is a relatively new and growing area; and it may have more fluctuations with who succeeds, given there are always new ones opening. And compared to companies in other economic sectors, creative businesses are more likely to grow. Fifty-six percent had reported growth in 2017, compared to only 45% of SMEs in the wider economy (Beckett, 2022). However,

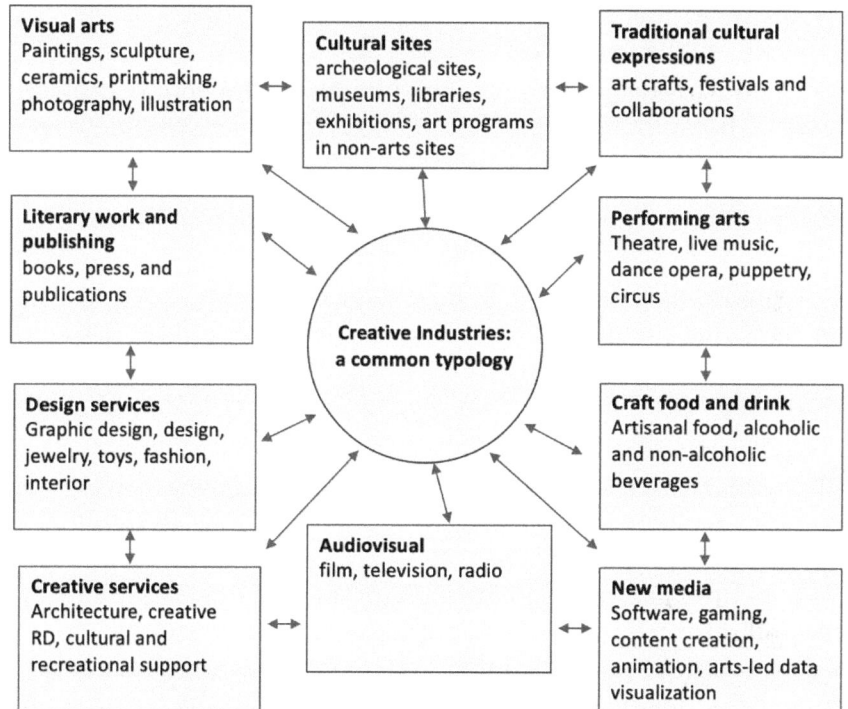

Figure 3.7 Examples of creative industries, created by Ashley.
Source: Adapted from UNCTAD

despite this growth, creative businesses find it difficult to access financing. The Creative Industries Policy and Evidence Centre at New Castle University share that the creative industries have these eight characteristics in the UK (Beckett, 2022, n.p.):

1. Creative businesses have a positive knock-on effect on the places around them (i.e. they generate spillover effects)
2. Creative business can be found in unexpected places (i.e. in addition to large clusters of activity they are also found in micro-clusters from rural to suburban areas)
3. A huge proportion of the creative workforce are freelancers
4. The Creative Industries has many higher-education graduates but suffers from skill shortages
5. A lack of diversity is holding the Creative Industries back

6. Investment in innovation is critical to success of the Creative Industries
7. Businesses in the Creative Industries are young, growing and ambitious—but poor access to finance means they risk running out of steam
8. The UK's Creative Industries are valuable and competitive on the global stage

Self-employed artists and creatives are also quite varied in terms of their business structures, the services and products they provide, and the different policies that may support their work (see Figure 3.7).

While there may be similarities with other countries—and there likely are—we also suggest that these kinds of studies and reports help provide a context and framing for how these industries materialize.

There are many ways to measure creative industries, and they all rely on various data sources that have strengths and weaknesses. The Americans for the Arts published *Creative Industries: Business & Employment in the Arts*, which draws on

Figure 3.8 Self-employed public mural artist Laci McCrea's traveling business run out of a truck and trailer.

Source: Photo by Amanda J. Ashley

Dun & Bradstreet business and employment data for nonprofit and for-profit organizations. Nationally, 673,656 businesses are involved in the creation or distribution of the arts, and they employ 3.48 million people (Americans for the Arts, 2017, 2023b). Their categories include museums and collections, visual arts and photography, film, radio and television, design and publishing, and arts schools and services. It's important to note that not all businesses register with Dun & Bradstreet; so, they have an underrepresentation. They draw on 644 9-digit Standard Industrial Classification to isolate their analysis. In another example, the National State Assembly of State Arts Agencies partnered with the National Endowment for the Arts (NEA) and the US Bureau of Economic Analysis (BEA) to develop an interactive dashboard that allows you to explore state-level data connected to arts and cultural production, as well as employment and compensation figures for the creative workforce (NASAA, 2020).

This section shows the commonalities and differences about how industries are understood, studied, and arranged at different scales and places. Now, we turn to focusing more on workers and the value of studying and planning for occupations and workers.

CREATIVE OCCUPATIONS

People typically focus on industries first when thinking about the creative economy; but that is just one component. There has been a seismic shift in recent years to also consider occupations and workers—the people that are the creators, makers, and doers of arts and creative activity (Ashley & Durham, 2015). This shift also helps us to understand artists as a labor force, or workers in their own right, rather than just as an amenity or draw for others. This occupational focus helps bring visibility to the breadth and depth of artistic activity. It also allows us to focus more on what workers need, rather than what industries need, given that industries are more likely to stay put rather than people. Artists can move in fluid ways not only in where they live and work, but also the commercial, nonprofit, and civic sectors in which they do that work. They often cobble careers together or curate diverse career experiences, which suggests a different set of strategies for support and investment to retain their talents and creativity. Some creative entrepreneurs harness their artistic expertise and talents within larger artistic spaces and districts. This pop-up fashion shop, by a local artist, is situated in the Baltimore Station North and Arts Entertainment District, which is also amplified by arts higher-education institutions like the Maryland Institute College of Art (see Figure 3.8). There is a cluster of arts activity in that space that is both permanent and ephemeral, leading to different opportunities for creative workers, businesses, and place-makers (Ashley, 2021).

A MOVEMENT FROM INDUSTRIES TO OCCUPATIONS

This push in the 2000s to not just think about an industrial perspective, but to consider the creative laborers, workers, makers, and similar occupations was profound. Florida (2002, 2005) popularized the idea of the Creative City, where one of

Figure 3.9 Pop-up fashion store in the Baltimore Station North Arts and Entertainment District.

Source: Photo by Amanda J. Ashley

the indicators focused on occupations. He estimated 15 million super-creatives and 23.3 million creative professionals in the United States, for a total of 38.3 million creative workers—translating to roughly 30% of the total US workforce. The super-creative class includes occupations across sectors: computer and math; architecture and engineering; life, physical and social sciences; education, training, and library; art, design, and entertainment; and sports and media. Creative professional occupations include management, business and financial operations, legal occupations, healthcare practitioners, technical operations, and high-end sales and sales. As you can see, not all are under an arts and culture umbrella; rather, they focus on higher education. This also leads to some concerns about inequity, as well as the reality that people bring lots of knowledge and expertise even if they do not have an advanced degree. In addition, there are also critiques that this term is far too broad given that not all these workers are creative.

Industrial analysis overwhelmingly underestimates the contributions of creative artists to a regional economy. It does not count self-employment, which is very high for artists. It does identify or count the ways that artists use their talents to help other sectors. It does demonstrate how artists may come up with new supplies or products that they need for their own work. It does not capture how artists use their incomes or forms of bartering to buy other local art products or services. It does not highlight how artists may provide entertainment and programming for people and consumers who would otherwise have to go out of their neighborhood, city, or region to access (Markusen & Shrock, 2006). In other words, industry analysis has many benefits, though it is incomplete when trying to ascertain the broader elements of the economy.

Scholars have sought to identify how these workers situate themselves geographically in the United States (Markusen & Shrock, 2006). They show that in reality, creators have different behaviors or attributes than industries, and they compellingly argue that artists choose a location to live and work based on an artistic and patron community, amenities, and affordable community. They think less about who may employ them, or what industry they are aligned with for employment. To test this,

Markusen and Shrock studied a distribution of artists across the largest US metropolitan areas, using data from the Public Use Microdata Samples, from the American Community Survey—for 1980, 1990, and 2000—which is a better data source for self-employed artists (Markusen & Shrock, 2006). They studied artists who were actors, directors, performance artists, dancers, musicians, composers, authors, writers, painters, sculptors, and photographers. They were primarily interested in those who self-identify as artists and have figured out how to pursue an arts career as their major or primary occupation. These workers and/or self-employed artists can do so through a variety of means, including employment, grants, commercial contracts, sale of their own original work, or other sources and support. They found that artists sort themselves in ways that are not closely tied to the patterns of city size or growth rates; this means that they need to be more thoughtfully targeted when creating and implementing economic development policy (Markusen & Shrock, 2006).

WHAT GETS INCLUDED AS A CREATIVE OCCUPATION? AND WHAT DO WE KNOW ABOUT THEM?

National governments are also interested in studying this occupational set. The US Bureau of Labor Statistics (BLS) reports that there were 2.57 million artists in the US workforce in 2020—representing 1.6% of all workers aged 16 and older. Their categories include 11 occupations: architects; art directors, fine artists, and animators; designers; actors; producers and directors; dancers and choreographers; musicians; announcers; writers and authors; photographers; and other artists and entertainers. While these categories only capture a portion of all artists in the workforce, this methodology has been used by the federal government for many decades, which makes it a valuable artist employment trend. Artist employment in this system does not cover art-connected jobs, including arts administrators, arts teachers, curators, technical staff, and fundraisers (Cohen, 2021). This information is helpful because it allows you to share broad trends, and to also say where data needs to be rounded out or fulfilled through other mechanisms.

When thinking through what occupations to include, the most common ones to consider are:

- Music artist
- Dance artist
- Writer or literary artist
- Performance artist (dancers, actors, and choreographers)
- Designer (fashion, architecture, landscape architecture, set, graphic, stage, and lighting)
- Visual artist (drawing, photography, painting, ceramics, illustration, printmaking, metals, and glass)
- Theater artist
- Film, television, or gaming artist
- Craft and heritage art

We also see artist censuses happening in practice at subnational levels. For example, Anchorage, Alaska released a census to count the number of amateur and professional musicians. They worked with MusicPortland and MusicOregon to develop the survey, so that they could use that information to build their music economy (Christopher, 2023).

As discussed in other chapters, there are a variety of economic development strategies for supporting artists as creative entrepreneurs. There are creative economy entrepreneurial loans, subsidized arts and workspace, incentives associated with developers building artist live-work spaces, friendly zoning and building codes that support different types of artistic processes, broad health insurance and mental health support, incubator spaces, and more. There are also developers and arts advocates outside of government entities that support artists and their needs throughout their career cycles. In addition, you will see these interventions pop up across public, nonprofit, and private sectors—given not only the need to address market failures, but also a recognition that some artists' activity leads to new products, innovations, and processes that generate economic growth and development. In Figure 3.10, you'll see an artist cooperative space—in the RiNo Arts District in Denver, Colorado—that offers studio and gallery space. This is a formal industrial space that once housed an ice factory and has gone through the process of adaptive reuse to take on a new economic activity.

Figure 3.10 Dry Ice Factory, an artists' cooperative, is in the RiNo Arts District and houses studios and gallery space.

Source: Photo by Amanda J. Ashley

OCCUPATIONAL UNIQUENESS IN COBBLING CAREERS AND CROSSING SECTORS

There's also been a push to understand how artists might be different from other occupations. For example, artists tend to have higher levels of self-occupation. They also have higher levels of education, compared to their earning power. They are also more likely, than other occupations, to have multiple jobs (Alper & Wassall, 1999). As Alper and Wassall (1999, p. 1) note:

> Webster's New World Dictionary defines moonlighting as "the practice of holding a second regular job in addition to one's main job." Unless otherwise noted, in this study a moonlighting worker's main, or primary, job is defined as the one in which he or she works (or usually works) the most hours. "It has been recognized for several decades that artists

as a group often hold multiple jobs throughout their careers, either by moonlighting or by switching among several short-term jobs." Although the term "moonlighting artist" implies that the artist job is the primary job, artistic jobs can also be, and often are, held as second jobs. For example, someone who is a graphic designer may work for a technology company as a coder while volunteering their graphic design skills for a local theatre company. A viola player may have a full-time position in their city's symphony, may also be managing bands through their own businesses, and may also play in an ensemble that visits K-12 education. These are more the norm than the exception.

Part of understanding artists is to consider the ways that they move across different sectors for their work and creative interests. The three primary sectors are commercial, nonprofit, and community (Markusen & Shrock, 2006, p. 7).

> The commercial sector encompasses for-profit firms that employ artists, contract with them for services, buy their work or process, and package and market their work for distribution. It also includes work that self-employed artists create and market directly, as in art fairs, on the web, via commissions, performances on tour, and individual teaching for pay.
> The not-for-profit sector encompasses work done for or with the support of the public sector or legally incorporated nonprofit organizations, such as museums, orchestras, opera houses, nonprofit presses, religious and social service organizations. It includes public art commissions and work supported by nonprofit foundation grants.
> The community sector encompasses forums and organizations often called informal, traditional, or unincorporated, where artists create and share their work unmediated by either markets or not-for-profit organizations, whether paid or not.
> (Markusen & Shrock, 2006)

In a study of Los Angeles and San Francisco artists, Markusen and Shrock (2006) found that crossing sectors was common rather than abnormal or rare. This connectivity mattered, as shared more in Chapter 5 of creative economy systems. A claim could be made that the wealthy Los Angeles film industry leaders should invest in the nonprofit theater scene, because that's where actors and actresses learned aspects of their craft that the film industry relied on for their workforce. These connections were not always about a financial benefit either. Sometimes artists were able to make a living and stayed connected or supported nonprofits they previously worked with, because they liked their mission, valued their work, or were grateful for their own experiences with that nonprofit.

We are also in a rapidly changing landscape of broadening the definition of who is an artist and a creator, as media influencers and content creators are gaining traction and marking a new kind of artistic sub-occupation. The rise of the internet has contributed to content creators who are responsible for the ideation, creation, and distribution of content to develop a target audience and brand. For example, 10-year-old Ryan Kaji is one of the most well-known content creators—one of the highest paid, with $30 million annually in 2021. He has nine channels on YouTube as well as shows on Amazon Kids+ and Nick Jr., which has led to product licensing (e.g. Skechers, Roblox), merchandising, and advertising. His animated superhero alter ego, Red Titan, has appeared in the Macy's Thanksgiving Day Parade balloon (Luscombe, 2021). With the advance of digital ad technology, advertisers have realized that they could get more with microtargeting by following everyday people, rather than a famous person or a celebrity. There are also some questions about whether this influencer and content creator is counted as an artist or as a creative; and these are fuzzy boundaries to consider.

Shapiro and Siddhartha (2019) studied nine major platforms with publicly available data: Amazon Publishing, eBay, Etsy, Instagram, Shapeways, Tumblr, Twitch, WordPress, and YouTube. These content generators earn income in multiple ways, including website ads, sponsorships, influencer compensation, revenue from social media traffic, gifts from fans, and direct sales. This study focuses on the growth in 2017 of one piece of the internet economic landscape that is often overlooked: a booming economy of new American creators. They (2019, n.p.) write:

Before the internet, an aspiring writer, photographer, filmmaker, musician, craftsperson or other type of artist had to depend on agents, managers or dumb luck to be considered by a publisher, music label, film studio or gallery to showcase their work. These middlemen and corporations were the gatekeepers of American popular culture. Today, those aspiring writers, musicians, filmmakers, and other creators—both aspiring professional and hobbyist—can reach national and even worldwide audiences by simply posting their creations on a range of internet platforms. And if people respond, they can begin to earn income from their creative activities. These creators are a growing part of a major segment of the American workforce who now operate as independent agents or workers on a part-time or full-time basis. The McKinsey Global Institute has estimated that 8 percent of working-age Americans, or some 12.6 million people, earn income from performing independent work on internet platforms.

To estimate these numbers, they collected and analyzed the most recent data provided by those nine leading platforms themselves and/or by financial and market analysts who follow them, since they could not use government statistics or private data. They did not cover music or fine arts here, which shows that there is insufficient information to demonstrate how to quantify this new creative economy, which is unsurprising given the new-ness of the field. As a result, their data is very conservative.

As Shapiro and Siddhartha (2019) note, these creators earn income in a range of ways such as posting on these platforms and sharing advertising revenues with the platform, based on their attracting substantial numbers of visitors or "eyeballs" to view their creations. In addition, platforms such as Etsy, Amazon Publishing, and Shapeways enable creators to directly sell their creations; Twitch shares revenues from monthly subscriptions to a creator's video game streaming or gaming comments, and creators on Instagram can earn income as "influencers" who promote a partner's brand or branded products.

However, among those accounts, there is an incredible discrepancy between the amount of money women and BIPOC creators make compared to their White, male counterparts. Adobe researchers reported that men make $55 per hour, while women make 20% less ($44). Meanwhile, White monetizers make an average of $62 per hour, while people of color make 21% less ($49) (Barr, 2022). These diversity, equity, and inclusion (DEI) issues are very important and need to be centered when thinking about creative economy policies at various scales.

WHAT'S CREATIVITY WORTH?

The United Nations Conference on Trade and Development (UNCTAD) predicted that the global valuation of the creative economy will reach 10% of global GDP before 2023 and is currently $985 billion (Buckholtz, 2021). This focus on creative industries, which consists of creative trade, labor, and production, is a tool for sustainable development, given that its growth outpaces all other industries. In 2021, UNCTAD proclaimed in the International Year of the Creative Economy for Sustainable Development:

> For the first time, G20 leaders have recognized culture and creative industries as drivers for sustainable development and in fostering economic resilience, and G20 ministers of culture have recommended including culture, cultural heritage, and the creative sector in post-pandemic recovery strategies.
> (Buckholtz, 2021)

UNCTAD shares examples of how robust the creative economy is, and how much potential remains. Phiona Okumu, Spotify's Head of Music for sub-Saharan Africa, suggests that streaming services and digital platforms are contributors, by explaining how African pop can be shared with global audiences in ways that they haven't been able to do so before. Bollywood, the Mumbai-base engine of India's film industry, and Nollywood, Africa's largest film (and private) employer in Africa, are able to reach more audiences using these technologies. The impact on South-South trade is significant because of its export potential (Buckholtz, 2021). These burgeoning creative economies are also working on ways to help new entrepreneurs access markets and confront challenges with labor inequities, piracy, and more. For example, the African Development Bank created a website and an app to help African entrepreneurs in the fashion and textile industries, particularly women and young people, connect to suppliers, buyers, and investors. In Latin America, IDB's Orange Innovation Challenge provides grants for creative and cultural activity business models that demonstrate a clear impact (Buckholtz, 2021).

MEASURING THE CREATIVE ECONOMY

Economic geographers, economic developers, and urban planning scholars search for data and proxy information to identify and scope activities, productivity, impacts, and flows of goods and services. Some of these focus on specific industries like film or fashion (Scott, 1996; Currid-Halkett, 2009). They are also interested in discovering the impacts and contributions of different arts and cultural programming and institutions, using different economic development assessment mechanisms. At the national advocacy level, for example, Americans for the Arts has used robust research methodologies to develop the *Arts & Economic Prosperity* project. This project helps US cities scope the impact of their nonprofit arts, cultural organizations, and audiences (Americans for the Arts, 2023a). It documents the economic contributions of the arts in 341 diverse communities and regions across the United States, representing all 50 states and the District of Columbia. In the most recent round, they found that nationally:

> The nonprofit arts and culture industry generated $166.3 billion of economic activity during 2015—$63.8 billion in spending by arts and cultural organizations and an additional $102.5 billion in event-related expenditures by their audiences. This activity supported 4.6 million jobs and generated $27.5 billion in revenue to local, state, and federal governments (a yield well beyond their collective $5 billion in arts allocations).
> (Americans for the Arts, 2023a, n.p.)

They argued that these findings "put to rest a misconception" that investments in the arts come at the expense of other economic growth areas (Americans for the Arts, 2023a, n.p.).

States and cities are also common publishers of economic impact studies. They may use the American for the Arts project mentioned earlier or their own data analysis systems. There are also other services that cities rely on when they don't have the capacity or knowledge to run the numbers themselves. For example, the Creative Vitality (CV) project is an increasingly popular scoping and comparative mechanism. This initiative grew out of the need for the public sector to share that their creative economy is more than just nonprofit arts. Through a subscription, cities can access the CVSuite, an online tool to help them understand their strengths and weaknesses, in comparison to other cities. The software was developed and is maintained by the Western States Arts Federation (WESTAF), which is a regional nonprofit arts service organization, dedicated to strengthening the financial, organizational, and policy infrastructure of the arts in the US American West, through their assistance to state arts agencies, arts organizations, and artists.

HOW TO MOVE FORWARD

Now that you have a better understanding of the creative economy, the rest of the book will help you think more about how to do actual design and implementation work. In preparation for this, we suggest beginning to consider what may be useful to help you move forward.

You may want to do scoping to identify the artistic disciplines, practices, and organizations that are part of your community or the areas where you'd like to see further development. You may want to collaborate with arts or arts-related leaders in your organization to determine what your arts assets are. It's important to make sure you have good representation; you may consider doing an arts asset map to help you see where your organic or planned clusters of activities exist or do not. For example, the City of Austin (TX) Economic Development Department and the Cultural Affairs Division curated a Cultural Asset Mapping Project (CAMP) that culminated in a report in 2018. They share that "cultural asset mapping is a form of community mapping—a participatory planning technique that uses collaborative exercises to collect citizen input on their surrounding environment" (City of Austin, 2018, p. 4).

The community mapping approach is meant to bring community voices to the front and center of city planning efforts and to provide a framework through which people can take an active role in identifying their own needs. But most importantly, it is meant to help expand a community's own understanding of their local assets and inform the effects of creating place-based solutions, in response to their community's specific needs (City of Austin, 2018, p. 4). For example, the CAMP project included focus groups, an online map and survey, a take-home kit for mapping exercises, and specific district sessions—to help identify ecosystems and concentrations, inform strategic investment, support planning, guide partnerships and collaborations, support creative placemaking, focus investments and resources, and empower people to organize.

Mapping is a very powerful tool. Cities and scholars are also trying other methods to make sense of their creative economies in ways that traditional metrics or mapping approaches do not. For example, Darwin, the capital city of Australia's Northern Territory, worked to see itself as a Creative City through a mental mapping exercise with Creative City workers. This approach, which culminated in a Geographic Information Systems map, unveiled hidden areas of clustered activity and spaces of inspiration, which would not have been captured normally (Brennan-Horley, 2010). This focus on "vernacular voices," created new ways of thinking about policymaking and intervention to help facilitate their creative economy agenda.

TAKEAWAYS

This chapter provided a big-picture look at the definitions of creative economy, including the following concepts:

- There is no consensus on how to define what "creative economy" means, which is both an opportunity and a challenge. However, there is a list of industries and occupations to consider.
- Creative economies and cultural economies are not the same. Cultural economies tend to focus on nonprofits and traditional art forms. Creative economies encompass for-profit enterprises, across design, television, film, gaming, animation, publishing, and other areas.

- Creative economies tend to focus on three parts: creative industries, creative occupation, and creative places. These have different profiles, forms of measurement, interventions, and programmatic structures.
- There are many ways to measure the creative economy and its components, drawing on varied data sources. These sources are not perfect; but they give you a sense of how to identify important elements.
- A good place to start, if interested in a creative economy approach, is to undertake creative and cultural asset mapping.

Discussion questions:

1. How do you define the creative economy? What are the advantages and disadvantages of having a universal definition?
2. What is the difference between a creative industry and a creative occupational approach? What economic development strategies would you use to support each?
3. What are anchor institutions? List one type and explain how it supports the creative economy.
4. Do you think content creators are artists? How are they reshaping the way we think about the creative economy?
5. What are the unique attributes of creative businesses and creative workers?

Activities

- Select one quote from the book. Share why you selected it, as well as how it contradicts, reinforces, or provides richness to what you know or assume.
- Identify an art, creative, and cultural plan in a community near you. Share to what extent they talk about the creative economy, as well as what recommendations you have for them to address it in greater depth.
- Search the internet for an infographic, blog, or podcast that is connected to the creative economy. Share it with a classmate or colleague and explain its connection to the course material.
- Draw a cultural asset map from your own personal experiences and knowledge. Compare this to those of your

classmates or colleagues. Share what is similar and different, on comparison? Design and explain a process for detailing a more robust map.

REFERENCES

Alper, N., & Wassall, G. (1999). More Than Once in a Blue Moon: Multiple Job Holdings. *American Artists*. www.arts.gov/sites/default/files/BlueMoon.pdf

American Artscape. (2023). "In Celebration of Artful Lives." November, 2023. https://www.arts.gov/sites/default/files/2023-american-artscape-no1-rev.pdf

Americans for the Arts. (2017). *The Creative Industries in the United States*. www.americansforthearts.org/sites/default/files/pdf/2017/by_program/reports_and_data/creative/2017_UnitedStates_NationalOnePager_Color.pdf

Americans for the Arts. (2023a). *Arts Economic Prosperity 5*. www.americansforthearts.org/by-program/reports-and-data/research-studies-publications/arts-economic-prosperity-5

Americans for the Arts. (2023b). *Creative Industries Business & Employment in the Arts: Measuring the Scope of the Nation's Arts-Related Industries*. www.americansforthearts.org/by-program/reports-and-data/research-studies-publications/creative-industries

Ashley, A. J. (2014). *Creating Capacity: Strategic Approaches to Managing Arts, Culture, and Entertainment Districts*. www.americansforthearts.org/sites/default/files/Culture-And-Entertainment-DistrictsManagement.pdf

Ashley, A. J. (2017). Strategic Planning for Arts, Entertainment, and Cultural Districts. In *How to Do Creative Placemaking*. Washington, DC: National Endowment for the Arts.

Ashley, A. J. (2021). The Micropolitics of Performance: Pop-up Art as a Complementary Method for Civic Engagement and Public Participation. *Journal of Planning Education and Research*, 41(2), 173–187.

Ashley, A. J., & Durham, L. (2015, March). *The Working Artist: Boise's Hidden Economy of Creators, Makers, and Doers*. https://ctycms.com/id-boise/docs/urban-research_mar-2015_final(7).pdf

Ashley, A. J., & Touchton, M. (2016). Reconceiving Military Base Redevelopment: Land Use on Mothballed US Bases. *Urban Affairs Review*, 52(3), 391–420.

Barr, K. (2022). Women and BIPOC Are Earning Way Less than White Men When Monetizing Online Content. *GIZMODO*. https://gizmodo.com/adobe-influencers-ad-revenue-tiktok-youtube-1849668326

Beckett (2022, June). *Eight Things to Know About the Creative Industries*. Creative Industries Policy and Evidence Centre. https://pec.ac.uk/blog/eight-things-to-know-about-the-creative-industries

Beyers, W., Bonds, A., Wenzl, A., & Sommers, P. (2004). *The Economic Impact of Seattle's Music Industry*. City of Seattle: Office of Economic Development.

Boston Redevelopment Authority. (2005). *Boston's Creative Economy BRA/Research*. www.bostonplans.org/getattachment/01decb82-3ba5-4dea-a8d1-fdeaa39495d6/

Brennan-Horley, C. (2010). Mental Mapping the "Creative City". *Journal of Maps*, 6(1), 250–259.

Buckholtz, A. (2021, December). *Creative Economy Takes Center Stage.* https://unctad.org/news/creative-economy-takes-center-stage

Callanan, L. (2022, January 31). *Defining the Creative Economy—Upstart Co. Lab.* Retrieved February 15, 2022, from https://upstartco-lab.org/creativity_lens/defining-creative-economy/

Christopher, B. (2023, August 29). *Music Census Aims to Count Alaska's Musicians and Measure Their Impact.* https://alaskabeacon.com/briefs/music-census-aims-to-count-alaskas-musicians-and-measure-their-impact/

City of Austin. (2018). *The CAMP Report.* https://drive.google.com/file/d/11LfexH2EovNkDSJnlTBqDxMVC2seUuR-/view

City of Philadelphia Office of Arts, Culture and the Creative Economy. (n.d.). *Mission. CreativePHL.* www.creativephl.org/about/mission/

Cohen, R. (2021). *Americans for the Arts Artists in US Workforce: 2006–2020.* www.americansforthearts.org/by-program/reports-and-data/legislation-policy/naappd/artists-in-the-us-workforce-2006-2020

Colorado Office of Economic Development and International Trade. (2020, October 21). *2020 Colorado Creative Economy Report Reveals Critical Role Creative Industries Play in State's Recovery and Resiliency.* https://oedit.colorado.gov/press-release/2020-colorado-creative-economy-report-reveals-critical-role-creative-industries-play

Colorado Office of Economic Development and International Trade. (2023). *History of Colorado Creative Industries.* https://oedit.colorado.gov/history-of-colorado-creative-industries

Colorado Office of Economic Development and International Trade. (n.d.). *Colorado Creative Industries.* https://oedit.colorado.gov/colorado-creative-industries

Coy, P. (2000, August 27). The Creative Economy. *Bloomberg.com.* Retrieved February 15, 2022, from www.bloomberg.com/news/articles/2000-08-27/the-creative-economy

Creative Industries Council. (2018). *CIC Access to Finance Research Report.* https://cic-media.s3.eu-west-2.amazonaws.com/media/471225/cic-access-to-finance-research-report-june-2018.pdf

Creative Industries Policy and Evidence Centre (PEC). (2022). *National Statistics on the Creative Industries.* https://pec.ac.uk/news/national-statistics-on-the-creative-industries

Currid-Halkett, E. (2009). *The Warhol Economy: How Fashion, Art, and Music Drive.* New York City: Princeton University Press.

DeNatale, D., & Wassall, G. H. (2007). *The Creative Economy: A New Definition.* www.nefa.org/sites/default/files/documents/ResearchCreativeEconReport2007.pdf

District of Columbia. (2019). *Title of the Cultural Plan: Executive Summary [PDF].* https://planning.dc.gov/sites/default/files/dc/sites/op/publication/attachments/FINAL%20CULTURAL%20PLAN%20exec%20summary%20%28Web%20Version%29.pdf

Florida, R. (2002). *The Rise of the Creative Class.* New York: Basic Books/Perseus Books Group.

Florida, R. (2005). *Cities and the Creative Class.* New York: Routledge.

Foord, J. (2009). Strategies for Creative Industries: An International Review. *Creative Industries Journal*, 1(2), 91–113.

Howkins, J. (2002). *The Creative Economy*. London: Penguin.

Ivey, B. (2008). *Arts, Inc.: How Greed and Neglect Have Destroyed Our Cultural Rights*. Berkeley, CA: University of California Press.

Killacky, J. R. (2022, December). Arts Commentary: Remembering the Culture Wars of the '90s. *Arts Fuse*. https://artsfuse.org/265769/arts-commentary-remembering-the-culture-wars-of-the-90s/

Liu, J. (2023, August). Hollywood Strikes Have Already Had a $3 Billion Impact on California's Economy, Experts Say: It's Causing "A Lot of Hardship". *CNBC*. www.cnbc.com/2023/08/09/hollywood-strikes-have-had-3-billion-impact-on-california-economy-so-far.html

Loh, C. G., Ashley, A. J., Kim, R., Durham, L., & Bubb, K. (2022). Placemaking in Practice: Municipal Arts and Cultural Plans' Approaches to Placemaking and Creative Placemaking. *Journal of Planning Education and Research*, 0739456X221100503.

Luscombe, B. (2021, November 12). How Ryan Kaji Became the Most Popular 10-Year-Old in the World. *Time*. https://time.com/6116624/ryan-kaji-youtube/

Markusen, A., & Shrock, G. (2006). The Artistic Dividend: Urban Artistic Specialisation and Economic Development Implications. *Urban Studies*, 43(10), 1661–1686.

Markusen, A., Wassall, G. H., DeNatale, D., & Cohen, R. (2008). Defining the Creative Economy: Industry and Occupational Approaches. *Economic Development Quarterly*, 22(1), 24–45.

McCarthy, K., Ondaatje, E., Zakaras, L., & Brooks, A. (2004). *Gifts of the Muse Reframing the Debate about the Benefits of the Arts*. www.rand.org/content/dam/rand/pubs/monographs/2005/RAND_MG218.pdf

Montana Arts Council. (2014). *Montana Arts Council Strategic Plan 2014–2021 [PDF]*. https://art.mt.gov/_docs/MAC-Framework-2014-2021-FINAL.pdf

National Assembly of State Arts Agencies (NASAA). (2020). *Creative Economy State Profiles*. https://nasaa-arts.org/nasaa_research/creative-economy-state-profiles/#nasaa_field_4

O'Connor, J. (2017, July 25). Not Jobs and Growth But Post-Capitalism—and Creative Industries Show the Way. *The Conversation*. https://theconversation.com/not-jobs-and-growth-but-post-capitalism-and-creative-industries-show-the-way-79650

Otis College of Art and Design. (2023). *The College of Art and Design*. www.otis.edu

Reed, B. (2023, July). Fran Drescher's Fiery Speech Against Hollywood Studios Goes Viral as Actors Strike. *The Guardian*. www.theguardian.com/culture/2023/jul/14/fran-drescher-speech-actors-strike-writers-strike-sag-aftra-hollywood-ceos

Rushton, M. (2015, April). Are Nonprofit Art Organizations Special? *Arts Journal*. www.artsjournal.com/worth/2015/04/are-nonprofit-arts-organizations-special/

Ryberg-Webster, S., & Ashley, A. J. (2018). The Nexus of Arts and Preservation: A Case Study of Cleveland's Detroit Shoreway Community Development Organization. *Change Over Time*, 8(1), 32–52.

Schulman, M. (2023). Why Are TV Writers So Miserable. *The New Yorker.* www.newyorker.com/culture/notes-on-hollywood/why-are-tv-writers-so-miserable

Scott, A. J. (1996). The Craft, Fashion, and Cultural-Products Industries of Los Angeles: Competitive Dynamics and Policy Dilemmas in a Multisectoral Image-Producing Complex. *Annals of the Association of American Geographers, 86*(2), 306–323.

Shapiro, R., & Siddhartha, A. (2019). Taking Root: The Growth of America's New Creative Economy. *Re:create.* www.recreatecoalition.org/wp-content/uploads/2019/02/ReCreate-2017-New-Creative-Economy-Study.pdf

Sheridan College. (n.d.). *Home Explore Your Possibilities.* www.sheridan.edu/

Sonneland, H. K. (2018, December 4). Explainer: What Is Colombia's Orange Economy? *AS/COA.* Retrieved February 15, 2022, from www.as-coa.org/articles/explainer-what-colombias-orange-economy

Stuckey, H. L., & Nobel, J. (2010). The Connection Between Art, Healing, and Public Health: A Review of Current Literature. *American Journal of Public Health, 100*(2), 254–263.

United Nations (n.d.). New Economics for Sustainable Development: Creative Economy. https://www.un.org/sites/un2.un.org/files/orange_economy_14_march.pdf

Wali, A., Severson, R., & Longoni, M. (2002). *Informal Arts: Finding Cohesion, Capacity and Other Cultural Benefits in Unexpected Places.* Chicago, IL: Chicago Center for Arts Policy at Columbia College. www.americansforthearts.org/sites/default/files/informal_arts_full_report.pdf

Wallis, C. (2011, July 6). *Arts Policy Library: Informal Arts.* https://createquity.com/2011/07/arts-policy-library-informal-arts/

Wilkinson, A. (2023, July 13). Hollywood's Historic Double Strike Explained. *Vox.* www.vox.com/culture/2023/7/13/23793828/sag-aftra-strike-wga-hollywood

Woltmann, S. (2023, July). *Everything You Need to Know About the SAG-AFTRA + AMPTP Negotiations Backstage.* www.backstage.com/magazine/article/sag-aftra-strike-negotiations-explained-76246/

Place and the creative economy

Chapter 4

INTRODUCTION

Studies of creative economies often focus on the flow of ideas, goods, and services, or on how production and labor force systems function. However, these flows and systems exist in space and interact with particular places in specific ways. Geographers think about "space" as the physical location and characteristics of a geographic area, whereas "place" is what gives a space personal, cultural, or historical meaning through the built environment and human activity (Low, 2017). This chapter will discuss how the creative economy intersects with a place in two primary ways. First, there are creative economic activities that are clustered or place-based in the same way that other basic industries have been historically. This concentration could be at the city scale like the motion picture industry in Hollywood, the country music industry in Nashville, or at the neighborhood or district scale like the 798 Beijing Arts District or the Brooklyn Navy Yards in New York City (see Figure 4.1). Second, cities and states have increasingly invested in economic development strategies that create or capitalize on a sense of place to draw residents and visitors; arts districts and placemaking are prominent strategies associated with this approach. So, the arts and artists can be amenities that draw others into a place, creators of products that have localized and spillover economic effects, or both. These strategies come from different motivations and economic theories. For example, a traditional large-scale performing arts district

Figure 4.1 Gallery in the *798 Beijing Arts District*.
Source: Photo by Leeluv, Wikimedia Commons

(e.g. Denver Performing Arts Complex, Philadelphia Avenue of the Arts) is driven by tourism. The Los Angeles film industry, and its concentration in Hollywood, is driven by innovation and export-based activity.

The creative economy encompasses activities and products that are not necessarily tied to any particular place. However, increasingly places have become critical components of the creative economy and may even be considered products themselves, leading to concerns about authenticity. As many cities in the western world have shifted from industrial production to service and amenity-driven economies—where many workers choose where to live based on the quality of life rather than the job location—creating a sense of place that attracts residents and tourists has become a vital economic development strategy. Public, private, nonprofit, and civic sector actors highlight existing or create new arts and cultural-driven activity—both to reinvent lagging or shifting local economies by generating jobs in new sectors and to capture knowledge workers and tourists who have many choices about places to live and visit as discussed in Chapter 3.

Although economic and industrial geographers have long focused on flows of goods, people, and services, these new creative economies demand a different theoretical approach, as they now rely heavily on socially constructed ideas of place. In other words, places' identities now come more from deliberate place branding and amenity construction than from being, say, the furniture capital of the world or a steel-making city. To be competitive in a globalized and virtualized economy—in which industrial production shifts to the lowest-cost location and knowledge workers and management can choose to locate wherever they want—places must be beautiful, exciting, unique, or particularly livable.

International place-based competitions increase the pressure to promote cities as celebrated cultural Meccas. Applications are due six years in advance for the European Capital of Culture Competition, hosted by the European Commission. The highly competitive application process asks cities to define how they use culture to foster development, diversity, and heritage, as well as what unique cultural features their city can offer to bring tourists to Europe. The three selected cities receive $1.5 million dollars to spend on events and cultural infrastructure over the course of one year. In 2022, the winning cities were Novi Sad, Serbia; Kaunas, Lithuania; and Esch-sur-Alzette, Luxembourg. Novi Sad used the theme of bridges as their moniker, highlighting the multiple bridges into their city; they hosted more than 1,500 cultural events in that year. Kaunas used the opportunity to boast about its historic architecture and create a new mythical beast of Kaunas as a narrative thread that ran through more than 600 projects and 1,000 events. Esch-sur-Alzette had been an industrial steel town, largely shut down in the 1970s; they featured redeveloped warehouses made into new concert halls, galleries, and cinemas.

The city identity-definition and branding, associated with these efforts, has only become more complex as social media used by both "regular people" and influencers impact locals' and outsiders' views of cities. Consequently, we've seen cities seek to label themselves as art or creative cities or develop this identity at sub-scales like neighborhoods or districts. In the City of Denver there are eight neighborhood art districts that formed organically through self-organizing businesses, nonprofits, and artists; they are now established and promoted places. Each one features something a little different. The Art District on Santa Fe is all about art galleries, artist studios, and restaurants. The Golden Triangle Creative District is home to eight museums as well as galleries, art studios, and specialty stores. River North Art District (RiNo) is a hot spot for furniture makers, sculptors, and other individual makers. 40 West Arts has a lot of public art installations and murals. The districts have received some capacity-building assistance from Denver Arts & Venues, the city and county arts agency; they operate independently otherwise.

In this chapter, we'll explore how place and the creative economy intersect in the ways mentioned earlier, some history of place-based arts economic development, and some of the benefits and pitfalls of these types of economic development strategies. We'll first discuss why and how place matters, and how arts and culture contribute to a sense of place.

SENSE OF PLACE

Humans are drawn to places they can recognize and to which they feel a sense of connection. Often, but not always, these places include memorable physical features and are built on a human scale. People's experiences of those places may include memorable events with friends, family, or strangers. This recognition and connection can be widely recognized, almost universally. For example, many older cities have a strong visual identity that makes it easy to identify them. Take for example, Venice, Italy; Xi'an, China; or Havana, Cuba. To elaborate on one of those examples, Venice's distinctive architecture style, street layout, and canal system make it instantly recognizable to people all over the world, even if they've never visited; this creates an instant sense of connection and familiarity, if they do visit. If you visit the Piazza San Marco, you know exactly where you are.

This recognition and connection, which we call "sense of place," can also be deeply personal and specific and associated with a place that is not well known at all. A particular city block, a bend in a country road, or the center of a village can all inspire a sense of meaning, familiarity, and belonging. This disconnect between a personal sense of place and a more universal sense of place was illustrated pointedly by one of our authors in a Ph.D. class in urban and regional planning. All the students had to make a presentation with photos about a place that was meaningful to them. One of the authors, a student in the class, had planned a visit back to her hometown, a typical small American suburb. While she was there, on a dismal, cloudy day in March, she took pictures for the presentation. After she presented, the professor commented on how uninteresting this place was, and how poorly it adhered to planning best practices. The student was a little taken aback. This was place, after all, where her parents still lived and where she had ridden her bike to the library, walked to get ice cream with friends, and learned to drive. She realized that even though there was nothing remarkable or even commendable about her hometown, that didn't matter to her; she still felt deeply attached to it and had expected the professor to understand that. Even though her hometown wouldn't spark a sense of recognition or connection in anyone who hadn't lived there (unlike, say, Venice), the sense of place she felt was real.

City leaders, however, can't just rely on longtime residents' sense of place to stay competitive. They know how important a sense of place is to attract new residents, workers, and visitors, because people seek out and return to places where they feel a sense of connection and comfort. As J.B. Jackson puts it, "A visit to one of [these places] is a small, but significant, event. We are refreshed and elated each time we are there" (Jackson, 1995, p. 24). The American cities of the 19th and early 20th centuries generally exhibited strong senses of place. Full of people and horses, and eventually some cars, they were characterized by over-the-top architecture, enormous signs, sidewalk sales, and entertainment venues (see Figure 4.2).

Unfortunately, standard planning, zoning, architecture, and development practices over the past century have often resulted in placeless geographies—with endlessly repeated stores, housing types, and freeways. These spaces are neither human scaled, nor do they offer any sense of recognition and connection. While they may be useful in some ways, they are utterly forgettable. People come to these spaces out of necessity, rather than seeking them out for enjoyment. William H. Whyte diagnosed this "lack of clear place identity" as early as 1968

Figure 4.2 Woodward Avenue, Detroit, Michigan, sometime between 1910 and 1920.
Source: Photo courtesy of Library of Congress, Prints & Photographs Division, Detroit

(Elsheshtawy, 2015, p. 401). To be clear, individual residents can still feel a connection to those types of places, out of familiarity and memory, as in the Ph.D. class example; but, those types of connections are unlikely to draw in new residents, workers, or visitors. Since the early 2000s, there has been an increasing emphasis on creating a sense of place in US cities, especially in downtowns. The hope is that these areas will start to feel like places where people feel that sense of attachment, memory, and recognition. However, creating a sense of place all at once is tricky; it may not result in as much attachment as is generated by places that have developed an identity over time and as a result of many people's care and attention. For example, some suburbs have created "city centers" that feel a little odd, because all the buildings are new and in the same architectural style, the location is a bit arbitrary (where there was land available), and there aren't independent, organic reasons that take people through the space in the course of a normal day.

ARTS AND CULTURE AS COMPONENTS OF A SENSE OF PLACE

Public art

Often funded by "Percent for Art" programs (which we discuss in greater detail, later in the chapter), public art (often, but not always, visual art), defined here as "works of art created explicitly for display in public spaces" (Kingwell, 2019, p. 584), has become a staple of public investment in cities as well as new private development. From large installations created by big-name artists to community-created murals and temporary pop-ups, public art appears in downtowns and city neighborhoods all over the world (Ashley, 2021). One of the stated objectives of including art in public spaces is to "humanize" modernist public areas that are otherwise not inviting or at a human scale (Hall & Robertson, 2001). Another objective is to create a sense of ownership over the space, which creates human connection and an ethos of care (in other words, the hope is that people will not vandalize or litter if they feel that ownership) (Sharp et al., 2005). Yet another objective is to create a sense of place. Public officials and private developers believe that public art contributes to a sense of place in two related ways. First, public art may try to connect to local history and culture to emphasize a place-based identity that has perhaps been lost over time. For example, Minneapolis's Mill Ruins Park contains remains of the foundations and infrastructure of demolished mills and their waterpower system, connected through walkways and interpreted through signage. This approach may employ local artists or craftspeople as part of an effort to make people feel more connected to place. This approach may (or may not) explicitly celebrate and involve marginalized communities whose histories have been hidden (Sharp et al., 2005). Second, public art often attempts to make place visually distinctive, so that people associate the artwork with the site. This approach can also include arts and cultural events that become identified with an area. In either case, art contributes to the city's public identity (Hall & Robertson, 2001). For example, Chicago's Millennium Park contains the metallic sculpture Cloud Gate ("The Bean"), by Anish Kapoor, a public art installation that has become an iconic symbol of the city (see Figure 4.3).

Figure 4.3 *Cloud Gate*, by Anish Kapoor, at Millennium Park, Chicago, IL.
Source: Photo by Brian Loh

Critics point out that people mostly just accept that art in public spaces is a good thing, either for aesthetic or social reasons, with little interest and even less funding available for evaluating its actual impacts. For example, if public art is meant to foster a sense of place, and it doesn't, it might be better to spend that public money on another intervention that would better further that goal. Art experts complain about the uneven quality of public art, saying that much of it is deliberately designed to be boring, so it doesn't offend anyone (Kingwell, 2019; Hall & Robertson, 2001; Phillips, 1988). In some instances, a public art fails to thread this needle and is ultimately modified or removed to end the controversy, as with Richard Serra's Tilted Arc (Hein, 1996), or is removed because the cultural conditions under which it was installed have changed so much that it is no longer acceptable, such as with US Confederate monuments (Rooney et al., 2021). There are also instances where a public art is "insurgent"—not authorized or funded by any public body; Banksy's stenciled graffiti art, largely painted on buildings in the UK, is one of the most prominent examples. This insurgent art is sometimes removed because it signals "disorder." Others contend that public art can be part of a project of gentrification and "neo-liberalized urban authoritarianism" (Harvey, 2000), whereby authorities impose a particular aesthetic and narrative on the city, in an attempt to control who belongs and what kinds of behavior are allowed (Sharp et al., 2005). Even public art that is meant to be inclusive in its cultural representation may fall short and engage in tokenism or even disrespect (Zitcer & Almanzar, 2020).

Finally, insofar as public art is meant to evoke a particular feeling or connection, there is not much understanding of how public art actually affects people's experiences of the city. The claim that "public art . . . is able to turn 'space into place,' investing the abstract with social meaning" (Hall & Robertson, 2001) doesn't take into account the social production of space; different people will experience that space differently and will take different meanings from the art experience. The individual nature of responses to public art may mean we should worry less about urban authoritarianism—people will interpret the art and interact with it on their own terms. Returning to the example of Cloud Gate, the moment it was installed, the artist, and even the City of Chicago, lost control of its meaning. In fact, by nicknaming the sculpture "The Bean," the public even overrode its original name. Public art, then, requires some humility on the part of the artist and the funder, because its meaning is ultimately determined by the collective (Hein, 1996).

However, even if public art does not produce a unitary experience for the public, or even the experience the artist intended, the art can still create an intellectual and emotional response that makes people interested and invested in place and give it character (Zitcer & Almanzar, 2020). Even the most mundane public art can, over time, become a valued part of the landscape (Sharp et al., 2005). Does The Bean produce a universal response in people who visit it? Probably not. But it certainly succeeds in creating a sense of place and contributing to the city's identity. This stronger sense of place and stronger identity through art creates economic value through art as an amenity, as tourism, and as community economic development.

Artist neighborhoods and the "right to the Creative City"

Artists have long sought out inexpensive and lightly supervised city neighborhoods that provide affordable and accessible spaces, in which to create and practice, which can accommodate the particular needs of artists. For example, artists may need to operate kilns or paint-spraying hoods or practice music at high decibels. These artist neighborhoods have become a common feature of deindustrializing and deindustrialized cities in North America and Europe, often arising in repurposed warehouses and factories with flexible architecture—well suited for adaptive reuse for live-work spaces, music/dance clubs, and performance spaces. When artists start to move in, the neighborhoods are often lightly populated, because they historically had few residential structures. For the artists, these neighborhoods are inexpensive because of their initial undesirability to "conventional" occupants, which can make the difference between being able to pursue their chosen career and not. Thus, creating new artist live-work spaces brings full-time residents and activity to areas whose original purpose is past. Artists may also find suitable spaces in low-income neighborhoods that already has residents. If the neighborhood has experienced abandonment, the artists' presence may not initially result in displacement of the original residents, since there is space to go around.

Over time, the character of these neighborhoods changes. Artists and their spaces become the amenity or what attracts others. The neighborhood gets busier, full of interesting people doing interesting things. With more "eyes on the street," the neighborhood feels safer. Small businesses open to serve the new residents. Suddenly, at some tipping point, others start to notice the neighborhood. It's still edgy, still affordable; but, the artists have laid the groundwork for others to want to move there, and they do. Buildings change hands, rents rise, and eventually there's a Starbucks—and all is lost. The artists get priced out and have to find their next undervalued neighborhood. The strong sense of place the artists have created, along with the new economic activity, is ultimately their downfall. Over time, the neighborhood becomes less different from other city neighborhoods.

The residents who supplant the artists are often the "creative class" or knowledge workers—well-educated, middle to upper middle class, with good transportation options, and with choices about where to live; these are precisely the kinds of residents most city leaders want to attract (Florida, 2002; Peck, 2005). The question is whether cities can accommodate these new, affluent residents and foster spaces that work for artists without continually enabling the cycle by which they are forced out. This displacement may even occur in neighborhoods where new residents are part of the same racial or ethnic group, as in the Boyle Heights Neighborhood in Los Angeles. Latino entrepreneurs want to capitalize on their culture and heritage to build the neighborhood's economy; but their success may make it harder for working-class Latinos to stay in the neighborhood (O'Brien et al., 2019). In some cases, such as in Berlin and Hamburg, Germany, artists have created urban social movements (USMs) to resist the gentrification of their neighborhoods, arguing that their investment in undervalued neighborhoods should be rewarded—not with higher rents, but with the ability to continue to occupy place they created; in other words, they assert a "right to the creative city" (Novy & Colomb, 2013).

PLACE-BASED CREATIVE ECONOMIC DEVELOPMENT

Of course, city leaders have long sought to differentiate places to attract residents, businesses, and investors. Planning and the interests of business leaders have also long been intertwined, such as the Commercial Club of Chicago commissioning prominent city planner (and Chicagoan) Daniel Burnham in 1906 to create a citywide plan. City leaders have often incorporated arts and culture into place-based economic development strategies (Ashley, 2014). While we do not pretend to include a comprehensive history of place-driven arts economic development, we'll talk about three historical categories of place-driven economic development, which had different motivations and different results, but which widely influenced subsequent urban design and economic development approaches. Importantly, all three examples used the arts as a component of their place-based revitalization approaches. We then explore contemporary creative placemaking strategies.

Historical examples of place-driven creative economic development

The ideas of the City Beautiful movement became popular in the late 19th century, as a reaction to the crowded, polluted, and, in many cases, hastily built cities of the Industrial Revolution. Architects, planners, and urbanists aligned with the City Beautiful movement believed that it was damaging on an individual level for people to live in such conditions. Moreover, it was damaging for the nation, as people who lived in hemmed-in, polluted conditions could not develop the civic consciousness that was important for the United States to thrive as a democracy. Making the city more beautiful and more humane would create a healthier, morally upright, civic-minded populace. The City Beautiful adherents believed firmly in environmental determinism—the idea that a person's surroundings influence their behavior and that changing people's surroundings can change their behavior. At the same time, of course, the public investment in city planning and the better-behaved residents would make the city more attractive to commercial interests.

To that end, City Beautiful architects and planners, in collaboration with and funded by city leaders, designed grand public buildings, parks, and civic centers meant to uplift and inspire. They explicitly drew upon classical Greek architecture, desiring to make a connection between ancient Greek democratic ideals and contemporary American democracy. These new civic buildings were often clustered in newly created cultural districts. The cultural districts included public arts facilities, such as museums, auditoriums, opera houses, and orchestra halls. These, again, were deliberately meant to expose regular working people to the most elevated art forms and to the kind of beauty that their daily existence otherwise lacked (see Figure 4.4).

The World's Columbian Exposition of 1893, in Chicago, showcased this grand civic style, with scores of enormous temporary Neoclassical exhibit halls, constructed out of plaster in a vast public park of lawns, walkways, and canals. While all but a handful of these buildings were meant to be demolished after the exposition closed, the 20 million people who visited the fair as well as those who were sent postcards or visited traveling exhibitions were exposed to this style of architecture and this vision of civic life. Countless smaller cities across the United States embarked on their own monumental placemaking endeavors. Many cities drew on international fairs and exhibitions to experiment with strategies that linked aesthetic and utilitarian purposes (see Figure 4.5).

Figure 4.4 Fountains and Grand Basin with exhibition buildings at *World's Columbian Exposition*, Chicago, IL, 1893.

Source: Photo by Frances Benjamin Johnston, The Library of Congress

Figure 4.5 *Detroit Institute of the Arts*, Detroit Historic Cultural District.

Source: Photo by Andrew Jameson, Creative Commons license

This embrace of a particular elevated version of the arts and civic life coincided with the era of reform and boosterism in city government, where city leaders aimed to root out corruption, promote their cities to gain new residents and businesses, and solve urban problems. But by the 1950s and 1960s, the optimism of the 1910s and 1920s had curdled into anxiety about urban decline. Inner-city neighborhoods were once again overcrowded and decaying, with Black residents hemmed in by de jure and de facto segregation and both Black and White city residents often unable to obtain financing to purchase or upgrade homes, due to redlining. City leaders and planners once again took bold action—although this time, without the neoclassical architectural emphasis. Once again, they put their faith in environmental determinism—the idea that changing people's environment will change their behavior. They gambled that obliterating Black neighborhoods, scattering some residents, and sending others to newly built public housing would decrease poverty and crime (and likely also disrupt civil rights organizing). They also thought that new freeways, civic buildings, and modern housing would change the behavior of Whites who had left the city for the suburbs, re-attracting them to downtowns.

Once again, city leaders and planners used the arts to anchor new civic spaces. One of the most prominent examples is the Lincoln Center complex in Manhattan (Ashley, 2014). Spearheaded by the controversial urban transformationist Robert Moses, and funded collaboratively by the city, state, and federal governments, the Lincoln Square Urban Renewal Project covered 14 demolished city blocks. 7000 low-income apartments were demolished and replaced by 4400 new apartments, 4000 of which would be for middle- or upper-income residents (Foulkes, 2010). The public spaces were vast and surrounded by multi-lane roads, creating a suburban-feeling auto-oriented cultural district in the middle of the densest city in the US. Lincoln Center was meant to have a regional—even global—impact, and its scale and style reflected that ambition.

The arts weren't just implicated in urban renewal economic development strategies as economic anchors; they were "used as compensation for the demolition and re-building of a neighborhood" (Foulkes, 2010, p. 414). At the same time as lower-income neighborhoods were being bulldozed and reconfigured as civic spaces and housing for higher-income residents, arts leaders made efforts to fund and expand programming that showcased a wider variety of art forms and cultures. Prominent jazz musicians, Black opera singers, and dance companies such as Alvin Ailey showcased America's racial and cultural diversity and attracted more diverse audiences. However, as the example of Lincoln Center shows, these arts-centered placemaking efforts of the urban renewal era largely failed to fit into the existing city fabric, because of their vast scale and, sometimes, forbidding architecture. In addition, they struggled to authentically connect to residents of the remaining nearby neighborhoods, with outreach often largely focused on school programs. Ultimately, these attempts at arts-based placemaking, driven by a desire to drum up tourism, did not reverse the course of mid-century disinvestment and suburbanization.

In the 1970s and 1980s, city leaders were still trying to crack the code of downtown and inner-city revitalization. Labor unions had been weakened, leaving both private sector and public sector workers vulnerable to layoffs and outsourcing. At the same time, globalization and stagflation had taken a toll on cities' industrial employment and tax bases. Wealthier city residents continued to move to the suburbs, leaving urban populations poorer and with higher social service requirements. The paradigm of economic thought, and therefore federal policy, shifted toward neoliberalism, with a belief in deregulation, open markets, and government in the service of supporting private enterprise (Grodach & Ehrenfeucht, 2015). Reeling from a loss of tax base and a concurrent loss of funding from the federal government, city governments retrenched, shedding public sector jobs and services that previous generations had taken for granted (Skidmore & Scorsone, 2011; Grodach & Ehrenfeucht, 2015).

As jobs and workers became more mobile, cities also started to try to compete for investment (knowledge jobs) and tourism (service jobs) in a way that hadn't been seen since the years of civic boosterism, at the turn of the 20th century. Many invested in strategies designed to replace traditional manufacturing and ancillary jobs with creative-class jobs. These workers are generally well compensated; and their industries tend to be less tied to a specific geography. The theory is that, if creative-class workers can theoretically work anywhere, any city has the potential to be a winner in the global competition for knowledge and creative workers (Sands et al., 2023). Those workers, in turn, create spillover service jobs. This shift in the type of industry and worker cities were trying to attract led to a shift in both economic development strategy and in the built environment. Economic geographer David Harvey observes that "American downtowns no longer communicate exclusively a monumental sense of power, authority, and corporate domination. Instead, they express the idea of spectacle and play" (1990, p. 266). This civic entrepreneurialism has encouraged the "architecture of festival and spectacle," where residents and tourists gather to shop and watch each other shop (1990, p. 265).

In the context of downtown decline and a rejection of the modernist approach to commerce and architecture, developer James Rouse had a new idea to try: the festival marketplace. Rather than relying on monumental civic buildings and large housing developments, cities would repurpose old buildings (or sometimes build new ones, usually in a postmodern architectural style) for small entrepreneurs. In some cases, these buildings showcased a particular version of local history. The individual retail spaces were usually very small and the stores very specialized, often including specialty foods, art galleries, and gift shops. Rouse also intended that the surrounding housing would be repurposed by artists and other creative-class residents and that the marketplace would primarily serve locals (Bloom, 2004). However, these festival marketplaces were not grassroots efforts to incubate small businesses, artisans, and artists—but rather carefully controlled environments, envisioned by one of the biggest suburban mall-builders in the US. The best-known and most successful examples of this approach are Faneuil Hall Marketplace in Boston, now a busy tourist attraction, and Harborplace in Baltimore (see Figure 4.6).

Inspired by these marketplaces' success, other cities tried to replicate the festival marketplace strategy. Most failed in spurring any kind of lasting revitalization, because they did not

Figure 4.6 *Faneuil Hall*, Boston, MA.

Source: Carol M. Highsmith, Carol M. Highsmith Archive, Library of Congress, Prints and Photographs Division

materially change the larger economic conditions under which the cities were operating. In 1984, the Rouse Company opened Portside Festival Marketplace in one of the author's hometowns, Toledo, Ohio, at a cost of $18 million. One of us visited there, as a child, and remembers going to the "fancy" seafood restaurant there with her parents and marveling at the kite store with its wares suspended from the tall ceilings. Portside incorporated arts and culture through an art supply shop, an art gallery for local artists, and an event stage with music and dance programming. Unlike Faneuil Hall and Harborplace, which endured through changes in the market, Portside had an exceptionally short unsuccessful run. The Rouse Company projected that 5 million people would visit Portside in its first year, spending $13-$15 million; but Portland's first year fell short of those expectations (Toledo Blade, January 31, 1985). By 1989, it was 25% vacant and had lost millions of dollars, leading its management company to end its management agreement

(Associated Press, September 23, 1989). The building was repurposed into an award-winning children's science museum; but that, too, struggled and closed. It finally reopened two years later, with the support of a countywide operating levy, and remains open today (see Figure 4.7).

As a created "place," Portside was absolutely a success. The building's postmodern design was light, bright, and inviting, reminiscent of the great glass pavilions of 19th-century public parks. It helped visually and spatially transform Toledo's riverfront, which was no easy feat. But as a vehicle for economic transformation, in a struggling downtown in the industrial Midwest, it was a total failure. Before and during Portside's brief life, Toledo's biggest downtown employers were shedding jobs. There was very little downtown housing to keep Portside busy in the evenings, leaving it feeling a bit creepy (Young, 1992) and abandoned. The convention center that was supposed to accompany Portside's opening was delayed by over two years, robbing it of necessary foot traffic. The retail mix of Portside was geared toward wants, not needs (such as the kite store, a store that sold only purple items, and a specialty nut store), which

Figure 4.7 Side view of *Portside Festival Marketplace*, Toledo, OH.
Source: Photo by Mark Snyder

didn't attract repeat customers in an economically struggling blue-collar city (Walters, 1990) and which left it even more vulnerable (see Figure 4.8). Finally, and sadly, all the beautiful glass made the building hugely expensive to heat and cool in Toledo's cold winters and warm summers.

The 1970s and 1980s saw many downtowns struggle to retain relevance and economic activity, as traditional economic bases changed and cities, overall, lost population. The festival marketplace concept was part of a set of strategies to reimagine downtowns as spaces for arts, entertainment, and creativity. In many cases, the festival marketplaces did not in themselves spur a sustained revitalization. However, city leaders kept trying to work toward the goals the festival marketplaces were trying to achieve.

Contemporary creative placemaking

The festival marketplace idea was one strategy to "make" places in spaces that had lost vitality or were not built at human scale, such as in cities and towns that had lost jobs and population

Figure 4.8 Kite store and atrium, *Portside Festival Marketplace*, Toledo, OH, July 18, 1984.
Source: Photo by Mark Snyder

after the restructuring of global manufacturing in the 1970s and 1980s, or in the postwar landscape, created by urban renewal, of the 1950s and 1960s (Schneekloth & Shibley, 1995). These cities and towns were struggling to compete in the global marketplace of cities; and leaders looked for ways to draw people (and their retail and tax dollars) back, often capitalizing on local cultural aspects or architecture to make residents and visitors feel like there was a "there" there. As it became clear that most of the large-scale geographic interventions of the 1950s through the 1980s had not succeeded in spurring lasting and widespread revitalization, city and neighborhood leaders tried a different set of tactics—once again connected to the creative economy—to draw people in. They called these strategies "placemaking."

Placemaking is the term for the economic development strategy of "creating quality places that people want to live, work, play, and learn in" (Wyckoff, 2014). This strategy is "driven by a recognition that unique places that feature cultural enrichment and a high quality of experience boost economic as well as social conditions" (Gilmartin, 2014). Placemaking can include streetscape and public space improvements, such as pedestrian-friendly street reconfiguration, street furniture, moveable tables and chairs, signage, and landscaping. Placemaking can also include programming and events that draw people to places and activate the space. Placemaking, then, addresses "the means of production"—the economic conditions of the locality—as well as "the production of meaning"—how place looks and feels, who feels that they belong, and what they do there (Lepofsky & Fraser, 2003, p. 128).

Placemaking does not necessarily include the arts; but in practice, as placemaking became a widely adopted practice, planners noticed the arts were often a critically important part of making a space feel like a place (Loh et al., 2022). In 2010, Ann Markusen and Ann Gadwa coined the term "creative placemaking." They explain:

> In creative placemaking, partners from public, private, non-profit, and community sectors strategically shape the physical and social character of a neighborhood, town, city, or region around arts and cultural activities. Creative placemaking animates public and private spaces, rejuvenates structures

and streetscapes, improves local business viability and public safety, and brings diverse people together to celebrate, inspire, and be inspired.

(2010, p. 3)

Just as with placemaking in general, creative placemaking could include physical or aesthetic improvements, like public art, or programming, like festivals and performances. Nationally known art shows and music festivals that are strongly associated with place such as Bonnaroo (Manchester, TN), Lollapalooza (Chicago), Glasgow Music Festival, Miami Visual Arts (Art Basel), and Treefort (Boise, ID), draw visitors in, create economic benefits, and create associations between these places and their arts and cultural activities that contribute to their distinctive identity. These creative placemaking efforts often take a broad view of arts and culture, including and celebrating local cultural traditions and food, such as the long-running National Cherry Festival in Traverse City, Michigan. Markusen and Gadwa Nicodemus explained that the benefits of creative placemaking included recirculating local income through local spending; re-using vacant and underutilized land, buildings, and infrastructure; creating jobs; fostering entrepreneurship; passing on cultural knowledge to younger generations; and attracting and retaining non-arts-related businesses (Markusen & Gadwa Nicodemus, 2010, p. 4). In other words, place-based public investments in arts and culture could have spillover effects that would help the private sector. And in keeping with the neoliberal era of local economic development, creative placemaking often involves public-private partnerships, which open additional avenues for funding; but this also means that the public interest may not be the foremost concern (Hackworth, 2007; Grodach & Ehrenfeucht, 2015).

City officials and planners embraced the concept of creative placemaking (Gadwa Nicodemus, 2013). National foundations (e.g. Kresge), government agencies (e.g. National Endowment for the Arts), and special interest groups (e.g. Project for Public Spaces) helped spread the word, leading to its widespread adoption as an economic development and revitalization strategy. Practitioners and advocates at the national and state levels released tool kits and provided technical assistance on how to do placemaking (Loh, 2019), while policymakers and arts and cultural leaders found a variety of ways to use it—to justify investments in arts and culture, to connect it to general planning practice, and to use it as a framework for cultural policy and programs. Over time, the distinction between placemaking and creative placemaking has blurred (Loh et al., 2022). In fact, many planners and officials use the terms interchangeably, mainly because when they talk about placemaking, they often include arts and culture as standard considerations. For example, the Michigan Municipal League's definition of placemaking is:

> The process of creating places that people care about and where they want to spend time. These high-quality places are active, unique locations that are interesting and visually attractive, people-friendly, safe, walkable, and bikeable provide mixed uses of businesses and housing, and offer creative amenities and experiences.
>
> (MML 2017, p. 4)

Thus, creative placemaking often connects city planners and officials, as well as arts and cultural organizations in ways somewhat reminiscent of the City Beautiful-inspired cultural districts of the 1920s, albeit on a usually smaller and more tactical scale. Creative placemaking often spurs collaborations across city departments and agencies. Such efforts can be directed from a city planning department, parks and recreation, economic development, a downtown development authority (DDA), an arts and cultural department, or a mayor's office; but they often require joining forces between more than one of these. Creative placemaking, while originally an economic development-focused approach, has also evolved into a tool for advancing social equity and community needs—including affordable housing and workspaces for artists, intergenerational creative opportunities, and galleries and incubator spaces for artists and other creative entrepreneurs (Redaelli, 2019). In Chapter 9, we highlight some examples of place-based, creative, equitable economic development.

Creative economic development critiques and pitfalls

Place-based creative economic development can provide many benefits to cities and towns. Investing in the local creative economy can help artists and other entrepreneurs gain a foothold in the industry and provide places for them to live and work affordably. Placemaking interventions in the form of physical structures and objects (such as buildings, streetscape improvements, and public art) and programming (such as festivals, pop-ups, and performances) can draw people back to spaces that have experienced disinvestment. Ultimately, they may really influence quality of life and change the way people view those spaces, downtowns, and neighborhoods. In turn, this change in perception and reality may spur new private investment and new in-movers. However, it's important to be aware of some of the potential downsides of place-based creative economic development. We'll talk about each of the major issues associated with place-based creative economic development in turn.

The most serious issue with any kind of economic development efforts at the city level, including creative economic development, is that cities exist in and are affected by global economic forces. They can take actions and make investments of public money to make their city more competitive and more attractive around the margins; but they can't materially change the regional, state, or national economic conditions in which they operate. Cities of the Midwest and Northeast that lost huge percentages of their good-paying manufacturing jobs—as industries such as auto, textiles, and steel restructured and sent most of their jobs overseas—can't suddenly revive or reinvent their economies by investing in streetscape improvements. Even Pittsburgh, PA, which pivoted from a steel-dominated economy to an education and medicine-focused economy, referred to as anchor institutions, more successfully than most, has less than half of its 1950 population. Further, David Harvey warns that this type of development can be a bit of a musical chairs game. He worries that this type of economic growth is largely built on highly compensated people buying real estate; the financial and real estate services needed to process those deals, all of it propped up by debt. It's fragile, and, as we are seeing in late 2023, highly susceptible to changes in interest rates. This is not a reason to throw up our hands and decide not to try anything; but it is a reason to temper our expectations and always consider the opportunity costs of public investments. In other words, if we spend money on place-based creative economic development, what are we not spending money on?

The second and third critiques are related to each other and have to do with gentrification, belonging, and authenticity. We will try to tease these three apart. When place-based creative economic development works as it is meant to, it usually changes the look and feel of place where the intervention occurs. These changes can take several forms. Perhaps more people are eating outdoors at sidewalk restaurant seating, or there is a weekly farmer's market with local food and artisans or a new art gallery for local artists. Eventually, perhaps under-occupied buildings are converted to apartments or condos. In all these cases, people are visiting, working, and, in some cases, living in spaces where they previously did not. Sometimes, prior to the economic development efforts, the neighborhood was essentially unoccupied, as when developers or arts buyers/renters convert former industrial spaces to artist live-work spaces. Other times, the neighborhood does have existing residents, but has lost population and is struggling economically. It is in these situations that the question of gentrification comes up.

Adding to the complexity around gentrification issues is that there is disagreement on what gentrification is, how to tell if it is happening, and who it benefits. For existing residents in a neighborhood experiencing public and private investment and new in-movers, some changes may be positive, at least at first. If there is enough vacant housing to accommodate the new in-movers, existing residents may not be displaced, especially if they are homeowners. In many cases, crime declines and accessibility to businesses and other amenities goes up (Freeman, 2006). However, even without displacement, these cultural changes in the neighborhood may make existing residents feel unwelcome or surveilled, leading them to leave even if they aren't technically priced out (Papachristos et al., 2011; Cornelissen, 2022). In gentrifying neighborhoods where there isn't enough vacant housing for in-movers, or where existing residents are mainly renters, there may be wholesale turnover in existing residents as newcomers are willing to pay higher rents. While gentrification can occur without any kind of intentional public action, it is often a feature, not a bug, of place-based creative economic development; and leaders need to take steps to avoid both physical and cultural displacement, as they work to improve quality of life and economic vitality.

The issue of cultural displacement brings us to the next critique or potential pitfall of place-based creative economic development: belonging and authenticity. A century ago, only the most elite forms of art were considered worthy of public investment. As we've mentioned, cities built grand museums, opera houses, libraries, and symphony halls in the neoclassical style, with the idea that they would elevate the public. Some of these buildings and experiences were explicitly meant to welcome everyone, especially libraries and museums, which were often free. But the type of art, music, and literature they showcased and shared was overwhelmingly White, western, and produced by elites. Today, while many place-based creative economic development efforts seek to be inclusive of diverse art forms and cultures, they often fall short. Leaders of these efforts may value diversity and inclusion as concepts, but lack much of an understanding of which people and which cultures already exist in the city or neighborhood—let alone truly include or even be led by people who are already there and who may be lower income and decidedly not elite (Ashley et al., 2022).

In areas with place-based creative economy interventions, two groups are most at risk for being priced out and displaced: artists and marginalized people (and there may be an overlap between the two groups). Artists, therefore, may contribute to gentrification, but also be harmed by it if they can no longer afford to live in the neighborhood that they made cool or attractive. Residents of color and those with fewer resources have a long history of being forcibly relocated to make way for development, creative and otherwise. The example of Lincoln Center earlier in this chapter illustrates that process well.

In contrast, Bedoya (2013) argues for what he calls a place-keeping or place-belonging approach that acknowledges that there are already people here, and this is their place, even if it doesn't look inviting to outsiders or generate as much economic activity as others think it should. Place-keeping works to integrate and incorporate the place's entire history, cultures, and peoples. Stern and Seifert (2010) also suggest making a shift in public investment toward naturally occurring arts and cultural districts that are distributed throughout neighborhoods, rather than focusing just on downtowns or large areas such as in the grand arts districts of the 1920s. Creative placemaking can certainly be organized from the grassroots up, with artists and neighborhood residents serving as social entrepreneurs, who creatively solve community-based problems (Redaelli, 2019).

Policy tools and strategies for place-based creative economic development

We've now talked about historical and contemporary philosophies of place-based creative economic development as well as some of the issues around gentrification, authenticity, and equity that this type of economic development can cause. Keeping in mind the historical successes and failures of these types of interventions and the need to be mindful of equity issues, how can city and neighborhood leaders work to revitalize their communities and strengthen their creative economies? City and neighborhood leaders can use a variety of tools to implement place-based creative economic development. In this chapter we'll talk about two broad categories of place-based policy tools and strategies: funding mechanisms and place-based policy interventions.

Creative economic development deals with funding both by capturing grants and tax dollars to fund programs and by disbursing grants to and arranging tax incentives for artists, nonprofits, neighborhood groups, small businesses, and entrepreneurs. Percent for Art ordinances are probably the most commonly used programs internationally to fund public art. These ordinances typically require that a percentage of the city's capital improvement or infrastructure budget is set aside to fund public art. To ensure that public art is chosen equitably, it is important to have a participatory process through the planning, selection, and installation phases that draws not just on those with arts expertise, but also those who are eventually going to interact with the art—a diverse group of ordinary people. This type of participatory process increases the odds that the art will align with community tastes and values and that people will be invested in and supportive of spending public money on it. It's also important not to require that the public art always be tied geographically to the project that triggered the spend, as disproportionate capital spending takes place in downtowns—potentially leaving other areas underserved with public art (Brennan, 2019).

Other funding mechanisms for arts and cultural and creative placemaking interventions include DDAs, downtown business associations (DBAs), and tax increment financing districts. These structures are set up to capture a portion of the growth of downtown or other district tax dollars over time to fund development activities in the district. To ensure that existing residents benefit from increases in property values in a revitalizing district, the city or other property owners may establish a community land trust, which is a nonprofit organization that owns and develops land for the benefit of the community. The profits from that development and increase in property values return to the community, and this may be used for affordable housing, community gardens and parks, arts and cultural amenities, or workspaces. Because the land and assets are held in perpetuity, the community land trust is one way to protect against physical displacement caused by gentrification (Community Land Trust Network, 2023). Finally, cities may negotiate with developers, as part of a planned unit development (PUD) approval, to provide arts and cultural amenities along with their project.

Cities or nonprofits then disburse these funds, as well as those received from state and federal grants, to individuals, businesses, and nonprofits. These grants can fund a diverse set of arts and cultural activities, including entrepreneurship and programming. Cities can also use tax incentives to spur the kinds of creative economic development they want to see in particular geographic areas, such as Enterprise Zones or Neighborhood Improvement Zones.

Cities can also use place-based policy interventions to incentivize and facilitate their creative economies. One prominent strategy is the formation of arts and cultural districts. These can be formed around "high" art, such as in the cultural districts of the early part of the 20th century; or they can form around an existing ethnic neighborhood, a cluster of artists, or a community of artisans or even food producers. Different types represent different urban economic theories about how to spur economic growth and/or development. Arts and cultural districts demarcate this creative economic activity, provide branding and marketing, and create programming to draw people to them (Ashley, 2015). Cities can become developers themselves and provide artist housing or artist live-work spaces on city-owned land. But city leaders can also use changes to existing zoning ordinances and building codes to make it easier and more affordable for artists to live and work in neighborhoods throughout the city. Zoning ordinances that allow live-work spaces or that allow residential uses in commercial and industrial districts open up additional land and buildings for arts activities and occupations. Changes to building codes that allow for more flexible arrangements, while still preserving safety, can make it cheaper to convert commercial and industrial buildings to living or working space. Land use designations that specifically allow or name activities that are associated with the arts as "principal permitted uses" can signal that such activities are welcome.

CONCLUSION

In this chapter we've explored the relationship between place and the creative economy. While facets of the creative economy operate independently from a place, much of its activity and effects are tied to particular places. We've especially focused, in this chapter, on efforts by city leaders and nonprofits throughout the 20th century and the early part of the 21st century to foster a sense of place, and its accompanying economic benefits, through arts and culture. We can see these strategies all the way back to the City Beautiful movement of the 1910s and 1920s, to the urban renewal era of the 1950s and 1960s, to the short-lived festival marketplace strategy of the 1980s, to today's smaller scale placemaking efforts. We've also looked at some of the potential problems that investing in pro-creative economy strategies can cause for artists and low-income residents. Finally, we've talked more about policy tools and strategies that cities use to foster place-based creative economic development. The policy tools mentioned in this section will be referenced again in Chapter 7 and put in context with additional policies employed by government and public-private partnerships to foster creative economy environments and practices. We'll also provide more specific examples to illustrate these policies in Chapter 9.

TAKEAWAYS

In this chapter, we shared connections between a place and the creative economy. The primary takeaways are:

- The creative economy intersects with place in two primary ways: as clusters of related economic activity and as a centerpiece of economic development strategies that aim to attract residents or visitors.
- Examples of place-based economic development strategies include arts districts, creative placemaking, public art, and creative economic development.
- A sense of place is a recognition and connection to a place that is personal and specific.
- There are historical precedents to place-based creative economic development, including the City Beautiful movement, emulation of examples seen at international expositions, urban renewal arts-based economic development projects, festival marketplaces, and the creation of place-based tourist attractions.
- Contemporary "creative placemaking" has been embraced by governments, national funders, and special interest groups and included concepts such as social equity, alongside aesthetic considerations.
- While place-based creative economic development can provide many benefits, potential downsides include gentrification, lack of authenticity, and potential displacement of artists and marginalized populations.
- Tools for place-based creative economic development include public funding strategies, tax incentives, public-private partnerships, the formation of arts and cultural districts, and zoning or code changes.

Discussion questions:

1 In your opinion, what factors contribute to a strong sense of place? Can those factors be created on purpose, or must they accumulate organically over time?
2 Are you aware of any local placemaking initiatives in your city? Some examples could include public art, pop-up retail, arts

programming, or streetscape improvements. How have those initiatives changed the way people think about and use space?

3   How can we ensure that placemaking doesn't send signals that only certain kinds of people are welcome in the space?

4   How would you define gentrification? How would you be able to tell if it's happening in a particular neighborhood?

Activity

- Recreate the Ph.D. student's assignment in this chapter. Take (or find) 4–6 pictures of a place to which you feel a strong connection, put them in a PowerPoint presentation, and write captions for them. Describe to your class what makes you feel that connection; and then analyze why this is so. Try to be objective (as the author was not) about whether it exhibits a strong sense of place and explain why or why not.

REFERENCES

Ashley, A. J. (2014). Negotiating Risk in Property-Based Arts Economic Development: Exploring the Innovative But Untimely Development Partnership Between the Seattle Art Museum and Washington Mutual. *Cities, 37,* 92–103.

Ashley, A. J. (2015). Beyond the Aesthetic: The Historical Pursuit of Local Arts Economic Development. *Journal of Planning History, 14*(1), 38–61.

Ashley, A. J. (2021). The Micropolitics of Performance: Pop-up Art as a Complementary Method for Civic Engagement and Public Participation. *Journal of Planning Education and Research, 41*(2), 173–187.

Ashley, A. J., Loh, C. G., Bubb, K., & Durham, L. (2022). Diversity, Equity, and Inclusion Practices in Arts and Cultural Planning. *Journal of Urban Affairs, 44,* 727–747.

Associated Press. (1989, September 23). Toledo's Riverfront Mall Is Dealt Another Setback: Management Firm Cuts Ties to Rouse Project. *The Washington Post.*

Bedoya, R. (2013). Placemaking and the Politics of Belonging and Dis-Belonging. *GIA Reader, 24*(2). www.giarts.org/article/placemaking-and-politics-belonging-and-dis-belonging

Bloom, N. D. (2004). *Merchant of Illusion: James Rouse, America's Salesman of the Businessman's Utopia.* Columbus: Ohio State University Press.

Brennan, J. (2019). Public Art and the Art of Public Participation. *National Civic Review, 108*(3), 34–44. www.jstor.org/stable/10.32543/naticivirevi.108.3.0034

Cornelissen, S. (2022). Remember, This Is Brightmoor: Historical Violence, Neighborhood Experiences, and the Hysteresis of Street Life. *Urban Affairs Review, 58*(3), 832–860.

Elsheshtawy, Y. (2015). Observing the Public Realm: William Whyte's the Social Life of Small Urban Spaces. *Built Environment, 41*(3), 399–411.

Florida, R. (2002). *The Rise of the Creative Class*. New York: Basic Books.

Foulkes, J. L. (2010, Winter). Street and Stages: Urban Renewal and the Arts after World War II. *Journal of Social History, 44*(2), The Arts in Place, 413–434. Oxford University Press. www.jstor.org/stable/25790364

Freeman, L. (2006). *There Goes the 'Hood: Views of Gentrification from the Ground Up*. Philadelphia, PA: Temple University Press.

Gadwa Nicodemus, A. (2013). Fuzzy Vibrancy: Creative Placemaking as Ascendant US Cultural Policy. *Cultural Trends, 22*(3–4), 213–222.

Gilmartin, D. (2014). Introduction. In E. Philips Foley, C. Layton & D. Gilmartin (Eds.), *The Economics of Place: The Art of Building Great Communities*. Ann Arbor, MI: Michigan Municipal League.

Grodach, C., & Ehrenfeucht, R. (2015). Urban Restructuring, Neoliberalism, and the Changing Landscape of Urban Revitalization. In C. Grodach & R. Ehrenfeucht (Eds.), *Urban Revitalization: Remaking Cities in a Changing World*. London: Taylor & Francis.

Hackworth, J. (2007). *The Neoliberal City: Governance, Ideology, and Development in American Urbanism*. Ithaca, NY: Cornell University Press.

Hall, T., & Robertson, I. (2001). Public Art and Urban Regeneration: Advocacy, Claims and Critical Debates. *Landscape Research, 26*(1), 5–26. https://blog.americansforthearts.org/sites/default/files/public%20art%20%2B%20urban%20regeneration%20advocacy%20claims%20debates_0.pdf

Harvey, D. (1990). Flexible Accumulation Through Urbanization: Reflections on "Post-Modernism" in the American City. In *Perspecta, Vol. 26, Theater, Theatricality, and Architecture* (pp. 251–272). MIT Press. https://arxiujosepserradell.cat/wp-content/uploads/2022/10/Flexible-Accumulation-through-urbanization_reflections-on-Post-Modernism-in-the-American-City-David-Harvey.pdf

Harvey, D. (2000). *Spaces of Hope*. Edinburgh: Edinburgh University Press.

Hein, H. (1996). What Is Public Art? Time, Place, and Meaning. *The Journal of Aesthetics and Art Criticism, 54*(1), 1–7. www.jstor.org/stable/431675

Jackson, J. B. (1995). A Sense of Place, a Sense of Time. *Design Quarterly, 164*, 24–27. www.jstor.org/stable/4091350

Kingwell, M. (2019). Editorial: Does Public Art Have to Be Bad Art? *Open Philosophy, 2*, 582–589. https://doi.org/10.1515/opphil-2019-0041

Lepofsky, J., & Fraser, J. C. (2003). Building Community Citizens: Claiming the Right to Place-Making in the City. *Urban Studies, 40*(1), 127–142.

Loh, C. G. (2019). Placemaking and Implementation: Revisiting the Performance Principle. *Land Use Policy, 81*, 68–75.

Loh, C. G., Ashley, A., Kim, K., Durham, L., & Bubb, K. (2022). Placemaking in Practice: Municipal Arts and Cultural Plans' Approaches to Placemaking and Creative Placemaking. *Journal of Planning Education and Research*. https://doi.org/10.1177/0739456X221100503

Low, S. (2017). *Spatializing Culture: The Ethnography of Space and Place*. New York: Routledge.

Markusen, A., & Gadwa Nicodemus, A. (2010). *Creative Placemaking*. Washington, DC: National Endowment for the Arts.

Michigan Municipal League. (2017). *A Decade of Placemaking in Michigan*. Ann Arbor, MI: Michigan Municipal League. https://mml.org/pdf/resources/publications/decade_of_placemaking_in_Michigan_book_final_2017.pdf

Novy, J., & Colomb, C. (2013). Struggling for the Right to the (Creative) City in Berlin and Hamburg: New Urban Social Movements, New "Spaces of Hope"? *International Journal of Urban and Regional Research*, 37(5), 1816–1838.

O'Brien, K., Vilchis, L., & Maritescu, C. (2019). Boyle Heights and the Fight Against Gentrification as State Violence. *American Quarterly*, 71, 389–396.

Papachristos, A. V., Smith, C. M., Scherer, M. L., & Fugiero, M. A. (2011). More Coffee, Less Crime? The Relationship Between Gentrification and Neighborhood Crime Rates in Chicago, 1991 to 2005. *City & Community*, 10(3), 215–240. https://doi.org/10.1111/j.1540-6040.2011.01371.x

Peck, J. (2005). Struggling with the Creative Class. *International Journal of Urban and Regional Research*, 29(4), 740–770.

Phillips, P. (1988, December) Out of Order: The Public Art Machine. *Artforum*, pp. 92–96.

Redaelli, E. (2019). *Connecting Arts and Place*. Berlin: Springer.

Rooney, S., Wingate, J., & Senie, H. F. (Eds.). (2021). *Teachable Monuments: Using Public Art to Spark Dialogue and Confront Controversy*. New York: Bloomsbury Publishing.

Sands, G., Reese, L. A., & Li, X. (2023). The Creative Class at 19: But What about Detroit? In A. A. Batabyal & P. Nijkamp (Eds.), *The Creative Class Revisited*. Philadelphia, PA: Basic Books.

Schneekloth, L., & Shibley, R. G. (1995). *Placemaking: The Art of Building Communities*. New York: Wiley.

Sharp, J., Pollock, V., & Paddison, R. (2005). Just Art for a Just City: Public Art and Social Inclusion in Urban Regeneration. *Urban Studies*, 42(5/6), 1001–1023. https://doi.org/10.1080/00420980500106963

Skidmore, M., & Scorsone, E. (2011). Causes and Consequences of Fiscal Stress in Michigan Cities. *Regional Science and Urban Economics*, 41(4), 360–371.

Stern, M. J., & Seifert, S. C. (2010). Cultural Clusters: The Implications of Cultural Assets Agglomeration for Neighborhood Revitalization. *Journal of Planning Education and Research*, 29(3), 262–279.

Walters, J. (1990, Fall). After the Festival Is Over. *Governing Magazine*.

What Is a Community Land Trust? (2023). *Community Land Trust Network*. www.communitylandtrusts.org.uk/about-clts/what-is-a-community-land-trust-clt/ (accessed 8 September 2023).

Wyckoff, M. (2014). Definition of Placemaking: Four Different Types. *Planning and Zoning News*, 32(3).

Young, M. (1992). Portside. *Carolina Planning*, 18(1).

Zitcer, A., & Almanzar, S. M. (2020). Public Art, Cultural Representation, and the Just City. *Journal of Urban Affairs*, 42(7), 998–1013. https://doi.org/10.1080/07352166.2019.1601019

Creative economy ecosystems

Chapter 5

INTRODUCTION

A city's cultural and creative economy ecosystem is a dynamic, organic structure with different types of leaders running various organizational entities, independent artists operating in multiple capacities, and audience members, patrons, and consumers participating in events. All these different actors connect through interwoven networks and foster interdependent partnerships that support their work, interests, and values (Comunian, 2011). The term ecosystem arose from anthropology and environmental sciences and is applied, in this context, in recognition that the creative economy is a complex adaptive system (CAS) guided by principles found in related network, systems, and complexity theories (Comunian, 2011; Cunningham & Flew, 2019; de Bernard et al., 2022). We introduce this chapter by sharing an example of creative entrepreneurs and the business they started to leverage their values and skills.

Kei Tsuzuki and Molly Luethi did not set out to be artists, nor do they comfortably refer to themselves as artists, even though they run a successful business in Albuquerque, New Mexico. Their company, Kei & Molly Textiles, sells a diverse array of products with images of their design. Although they had experience in the nonprofit sector, teaching English as a second language and advancing women's economic development, they chose a for-profit model for their business. They believed this

DOI: 10.4324/9781003147688-5

model would best allow them to advance their true mission, which is to use a screen-printing business to create meaningful jobs for new immigrants and refugees and orient them to being a part of the American workforce (see Figure 5.1). We'll explain later in the chapter why this is. While their organization is a commercial business, framed by community engagement and social justice purposes, they concurrently identify as a creative enterprise, because of their unique designs printed on merchandise and small-batch hand-production methods.

Kei reflected:

When we first started, we were doing all these art fairs, and selling at the grower's market with artists and vendors. We really got a sense of artists making their living through their art. And for me, that's what the creative economy is. It could be a smaller ceramicist just going to the growers market every weekend and putting out their wares or it could be people like us who have art as the basis of their production.

(interview 3/10/2023)

Figure 5.1 Kei & Molly Textiles' staff printing blankets.
Source: Photo by Matilda Rose Bubb

Creative entrepreneurs like Kei and Molly are actors willing to use their agency, resources, and relationships to innovate solutions to address a problem and step into leadership roles in their city (Kingdon, 2011). In the coming pages, we will hear from more leaders and learn what they are doing to respond to community problems with creative solutions.

In this chapter, we share methodological details and establish a theoretical frame around ideas related to ecosystems. Then, we explore several topics related to the creative economy environment, including arts entrepreneurship. We also examine how leaders and entrepreneurs employ different organizational structures to leverage their creative practices and how the government works interdependently with these entities. Specific attention is paid to participating actors, by including vignettes to provide context to what actors do in the creative economy.

METHODOLOGY AND VALUE MEASUREMENT

We explore the creative economy ecosystem by drawing on international literature and semi-structured interviews. We interviewed leaders, from thirteen cities, who were identified as highly creative, of varying populations, spread geographically across the United States. The cities and those interviews were carefully selected by considering different systems of cultural and creative measurement, which we will explain. We supplement this material with contextualized information from reports, organizational documents, and websites. We conclude by discussing how the gig economy, shifting demographics, and independent artists are impacting cultural and creative ecosystems.

As noted in Chapter 3 when discussing the evaluation of creativity's worth, since the 1970s scholars and practitioners have searched for comprehensive ways to measure the cultural development and health of the cultural sector in cities, and, more recently, the value generated by creative businesses (Ortega-Villa & Ley-Garcia, 2018). The fundamental underlying issues are how to assign value to arts, culture, and commerce and a focus on evaluation and measurement that provides quantifiable, categorical, comparative evidence for cultural policy and administration decision-making processes (MacDowall et al., 2015). Because of varying definitions of culture, the addition of the creative industries, and different objects of measurement, there is no single national or global explanatory index for culture or creative industries (Ortega-Villa & Ley-Garcia, 2018) as we note in Chapter 3. This makes it difficult to know who to look to as leaders in the field.

In the last two decades, several different systems of measurement have been developed, operating with different targets on various geographic scales, aiming to evaluate and rank cultural vibrancy; there has also been a corresponding increase in academic publications on this topic (Montalto et al., 2019). Examples of noted creative economy measurement practices include nonprofit advocacy group Americans for the Arts' "Arts & Economic Prosperity" studies that focus on nonprofit arts and cultural organizations and their audiences in specific cities or regions; national-level economic data and reports prepared by international organizations, such as the UNCTAD; or The Culture, Arts, Heritage and Sport Economic Impact Model produced annually by the Canadian Government. Each index measures something different; but all try to communicate what makes a place more creative than others and how culture and creativity contribute to economies or social environments.

In looking at possible ways to select cities where we might learn the most about who is advocating for and defining creative economy initiatives and programs, we considered several of the measurement practices and ranking systems identified earlier. We wanted to identify cities that were considered highly creative locations as we thought this would increase the likelihood that we would find recent policy innovations and policy entrepreneurs in these locations that would provide rich data to explore and share with readers.

We decided to use the Cultural Vitality Index (CVI) developed by Cultural Vitality Suite and funded by the Western States Arts Federation, which is a dataset that cities use to inform policy arguments, articulate the value of culture in regions, and compare Metropolitan Statistical Areas (MSAs). The CVI is a statistical metric of creative activity per capita within an identified region. According to their website (https://cvsuite.org/), the CVI compares the per capita concentration of creative activity, based on data representing creative-industry earnings, industry sales, creative occupations, and cultural nonprofit revenues.

Out of the top 55 cities identified as most creative, the authors selected thirteen cities of varying populations, spread geographically across the United States, from which to interview cultural and creative leaders. We also looked at the structural nature and location of the local arts agency within the city; and we found that cities ranked higher in the CVI tended to have independent departments of art or were divisions of the mayor's office (which denotes some importance, value, and greater power) rather than arts agencies that were embedded in their parks and recreation or library divisions (see Table 5.1). Larger cities that have received more attention in the literature and are thus more known, such as New York, Los Angeles, and Austin, were purposely excluded from interviews.

THEORETICAL FRAMEWORK: NETWORK, SYSTEMS, AND COMPLEXITY THEORIES

Scholars have been turning to network, systems, and complexity theories in the past twenty years to explore concepts of how different types of individuals and organizations interact, form relationships, and evolve in cultural and creative economy environments, (Comunian, 2011, 2019; Colavitti et al., 2018; Dovey et al., 2016; Jung & Vakharia, 2019). These theories originated in physical science fields such as biology, engineering, and physics, but began migrating into the social sciences in the late 1990s to fields such as urban and organizational studies, computer science, economics, and, more recently, cultural studies (Allen, 1997; Comunian, 2011, 2019; Byrne & Callaghan, 2023).

The similarities between these theories are that they recognize the interconnectedness and interdependencies of elements within a system, which could be individuals, organizations, funders, or places in the creative economy (Morcol & Wachhaus, 2009). They each emphasize the concept of emergence and self-organization, where complex patterns arise from interactions between components such as new ideas or trends, and then reorganize into new structures such as independent artists building a studio collective or musician friends creating an annual jazz festival. Lastly, these theories

Table 5.1 High-performing creative economy cities selected for cultural leadership interviews.

CVI rank	City	State	2021 Population	Name of City Cultural Organization	Structural Location
Quadrant A WEST					
18	Seattle	WA	776,555	Office of Arts & Culture	Independent department
36	Sacramento	CA	525,398	Convention & Cultural Services—Arts, Culture, and Creative Economy Commission	Independent department
19	Denver	CO	749,103	Arts & Venues Denver	Independent department
32	Albuquerque	NM	562,281	Arts & Culture Department	Independent department
Quadrant B MIDWEST					
38	Kansas City	MO	501,957	Municipal Art Commission	Planning Department
46	Minneapolis	MN	439,012	Department of Arts & Cultural Affairs (just approved in July 2021); The Office of Arts, Culture, and the Creative Economy; Minneapolis Arts Commission	The new one is an independent department; Arts, Cultural, and Creative Economy is under the Mayor's Office
26	Detroit	MI	664,139	The Office of Arts, Culture, and Entrepreneurship; Detroit Entertainment Commission	The Office of Planning and Development Department; Commission Advisory to City Council
Quadrant C NORTHEAST					
6	Philadelphia	PA	1,585,010	The City of Philadelphia Office of Arts Culture and the Creative Economy	Program of the City Managing Director
21	Boston	MA	695,448	Tourism, Sports, & Entertainment	Independent department
Quadrant D SOUTH					
7	San Antonio	TX	1,581,730	Department of Arts & Culture	Independent department
53	New Orleans	LA	388,424	Mayor's Office of Cultural Economy; also New Orleans Tourism and Cultural Fund	Mayor's Office
23	Nashville	TN	678,448	Metro Arts/Nashville Office of Arts & Culture	Independent department
42	Miami	FL	478,251	Miami Film and Entertainment Office	Film is an independent department

perceive non-linear dynamics as driving forces, where small changes anywhere in the system can lead to large effects, rather than the traditional cause-and-effect impact of linear dynamics (Comunian, 2019).

There are also significant differences between these theories. *Network Theory* is mostly focused on relationships and connections between individual entities. Its key concepts are connectivity, clustering, network structure, and patterns of how information spreads (Dovey et al., 2016). Network theory could be used to study consumer and producer relationships, artist collaborations, or how and why talent moves from one place to another.

Systems Theory looks at the creative economy as a holistic system of interrelated parts, knowing that a change in one component affects the overall system, such as a policy shift or introduction of a technology innovation like artificial intelligence; its key concepts are feedback loops, equilibrium shifts, boundary definition, and system behaviors (Jung & Vakharia, 2019). We'll briefly define these concepts.

A *feedback loop* is a system to respond to negative or positive user comments to guide future product or service developments. A simple example is an audience member telling a theater manager that the room was too cold, and the theater manager increases the temperature. A more complicated feedback loop could be the theater conducting surveys or qualitative interviews about how audience members enjoyed the previous year's season, analyzing the results, and changing organizational behavior or choices of plays because of the feedback received.

Equilibrium in an economic system is when supply and demand are balanced. An *equilibrium shift* in the creative economy is similar, but refers to changes that impact the stability of creativity, innovation, or market dynamics in a particular sector. Equilibrium shifts can be caused by technology advances, cultural trends, economic changes, or consumer behavior. An example is how the streaming of music changed consumer behavior regarding how the public spends money on music and the impact this had on music, in terms of product development and revenue models for artists.

Boundary definition refers to defining what is inside or outside of a system or project. Boundary definition adds scope clarity and provides a foundation for understanding, analyzing, and optimizing interactions and resources in a complex system. This can be applied in the creative economy by thinking about the scope of work for a creative project, timeline, project goals and objectives, and roles and responsibilities that govern who does what. Particularly when working on a task basis, having clear shared understanding between the client and the creative regarding what is expected is necessary for managing expectations, preventing scope creep, and ensuring project success.

System behavior is about the complex patterns of interactions, processes, and outcomes in a system. In the creative economy, it could be studying the interactions between designers, manufacturers, distributors, and consumers in the fashion industry.

Overall, Systems Theory might be applied in the creative economy by studying the supply chain dynamics in film or music distribution or the legal and regulatory framework of intellectual property, and how these facilitate the sale of creative works.

Complexity Theory focuses on the overall system as a complex adaptive system that is evolving and reorganizing, based on the emergence of new factors such as artistic genres, trends, or technologies; its key concepts are that systems are open and operate far from equilibrium, consist of non-linear interactions, have distributed connectivity, are prone to path-dependence, and engage in self-organization as a primary mode of operation (Comunian, 2019). Again, we'll briefly define these key concepts and provide relevant examples inspired by Comunian's research (2011, 2019).

Far from equilibrium means that the system is never completely stable but instead is in a constant state of change. If you think about the creative ecosystem of a city, it is always changing. When one organization closes, another opens. Staff moves from one place to another or leaves town. Artists emerge out of youth culture and have different interests and preferences than the generation before, prompting new types of organizations to form.

Non-linear interactions refer to the condition where changes that happen at any point in a system, small or large, can have an outsized impact on a place or system. The chance meeting of two people, from very different backgrounds, who then go on to create a leading nonprofit cultural organization that changes the discourse in the art world, is an example of one of our author's experiences working at Exit Art in New York City in the 1980s and 1990s. Jeanette Ingberman, daughter of Polish Holocaust survivors and art historian, educated at Columbia, met Papo Colo, a path-breaking, self-identified trickster, Puerto Rican-born artist, at the Bronx Museum of Art, where she was the curator (Fox, 2011). Ingberman and Colo started Exit Art in 1982, a gallery that featured marginalized artists, including women, minorities, foreigners, gays, and lesbians. It closed in 2012 after Ingberman's death from leukemia; but the artists and ideas they launched reverberate to this day.

Distributed connectivity is about how large numbers of human and non-human elements interact with each other across different scales, with no centralized control over the overall system. An example of this could be how talent is discovered in contemporary times. While someone may be found through the traditional agent reference, they may also be found via an online social media or video-sharing platform, or from a global pool of content being made by filmmakers, shared in the festival circuit.

Path dependency is defined as the quality of earlier events affecting the trajectory and equilibrium of later events (Djelic & Quack, 2007). Applied, we might think about how current cultural conditions of a place are impacted by who lived in that place before and what organizations preceded the ones that are there now.

Overall, Complexity Theory might help us understand unintended consequences or externalities of well-intentioned policies, the emergence of trends or fads that arise from unexpected places, or how a bottom-up artist-organized cultural institution can become central to a regenerated creative district, as this theory is being applied in the social sciences with increasing frequency and success (Byrne & Callaghan, 2023).

Taken together, these three theories share foundational concepts, but offer different lenses through which one might understand the complexities of cultural and creative economy. Each theory operates in a multidisciplinary environment and provides insight into various aspects of relationships, creative innovation, and varied social interactions. Their application to the creative economy is recent and limited, in relation to other industries, which presents opportunities for practitioners and scholars to conduct research that explores these theoretical applications in concert with emerging patterns of the cultural and creative economy in real-world environments (Jung & Vakharia, 2019; Comunian, 2019).

CREATIVE ECONOMY ACTORS

Many different actors, organizations, institutions, and individuals participate in furthering creative economy agendas. Ashley (2014) notes a variety of different contributors and players among government, private effort, nonprofit, civic, and advocacy entities (see Table 5.2).

Within government, there is an impressive range of government or quasi-government participants that include economics development staff, urban planners, cultural planners, arts and cultural staff, state-level arts and creative district agencies, parks and recreation staff, cultural planning agencies, arts commission volunteers, hired Creative City consultants, planning and development service staff, state labor and commerce agencies, and national organizations, to name a few. There is also a plethora of quasi-governmental agencies involved, including redevelopment authorities, business improvement districts, and other types of taxing authorities.

On the nonprofit side, there is robust representation. It is common to see national advocacy organizations, state and local arts organizations, arts discipline-specific groups, international coalitions, and more. On the private side, we see real estate developers, arts journalists, economic development lobbyists, marketing firms, downtown business associations, and small and large business owners, for example.

At the international level, one of the powerful coalitions advancing the "Creative City" agenda is the United Nations Educational, Scientific, and Cultural Organization (UNESCO) Creative Cities Network (UCCN), where 300 cities around the world currently make up this network, working together toward

Table 5.2 Scale of creative-economy actor organizations

Neighborhood	City	Region	State	Nation
Neighborhood association	Municipal arts and culture agency, division, or department	Regional arts agencies	State arts agency	National division on arts and culture
Arts center	Municipal economic agency, division, or department	Regional economic development agency	Creative economy division	
Community-based organization	Film &/or television coalition	Multi-country or country alliance organization (UNESCO)	Commerce Division	
Arts organization	Universities, colleges, technical schools, or arts colleges	Universities, colleges, technical schools, or arts colleges	Department of labor	
Arts and cultural district alliance	Planning departments	Consultants	Planning departments	
Business improvement district	Environment and energy departments		Transportation departments	
Real estate developers	Arts commissions			
Consultants	Consultants			
	Libraries			

a common objective: placing creativity and cultural industries at the heart of their development plans at the local level and cooperating actively at the international level. UNESCO and other international-level champions like them will be discussed more in Chapter 8. This list of actors gives you an idea of the many different roles people are playing in this complex ecosystem.

Here are five examples of initiatives and programs with different types of actors at different scales that show the complexity of support for the creative economy. First, many cities and states have incentives for film and television production. For example, the City of Austin (TX) has a "Creative Content Incentive Program," where they provide a maximum incentive of 0.50% of the wages paid to residents (Visit Austin, 2023). They offer additional incentives if the project promotes Austin in greater ways, such as having its headquarters and majority of employees located in Austin. The implementation of this government incentive attracts and affects private sector arts and cultural jobs. Individual local artists, be they actors, set designers, costume designers, or filmmakers, are employed to meet the needs of the project and help the financiers recoup some of their investment through incentives.

In another site-specific project led by the government, the City of Los Angeles Department of Cultural Affairs (DCA) spearheaded the "Cultural Quarter" initiative to create a mixed-use facility, featuring 100% affordable artists' housing, a black-box theater, an art gallery, and a satellite campus for the California Institute of Arts (National Endowment for the Arts, 2023). The initiative was designed to provide greater access to creative-industry jobs, for a more diverse group of Angelenos, through internships and training opportunities. It was focused in areas called Promise Zones, which are vulnerable areas that have high rates of poverty. This initiative supports artists who are small-business owners in their own right. The clustering of the different creative uses makes the ecosystem denser, where creative collisions can occur between people from different creative practices. These collisions birth new relationships, spawn new projects, and spur innovation.

Individual artists who self-organize with other artists are also important actors in the creative economy. In Boise, Idaho, a group of women looking for support and camaraderie started a monthly meetup called Creative Women's Collective. The stated purpose of the group is to make friends with like-minded artists and creatives, working across different fields. Collaborations, work opportunities, inspiration, and support for each other emerge out of this organic, self-selected network of over eighty women. In a panel discussion, one of the founding organizers reflected that she gained a sense of creative permission from her employers at Visionkit Studio, a creative production studio. The owners, Matthew Wordell and Aaron Rodriquez, developed their philosophy of creative permission for their own work, to erase the impediment of imposter syndrome and allow themselves to expand past imagined barriers. Now, they extend this permission to their employees and colleagues, so that they may step into their own personal and professional power as well. Networking events like this one and informal events organized around creative activities, like having a music jam session or a crafting circle, facilitate self-efficacy in artists and creatives (see Figure 5.2).

Figure 5.2 Irish musicians come together in a Copenhagen pub for an informal jam session.
Source: Photo by Matilda Rose Bubb

Our next example shows how far reaching the impacts of one actor in the ecosystem can be. The Greenpoint Manufacturing and Design Center in Brooklyn is a nonprofit industrial developer. Since 1992, it has rehabbed eight manufacturing spaces, so that small manufacturing enterprises, artisans, and artists would have a place to work in a city that is increasingly pushing out creative work for residential uses. This has been a particularly important strategy for offering affordable, flexible production space for small and medium-sized creative manufacturers (Greenpoint Manufacturing and Design Center, 2023). That space houses custom fabrication in such areas as model making, home goods, textiles, glass, ceramics, and more. There is wood working with furniture, frame making, and antique restoration. There is also fine art, including painting, sculpture, and photography. When one of the authors visited the site in 2020, jewelry makers were making custom work for Nordstrom's and model builders were constructing displays to support exhibitions in the Natural History Museum. This nonprofit supports artist entrepreneurs, who then interact with the for-profit world as well as large established cultural institutions.

Finally, dual nonprofit partnerships are also an example of how these ecosystems materialize. In Seattle, the Trust for Public Lands worked with the Seattle Art Museum to develop the Olympic Sculpture Park as a Creative City urban redevelopment project. These organizations brought different skills, resources, and knowledge to the project to implement their new ideas (Ashley, 2014). Coming back to the concepts of network or systems theories, it is important to note that it is not just who or what skills the individual players may have but, importantly, how they work together. It is in these interactions where they experience changing equilibrium, feedback loops, and self-organization—identified in complexity theory as the elements that lead to the emergence of new ideas and creative structures (Comunian, 2019). A feedback loop drawn from these examples may be determining if people are applying for the film incentives in Austin, filling up the spaces in the Cultural Quarters, or using the custom fabrication spaces at the Greenpoint Manufacturing and Design Center. If they are, then a need is being met for the right population at the right price point. If not, then what conditions need to change? In all of these projects, there is a constant organic evaluation of conditions to determine what is serving artist producers, their audience of consumers, the supporting government, and the multitude of other actors involved in the capital transactions necessary to make these projects happen.

POLICY ENTREPRENEURS

Who are the creative economy policy entrepreneurs? Why do they do what they do? And where are the policies that they are supporting coming from? *Policy entrepreneurs* are actors willing to use their agency, resources, and relationships to disrupt the political status quo with policy innovations (Petridou & Mintrom, 2021; Kingdon, 2011). They actively survey the field for available policy solutions that can be adapted and applied to their local problems; and they are willing to make the arguments—to policymakers, the community, and the public—that are necessary to get them considered and passed (Goldberg-Miller, 2015). Policy entrepreneurs may come from within or outside the government and could be any policy-relevant actor, such as elected officials, appointed administrators, or those leading interest groups or research organizations (Kingdon, 2011).

The creative-city leaders we interviewed came from various backgrounds and perspectives. Some are career arts administrators, who have been part of policy formation, passage, and implementation for many years and are driven by a passion for the civic arts. Others had backgrounds in diverse fields, including urban or cultural planning, film, economic development, business management, marketing and communication, museum education, public policy, performing arts, nonprofit organizing, and product development in corporate environments.

The strategies they use to advance policy ideas include storytelling, problem framing, developing interdisciplinary teams, networking, and building advocacy coalitions (Petridou & Mintrom, 2021). Policy entrepreneurs may have strong solution preferences that may not be based on rational arguments, but are instead based on personal preferences, concepts pre-existing to the new problem, and emotional ideas about their solution (Cairney, 2018; Weible & Sabatier, 2018). For instance, when we interviewed an arts leader in Albuquerque, she mentioned the problem of vacant storefronts in a section of the downtown. Her response to this problem is to bring in artists and creatives to activate those spaces and make an otherwise empty area more fun (interview 11/21/23). This may be the solution Albuquerque's downtown needs. But it may also be an opportunity to apply a preferred policy idea to a problem area. Policy entrepreneurs may have solutions that precede the problem they are advanced to fix, and they may then work to get those solutions into the political system (Cairney, 2018). There are instances of policy entrepreneurs such as developers, politicians, leaders of nonprofit arts organizations, and artists who choose to champion creative economy policies in their respective cities—because they believe they will promote funding for the arts and artists that may not be there otherwise.

CREATIVE ENTREPRENEURSHIP

Let's return to the question of why Molly and Kei chose to start a for-profit business over a nonprofit model for their screen-printing business, even though they had humanitarian motivations and were engaged in an arts-related practice. When asked, they reflected that they didn't want to spend their time managing a board, chasing after grants, and writing reports—functions that would be required due to the structure of a tax-exempt organization whose funding mechanisms are rooted in the philanthropic and government environments. They expressed that they find it rewarding to generate earned income that pays for their business expenses and unique employee services, such as language acquisition and assistance navigating the bureaucracies of school enrollment, home rental, and acquiring social security cards. "We can make our own decisions. We don't have to go back to a grant outline and figure out that we can only spend the money this way," said Kei (see Figure 5.3). Their impetus to be for-profit entrepreneurs is to use their own creativity and skills to act independently as an economic engine that supports themselves, creates jobs, and provides a welcoming work environment for a specific population (interview 3/10/23).

Figure 5.3 Kei & Molly Textiles' products in their Albuquerque storefront.
Source: Photo by Matilda Rose Bubb

ARTS ENTREPRENEURSHIP

Stepping back to consider the creative entrepreneurs who are founding these types of organizations and why they might choose one structure over another, we find the term "arts entrepreneurship" as a focus of arts management research in the literature (Essig, 2015; Chang & Wyszomirski, 2015; Goldberg-Miller & Xiao, 2018). Researchers have different definitions of arts entrepreneurship. Essig defines it as a process by which someone converts the means to a desirable end through a structure, which could take various forms or scales (2015). Arts entrepreneurs have ideas that take a multitude of artistic expressions or symbolic forms as products, which are then shared with an interested public, through an organizational structure or process, such as their online commerce website or physical store—resulting in, ideally, a profitable end and a meaningful or socially impactful result for them as entrepreneurs (Essig, 2015). Artists, then, are business owners.

Chang and Wyszomirski (2015, p. 24) identify arts entrepreneurship as "a management process through which cultural workers seek to support their creativity and autonomy, advance their capacity for adaptability, and create artistic as well as economic and social value." Creative arts entrepreneurs, like Kei and Molly, are leaders who balance risks in the market environment, their personal career, and creative pursuits to create a new venture, identify financial capital, and develop a market or audience to a profitable end (Chang & Wyszomirski, 2015; Tremblay, 2008). They respond to an unstable and ever-changing environment that requires them to deal with economic disruptions, changing economic climates for public and private arts funding practices, new consumer demands, demographic shifts, technological pressures, and wage gaps (Chang & Wyszomirski, 2015; Santos Vieira de Jesus, 2021). The precariousness of creative work was laid bare during the COVID-19 global pandemic, affecting nonprofits, musicians, performers, venue, and business owners in this labor market particularly hard (Comunian & England, 2020; World Economic Forum, 2022).

People enter the creative marketplace for varied reasons. Their choices may be governed by a desire to make money, act on social values to make a difference, contribute their own aesthetic voice to the public conversation, or a combination therein (Hewison, 2004). How an entrepreneurial producer might engage with their potential consumers or audience has shifted dramatically, in part, due to the move online during the pandemic and the expansion of digital technology advances, such as social media and e-commerce sites like Etsy, crowdfunding, cryptocurrency, gig employment platforms, NFTs, and streaming platforms (Chang & Wyszomirski, 2015). Varied tactics and technology choices also change how markets are developed, reached, or monetized, making it easier for individual artists and creators to be sole-proprietor entrepreneurial actors (see Figure 5.4). An artist and creator can earn a living piecing together various micro-enterprises or contracting out their creative labor through the gig or freelance economy of short-term government and private projects in design, as writers,

Figure 5.4 Arts entrepreneur Randy Van Dyke in his *Capital Contemporary Gallery* and Van Dyke Frame Design storefront, Boise, ID.

Source: Photo by Matilda Rose Bubb

photographers, or as sound engineers (Kuhn & Galloway, 2015; Ellmeier, 2003; Woronkowicz & Noonan, 2019). We will take another look at arts entrepreneurship in the next chapter, focusing on individual artists.

Let's examine, more closely, the different organizational models or working practices an arts entrepreneur may choose from.

CULTURAL AND CREATIVE ORGANIZATIONAL MODELS

The cultural and creative ecosystem is a multifaceted domain of intersecting actors, nonprofits, businesses, and government entities, each serving stakeholders differently. From an economic perspective, nonprofit and for-profit entities occupy different market spaces and are not competitive—resulting in complementary relationships (Abzug & Webb, 1999). Arts nonprofits interact with for-profit and government organizations in various ways, such as serving as contractual agents for the government, for example in education; contracting with businesses to provide services; operating fundraising campaigns; and engaging corporate or government leaders as volunteers and board members (Abzug & Webb, 1999).

Cultural nonprofit institutions develop in the context of professionalized organizational fields and are driven by cultural and educational policy formed by social values. Creative industries, in contrast, are made up of businesses based on the concept of an industrial system, where symbolic goods with intellectual property are mass-produced and governed by economic policy and a profit motive (Redaelli, 2008). The government assumes a regulatory and supporting role, crafting policies that fuel prosperous property development, funding cultural programs and nonprofit organization grants to develop content for cultural consumption, and convening conversations that direct the growth and development of the cultural and creative sectors (Grodach, 2017). These organizations operate in private, nonprofit, and public sectors, each organized around different priorities, laws and policies, and economic demands that are not fixed, but are continually evolving (Markusen et al., 2008). Within these sectors, there are distinct business models that operate interdependently (Comunian, 2011).

Following are outlines of nonprofit, for-profit, and public creative organization business models and examples of their interdependencies.

NONPROFIT CULTURAL BUSINESS MODEL

There are approximately 125,600 arts nonprofits in America, ranging from presenting organizations, such as museums, performing arts facilities, literary publishers, television broadcast companies, and radio broadcasters, to cultural production groups, such as ballets, operas, theaters, and symphonies (causeiq.com accessed 2/26, 2023).

A nonprofit organization is, as designated in the United States by the Internal Revenue Service, exempt from federal and some state or local taxes and authorized to provide charitable tax deductions to donors (Cherbo et al., 2008). Nonprofit organizations are created and managed by "demand-side stakeholders," who want a product or service for themselves or for the good of others, but are not built around producing profit (Abzug & Webb, 1999, p. 421). Cultural nonprofit organizations form around mission-based purposes and operate with funding through government subsidies, earned revenue, and contributed revenue (Cherbo et al., 2008).

Nonprofits typically derive a small portion of their income from earned revenue, fees, or services (Abzug & Webb, 1999). Earned revenue may be ticket sales, space rentals, product sales, memberships, benefit income, or contract work. Contributed revenue comes from philanthropic foundations, government grants, donations from individuals, and corporate sponsorship (Cherbo et al., 2008). The reasons a person or business might donate to a cultural nonprofit range widely, including as an expression of shared values and preferences, perceived public-good benefits, market failure arguments, upholding heritage or identity, supporting excellence, improving the local cultural environment, providing equity and access to cultural resources, or shaping cultural tastes (Ashley, 2015; Craik, 2005). Corporate sponsorships to nonprofits are viewed as patronage, which is a gift or donation; marketing, which is understood as a business transaction deal; or a partnership, which is an alignment of mission and values that reinforces mutual brand or image projections (McNicholas, 2004).

In Europe, more so than the United States, many cultural institutions are funded primarily from direct government subsidies. But, in recent years, even these have increased fundraising efforts, so they might purchase art, pay high-profile performers, or cover escalating operating costs (Bille et al., 2020).

FOR-PROFIT CREATIVE BUSINESS MODEL

For-profit creative firms are founded and run by those who have a monetizable idea with potential intellectual properties, capital or investors with capital, and a desire for financial return on their investment (Abzug & Webb, 1999). Firms are part of larger industries or sectors, each having their own shared systems of suppliers, regulations, resources, and consumers; and they operate at a range of scales, from the very small to the very large (Redaelli, 2008). For example, a creative commercial company could be a single entrepreneur selling hand-made products, such as paintings, or contracting out their creative services by performing skills, such as writing, designing, or editing. On the other end of the spectrum are large, international media corporations producing blockbuster movies; publishers releasing thousands of books; or the video game industry churning out new entertainment engagement offerings by employing technology advances, such as virtual or augmented reality (Cherbo et al., 2008). Creative industries are known as commercial businesses that generate intellectual property, experiences, and products through their work, such as architecture and other design fields, the publishing industry, the music industry, theater, dance, visual arts, film, games, or software (Peltoniemi, 2015).

PUBLIC SECTOR MODEL

The government identifies arts, culture, and creative businesses as valuable community assets and economic drivers and uses tools, such as planning and policy, to direct resources to support the public good and align with leaders' political and economic interests (Ashley, 2015; Redaelli, 2013). From a systems perspective, the government performs several functions in relation to nonprofit cultural and for-profit creative organizations and industries. Local, regional, and national governments act as regulators and gatekeepers through the management of permits, regulations, and grants; they promote social capital by conducting planning, convening, and organizing around interests or field information; they provide financial capital through grants and service contracts; and they offer political capital by directing tax resources and social connections (Grodach, 2017).

The government also influences the spatial development and clustering of creative organizations in cities through zoning, the formation of cultural districts, building of cultural facilities, or other forms of capital investment in neighborhoods (Stern & Seifert, 2010). These urban development strategies are seen as ways to build economic revenue through tourism, attracting residents, ticket sales, and generation of identity markers (Grodach & Loukaitou-Sideris, 2007).

For example, Denver Arts and Venues is a city and county agency that manages multiple cultural facilities, including Red Rocks Amphitheatre, Denver Performing Arts Complex, Colorado Convention Center, Denver Coliseum, Loretto Heights, and

McNichols Civic Center Building. These enterprises generate their own revenue from event rental, beverage sales, parking, ticketing fees, and sponsorships—which is then re-invested in running the facilities and funding cultural programs such as public art and cultural grants. The executive director of Denver Arts and Venue referred to the organization as "a social cultural enterprise," which operates more like a nonprofit or business than a government (interview 11/21/22).

Outside of managing cultural facilities, Denver Arts and Venues has a spatial impact on the city's nonprofit and for-profit creative organizations through policy actions. They support cultural districts and do-it-yourself artist-run creative spaces with internal advocacy and external technical support. In the case of the city's eight organically developed cultural districts, Denver Arts & Venues provides capacity-building technical assistance, strategic planning resources, and targeted program funding that help those districts coalesce, market themselves, and plan for sustainability. For artist-run creative spaces, the agency partnered with Denver Community Planning and Development department to provide temporary occupancy waivers, while the spaces worked to update infrastructure, like crash bars on doors and sprinkler systems, to meet code requirements (City and County of Denver Community Planning & Development, 2017). These are examples of the interdependencies of the sectors and how each sector helps the other to meet their goals and objectives.

ANCHOR INSTITUTIONS

Anchor institutions are another way that the creative economy work advances in meaningful ways. There's a significant body of scholarly literature in urban studies and urban planning around the idea, importance, and evolution of the "anchor institution," which denotes an institution with significant assets that is unlikely to move. Universities, hospitals, and some large nonprofit institutions (foundations, churches, cultural institutions, and sport teams) became anchors, either consciously or unconsciously in regional economic development, due to corporate consolidation and the globalization of industries that created footloose companies and organizations that were no longer so heavily tied to place (Community-wealth, n.d.; Ehlenz, 2018; Birch et al., 2013). In response, scholars began to identify the traits and characteristics that university anchors and their "sticky capital" possess: they are major employers and support career ladders; they have sizable landholdings and invest in infrastructure; and they are centers of knowledge and innovation (Maurrasse, 2001). In some cases, they also anchor intra-urban collaboration and competition, creating broader networks throughout the region (Addie, 2020).

Anchor institutions are connected to arts and culture at different scales. Arts and cultural districts perform as urban anchors in place-based economic development in many cities, including Dallas, Denver, Pittsburgh, Philadelphia, and Seattle (Ashley & Durham, 2021). Birch et al. (2013) and Johnson (2018) identify how nonprofit arts and cultural organizations perform as urban anchors through their involvement in arts education, arts public participation, and neighborhood revitalization, as well as in how they develop and navigate public-private partnerships to fulfill their missions. Community arts organizations, which are artist service organizations in neighborhoods, act as smaller but important anchors in their neighborhoods by supporting microlocal arts activities (Markusen, 2014).

Larger regional and state arts anchors are often higher-education institutions. We may not immediately think of universities as arts organizations, but universities are likely the greatest arts patrons in the United States. Universities house art museums, theater companies, symphony orchestras, film studios, and publishing outlets, just to name a few arts organizations and brick-and-mortar investments that live under the higher-education umbrella. But universities in the twenty-first century are more than just arts patrons of physical structures; they are potential collaborators and partners in the regional arts and cultural ecology through their work on entrepreneurship, innovation, and knowledge transfer in economic, social, and community development. They are places where most emerging artists receive their artistic training and skills (Ashley & Durham, 2021). Universities support and invest in faculty and staff that oversee arts curricula, fund scholarships, pay faculty who are artists in their own right, and provide the research support and infrastructure needed for arts economic development. They hire faculty who bring ideas of organizational change for arts and culture; and they consider how to fund and finance those ideas. They are also important public art and community art partners in arts and cultural districts, where they may be connected in other ways, such as having a working studio there or acting as mentors for younger artists.

BLURRED BOUNDARIES

Outside of the binary choices, of for-profit and nonprofit, exist hybrid organizational models that blur boundaries (Whitaker, 2023). Examples include nonprofits that use market-driven revenue tools or commercial entities led by public-good outcomes or partnerships that bring together government, business, philanthropy, and creative entrepreneurs to execute projects. These are examples where legal boundaries and purposes cross over our traditional understanding of organizational models (Whitaker, 2023).

For-profit businesses may be structured around social values, as exemplified by those who obtain B Corp Certification—an assurance that a business meets identified criteria centered on social and environmental performance, legal commitments to stakeholders, and performance transparency. To be a B Corp is a commitment to achieve positive impacts on society, participants, employees, the local community, and the environment—in addition to generating profit (Ballard, 2021). B Lab, based in the United States, was founded in 2006 to act as a nonprofit network, working to transform the global economy to benefit all people, communities, and the environment. In the first year of their operation, in 2007, they certified 82 corporations as B Corps; and as of May 2023, there are 6,856 certified B corporations in 161 industries and 90 countries (Ballard, 2021).

The advantages of a B Corp certification are: building trust with consumers, communities, and suppliers; attracting and holding on to employees; and attracting investors who support the mission (Daugherty, 2023). The disadvantages are: a higher level of scrutiny on the organization to make sure they live up to the standards; the laborious process of certification; and the need for, often expensive, systems to track requirements (Daugherty, 2023).

Treefort Music Festival, founded in 2012 in Boise, Idaho, is a successful B corporation that delivers a five-day independent music festival every March and a three-day music festival in September. According to its founders:

> We have often stated that we are a "for profit entity run like a non-profit" because we have always been a values-based project, driven by a purpose much more than the lure of profit. In the summer of 2014, we were presented with a legal option for which we could best represent who we are as a festival, as community members and as a business—the Treefort Leadership Team officially formed Treefort, LLC and began seeking B-Corp certification to lock in and protect the legacy principles the festival was founded upon. Treefort became the first certified B-Corp music festival in 2015.
>
> (Treefort, 2023)

Two of the authors of this book happen to live in Boise, Idaho; so, we have great familiarity with the Treefort Music Festival and how it operates in the community. The founders designed it as a festival of discovery, featuring emerging bands from all over the world. In 2012, it had 137 bands. Each year it has grown significantly; in 2022, it had 470 bands and drew over 25,000 participants. As stated, it is a for-profit company that aspires to live up to the values of a nonprofit, with a focus on community values and environmental stewardship. They have rejected advertising overtures from large commercial beverage companies to prevent stages being named after products. They have an active Green Team that separates garbage for the landfill, recycling, and compostable waste; staff tracks the festival's carbon footprint, making efforts to reduce it; bands use gas generators for power; and vendors sell reusable cups for all beverages (Ballard, 2021). They also have an anti-racism statement, expressing that the event is for everyone, with a commitment to their own focus on being an anti-racist organization. The strong community relationships, built intentionally over time, came through during the pandemic. To cover losses, help keep the organization afloat, and support musicians, Treefort raised $350,000 in 2021 from nearly 1,000 private investors through a WeFunder campaign (Nows, 2022).

This fundraising effort is identified as an "equity crowdfunding" campaign, as it was billed and perceived as an effort to save a trusted and valued community partner—not just to save a business organization (Nows, 2022). In 2023, Duckclub, the parent organization that organizes Treefort, became a venue operator with the building of state-of-the-art Treefort Music Hall and the purchase of a historic Shriner Hall, as all-ages music venues. Private investors backed the purchases, because they believe in the Treefort mission (see Figure 5.5).

THE GIG ECONOMY DEFINITIONS AND SKILLS

The gig economy can be defined as the exchange of labor for money between individuals or companies on a short-term or freelance capacity and payment by task basis (Lepanjuuri et al., 2018). As per a 2018 study in Great Britain, 4.4% of the population, or 2.8 million people, worked in the gig economy in the previous year; gig workers were found to be primarily younger—ages 18 to 34—and similarly educated to the general population; examples of general jobs in the gig economy,

Figure 5.5 Treefort Music Hall hosts Tito Puente Jr. and his band.
Source: Photo by Matilda Rose Bubb

many of them part-time, include music or theater performers, couriers, transportation workers driving for companies like Uber or Lyft, food delivery drivers, and task-driven services as provided through online platforms (Lepanjuuri et al., 2018). Cultural or creative people working in the gig economy often act as arts entrepreneurs, running sole-proprietorships that are connected to their personal brands and unique skills as performers, writers, filmmakers, or visual artists (Venalainen, 2021). Some choose the freelance lifestyle, so that they have more independence, flexibility, and varied opportunities, as well as a way to capitalize on their creative skills with different employers (Petriglieri et al., 2019). Additional skills needed include the ability to communicate clearly, negotiate bids and bills, juggle multiple projects, time management, scheduling, budget management, and conflict management (Venalainen, 2021). Strategies for success include identifying or creating comfortable places to work if they are using computers or doing creative development work; developing a routine that keeps the workflow going; staying focused on a broader purpose that encompasses all their skills and talents; remaining connected to a network of mentors, collaborators, and friends; and redefining what work means and how to balance it with the rest of life (Petriglieri et al., 2019) (see Figure 5.5).

DOWNSIDES TO THE GIG ECONOMY

While the gig economy can provide benefits, it also has some serious downsides for cultural and creative workers. Gig work as a dancer, actor, designer, or musician can lead to low wages or irregular and unpredictable incomes, resulting in financial instability (Guerra & Lamontagne, 2023). To develop security, artists and creative workers must often develop a portfolio of assets that can be organized into different domains or side hustles, such as the musician/blogger/caterer (Baldini, 2022). Difficulties can arise around bargaining for intellectual property rights and retaining ownership of creative output in work-for-hire situations. Most of these roles lack health insurance, retirement benefits, and sick or vacation leave —all that traditional employees enjoy. Burnout and managing work-life balance can be challenging, since the entrepreneur is managing themselves and often multiple projects. Access to larger global

Figure 5.6 Gig working artists drawing caricatures in Seattle's Pike Place Market.
Source: Photo by Matilda Rose Bubb

markets can be difficult for independent contractors. The opportunity to pause for professional development or additional education may be missed due to the precarity of finances or timing of work opportunities (Guerra & Lamontagne, 2023; Kaiser-Schatzlein, 2021).

WORKFORCE PRECARITY

The COVID-19 pandemic impacted the creative economy in significant ways. In the United States, we lost an estimated 2.7 million jobs and more than $150 billion in sales of goods and services for creative industries nationwide. The fine and performing arts industries were hit hardest, suffering estimated losses of almost 1.4 million jobs and $42.5 billion in sales (Florida & Seman, 2020). Work was completed by government, advocacy, and private organizations to not only document the extent of the damages, but to also come up with strategies to support creatives. For example, The Colorado Creative Industries helped establish the Colorado Arts Relief Fund that provided

$7.5 million to artists and arts organizations across the state. Be An ArtsHero[1]—a grassroots campaign of arts and cultural workers, unions, and institutions—worked to successfully lobby for more relief for the creative economy, during the pandemic.

Many cultural and creative gig workers found themselves in particularly precarious conditions during and after the COVID-19 pandemic, due to canceled contracts and a lack of social or economic guarantees such as unemployment (Comunian & England, 2020; Santos Vieira de Jesus, 2021). Virtually overnight, lockdowns prompted closure of venues such as galleries, theaters, music halls, and recreation centers, which led to widespread job termination, layoffs, and canceled contracts (Jeannotte, 2021). A Canadian group called ArtsPond initiated a survey and resulting website called "I lost my gig"—reporting that between March 30th and August 15th, 2020, with 1,037 respondents, a total of 29,232 gigs had been canceled with a loss of over $20 million (ArtsPond, 2023). This catastrophic health event demonstrated the precarity of cultural workers in a gig economy and some of the unsustainable work practices that exist in the creative economy (Comunian & England, 2020). While, around the world, there were efforts by governments to offset these losses with special programs aimed at artists and cultural workers, these programs were limited and short-lived (Jeannotte, 2021).

As referenced in Chapter 3, the 2023 film and television writers' strike demonstrated that a pandemic was not the only threat to creative workers. Representatives of the Writers Guild of America union expressed that bad working conditions, unfair pay, fear of losing work to artificial intelligence, and the insecurities of working from job to job were at the forefront of their concerns (Browning, 2023). Writers were seeing their secure employment—with health benefits and annual, renewed television shows guaranteeing them good wages and predictable working conditions—devolve into day-to-day employment, in some cases, with none of the securities previously offered, drawing parallels with the gig work of an Uber driver (Browning, 2023).

SHIFTING DEMOGRAPHICS, CULTURAL INEQUITIES, AND COMMUNITY TRAUMA

American culture is transitioning through profound demographic changes and new migration patterns

(Mordechay et al., 2019). The 2017 US Census Bureau's race and age statistics reveal an aging White population and an increasingly diverse younger population, with projections that by 2045 the nation will become minority White (Frey, 2015). In Canada, Australia, and the United States, governments are reckoning with the genocide of indigenous populations and their relationships are reorienting around reconciliation at the policy, legal, and social levels in various capacities. African Americans, Latinos, Asians, Native American, and multiracial Americans are reinvigorating communities across the country, while facing difficult realities of racism, politicization of history, and devaluing of their contributions to arts and culture (Frey, 2015). The challenges, sometimes violent, that people of color face daily in society can't be ignored by the cultural field.

In 2020, in Minneapolis, a creative economy leader reflected that artists who were on contract for the city's Creative City Making Program were on the front lines of the protests responding to the death of George Floyd at the hands of a police officer, using their art to help people process what was happening. Even before Floyd's death, Black Minneapolis residents were disproportionately affected by police uses of force. Living with this everyday risk of violence affects people of color disproportionately and is felt by the creative community, many of whom are people of color. The projects the artists were doing for the city ceased while the artists responded to and participated in the aftermath of the community trauma of Floyd's murder. The arts administrator worked to extend the city program timelines, asked for additional resources, and supported the artists while they were in crisis around this issue of racism and police violence on Black people (interview 10/28/2023).

In the beginning of this chapter, we introduced Kei & Molly Textiles, whose workers are primarily incoming refugees from various parts of the world. Immigrants are another important demographic group to consider when discussing the changing face of the creative workforce. Immigrants bring their own cultural experiences, skills, and perspectives to the mix in their new home locations. When Kei and Molly created their business plan, they integrated into it the importance of treating their immigrant workers as whole beings and recognized that they had challenges that others did not.

> A lot of our staff came here [to America] with health issues; they've been living in refugee camps in Rwanda, don't have access to real medical care or dental here and they come here and realize they have diabetes. Or they have had certain things happen to them that have been very difficult, health wise. We help them navigate the health system. We've given them a job, but we also know that people need social support. We have a volunteer who helps with registering kids in the public school system, goes to doctors' visits with them so they understand what is going on and what medications they have to take. Molly and I used to do that ourselves. We'd go to the hospital and talk to the doctors. Because of that we'd all miss work. Sometimes their kids are sick or in trouble. They are afraid they can't take time off to figure that out. We have a lot of patience with our staff because we understand the reality of their lives.
>
> (interview 3/10/2023)

Another aspect that they work, with their staff, on is learning English. They have a box with questions in it (see Figure 5.7).

> It's just to get us going when we're all standing around here. We try to keep them kind of simple because some of them speak English well and wow, that's awesome. We always get new stories. One of the questions was something like what is your most treasured possession. We Americans think about an object of some sort. One of them said my most treasured possession is my passport. I'm free. Another one said my car because it gives me freedom. So it was interesting because it then leads to more interesting discussions about what it means to be here and what it means to be away from their original countries.
>
> (interview 3/10/2023)

The inclusion of demographic information is increasingly being added to applications for projects, although this is a contested practice with the Supreme Court's 2023 ruling against racial

Figure 5.7 Kei and Molly use question prompts to help their staff learn English.
Source: Photo by Matilda Rose Bubb

consideration for college admissions;, this brings into question one of the primary tools used in the post-civil-rights movement to ensure diversity in various environments (BBC, 2023). A public art manager from Albuquerque shared with us that they added demographic information to their calls for artists, which helps the selection panel be aware of their own internal biases that factor into their choices (interview 3/10/2023).

The valuing of diversity, equity, and inclusion is increasingly showing up in city cultural plans; although, more work still needs to be done in this area (Ashley et al., 2021).

CONCLUSION

This chapter introduces examples of actors, entrepreneurs, and organizations that make up the creative economy ecosystem and places them in the context of organically changing, complex adaptive systems. Using networks, systems, and complexity theories, practitioners and students can consider the intricate and evolving relationships between producers, consumers, regulatory bodies, and the public. It is our intent to prompt practitioners and scholars to think about how these concepts may be applied in their own communities. You can use these understandings to track and influence policy, condition change, or conduct research studies that help others understand what is going on in shared creative ecosystems. It is through careful observation that we might decode the existing or emergent interconnections in the creative economy ecosystem; we can then identify strategies to help these individuals and organizations ensure their resilience and inclusivity and respond to the new conditions sure to come our way.

TAKEAWAYS

From Chapter 5 we have the following takeaways about the creative economy ecosystem, its actors, and organizational models:

- A city's *arts and creative ecosystem* is a dynamic complex adaptive system—made up of networks of actors, organizations, institutions—which work interdependently to further creative economy agendas.
- Individual and organizational *actors* are engaged at various scales, including the neighborhood, city, region, state, and national level.
- *Arts entrepreneurship* is a management process used by creative leaders who seek to support their own or others' creative products or services, retain independence, and create artistic, economic, and social value.
- *Cultural nonprofit organizations* are developed in the context of professionalized fields, such as dance, visual arts, or literature; are mission-driven; and support the creation of aesthetic symbolic goods with intellectual property value.
- *Creative for-profit businesses* are founded and run by those who have a monetizable idea with potential for intellectual properties, capital or investors with capital, and a desire for financial return on their investment.
- *The gig economy*, which is the exchange of labor for money between individuals or companies, for tasks, on a short-term or freelance capacity; while it provides independence

and flexibility to creative workers, it can also be financially precarious.
- *Workforce precarity* is a reality for many working in the gig economy, prompting us to consider the employment practices at play and the support nets for creatives working in the gig economy.
- *Demographics* are shifting and communities are becoming more diverse. Equity, diversity, and inclusion are critical to consider in the future of emerging creative economies.

Discussion questions:
1. What type of creative businesses or organizations does your community need (that it doesn't have or have enough of)?
2. If you, as an arts entrepreneur, were to start a creative organization, which organizational model would you use? Would it be a commercial, for-profit business? Would it be a nonprofit? A partnership? What creative sector would it be in? And what products or services would you provide? Who are your customers?
3. Are there any B Corp businesses in your community? If so, what are they? And how does being a B Corp change how they do business?
4. What would you consider as the "anchor institutions" in your community? What purposes and populations do they serve?
5. Who has worked in the creative gig economy as an actor, musician, writer, filmmaker, costumer, visual artist, production team member, or something else? What were your experiences? What upsides and downsides did you experience?

Activities
- In your community, identify an example of meaningful cultural partnership between a for-profit commercial company, a nonprofit organization, and/or government entity. Explain their shared purpose and how their interests intersect and diverge?
- Write a mock business plan for the new creative organization you brainstormed on during the discussion. What kind of capital do you need to start? Where will it be located? What are your short- and long-term goals?

Note
1   https://beanartshero.com/.

REFERENCES

Abzug, R., & Webb, N. (1999). Relationships Between Nonprofit and For-Profit Organizations: A Stakeholder Perspective. *Nonprofit and Voluntary Sector Quarterly*, 28(4), 416–431.

Addie, J. P. D. (2020). Anchoring (in) the Region: The Dynamics of University-Engaged Urban Development in Newark, NJ, USA. *Geografiska Annaler: Series B, Human Geography*, 102(2), 172–190.

Allen, P. M. (1997). *Cities and Regions as Self-Organizing Systems: Models of Complexity.* London: Routledge.

ArtsPond. (2023). *I Lost My Gig.* https://ilostmygig.ca/ (accessed 23 August 2023).

Ashley, A. J. (2014). Negotiating Risk in Property-Based Arts Economic Development: Exploring the Innovative But Untimely Development Partnership Between the Seattle Art Museum and Washington Mutual. *Cities*, 37, 92–103.

Ashley, A. J. (2015). Beyond the Aesthetic: The Historical Pursuit of Local Arts Economic Development. *Journal of Planning History*, 14(1), 38–61.

Ashley, A. J., & Durham, L. (2021). Universities as Arts and Cultural Anchors: Moving Beyond Bricks and Mortar to Entrepreneurship, Workforce, and Community Development Approaches. *Artivate: A Journal of Entrepreneurship in the Arts*, 10(2), 1–41.

Ashley, A. J., Loh, C. G., Bubb, K., & Durham, L. (2021). Diversity, Equity, and Inclusion Practices in Arts and Cultural Planning. *Journal of Urban Affairs*, 1–21.

Baldini, A. (2022). Artist as Workers: Rethinking Creativity in a Post-Pandemic World. *Aesthetics of Contemporary Work*, 33.

Ballard, B. (2021). There Is No Planet "B"—How US Music Festival Production Companies Can Reduce Their Negative Environmental Impact by Incorporating as a Benefit Corporation. *William & Mary Environmental Law and Policy Review*, 45(3), 957–976.

BBC. (2023, June 29). *Court Overturns Race-Based College Admissions.* www.bbc.com/news/world-us-canada-65886212 (accessed 1 August 2023).

Bille, T., Mignosa, A., & Towse, R. (2020). *Teaching Cultural Economics.* Cheltenham & Northampton, MA: Edward Elgar Publishing.

Birch, E., Perry, D. C., & Taylor, Jr. H. L. (2013). Universities as Anchor Institutions. *Journal of Higher Education Outreach and Engagement*, 17(3), 7–15.

Browning, K. (2023, May 28). Hustle Till It Hurts: Gig Work's Luster Dims. *The New York Times*.

Byrne, D. S., & Callaghan, G. (2023). *Complexity Theory and the Social Sciences: The State of the Art* (2nd ed.). New York, London: Routledge.

Cairney, P. (2018). Three Habits of Successful Policy Entrepreneurs. *Policy & Politics*, 46(2), 199–215.

Chang, W. J., & Wyszomirski, M. J. (2015). What Is Arts Entrepreneurship? *Artivate: A Journal of Entrepreneurship in the Arts*, 4(2), 11–31.

Cherbo, J. M., Vogel, H. L., & Wyszomirski, M. J. (2008). Toward an Arts and Creative Sector. In J. M. Cherbo, R. A. Stewart & M. J. Wyszomirski (Eds.). *Understanding the Arts and Creative Sector in the United States* (pp. 9–27). New Brunswick, NJ & London: Rutgers University Press.

City and County of Denver Community Planning & Development. (2017). *Compliance Plan and Conditional Certificate of Occupancy.* www.denvergov.org/content/dam/denvergov/Portals/696/documents/Denver_Building_Code/2016_Code_Policies/Safe_Occupancy_Policy.pdf

Colavitti, A. M., Usai, A., & Serra, S. (2018). Towards an Integrated Assessment of the Cultural Ecosystem Services in the Policy-Making for Urban Ecosystems: Lessons from the Spatial and Economic Planning for Landscape and Cultural Heritage in Tuscany and Apulia (IT). *Planning Practice & Research, 33*(4), 441–473.

Community-wealth.org. (n.d.). *Overview: Anchor Institutions.* https://communitywealth.org/strategies/panel/anchors/index.html

Comunian, R. (2011). Rethinking the Creative City: The Role of Complexity, Networks and Interactions in the Urban Creative Economy. *Urban Studies, 48*(6), 1157–1179.

Comunian, R. (2019). Complexity Thinking as a Coordinating Theoretical Framework for Creative Industries Research. In S. Cunningham & T. Flew (Eds.), *A Research Agenda for Creative Industries* (pp. 39–57). Cheltenham & Northampton, MA: Edward Elgar Publishing.

Comunian, R., & England, L. (2020). Creative and Cultural Work Without Filters: COVID-19 and Exposed Precarity in the Creative Economy. *Cultural Trends, 29*(2), 112–128.

Craik, J. (2005). Dilemmas in Policy Support for the Arts and Cultural Sector. *Australian Journal of Public Administration, 64*(4), 6–19.

Cunningham, S., & Flew, T. (Eds.). (2019). *A Research Agenda for Creative Industries.* Elgar Research Agendas. Cheltenham & Northampton, MA: Edward Elgar Publishing.

Daugherty, G. (2023). B Corp: Definition, Advantages, Disadvantages, and Examples. *Investopedia.* www.investopedia.com/b-corp-7488828#:~:text=B%20corps%20are%20for-profit%20companies%20that%20have%20received,90%20countries%20worldwide%20as%20of%20late%20May%202023 (accessed 20 September 2023).

De Bernard, M., Comunian, R., & Gross, J. (2022). Cultural and Creative Ecosystems: A Review of Theories and Methods, Towards a New Research Agenda. *Cultural Trends, 31*(4), 332–353.

Djelic, M.-L., & Quack, S. (2007). Overcoming Path Dependency: Path Generation in Open Systems. *Theory and Society, 36*(2), 161–186.

Dovey, J., Moreton, S., Sparke, S., & Sharpe, B. (2016). The Practice of Cultural Ecology: Network Connectivity in the Creative Economy. *Cultural Trends, 25*(2), 87–103.

Ehlenz, M. M. (2018). Defining University Anchor Institution Strategies: Comparing Theory to Practice. *Planning Theory & Practice, 19*(1), 74–92.

Ellmeier, A. (2003). Cultural Entrepreneurialism: On the Changing Relationship Between the Arts, Culture and Employment. *The International Journal of Cultural Policy, 9*(1), 3–16.

Essig, L. (2015). Means and Ends: A Theory Framework for Understanding Entrepreneurship in the US Arts and Culture Sector. *Journal of Arts Management, Law and Society, 45*(4), 227–246.

Florida, R., & Seman, M. (2020). *Lost Art: Measuring COVID-19's Devastating Impact on America's Creative Economy.* Metropolitan Policy Program at Brookings.

Fox, M. (2011). Jeanette Ingberman, a Founder of Exit Art, Dies at 59. *The New York Times.*

Frey, W. H. (2015). *Diversity Explosion: How New Racial Demographics Are Remaking America.* Washington, DC: Brookings Institution Press.

Goldberg-Miller, S. B. D. (2015). Creative Toronto: Harnessing the Economic Development Power of Arts & Culture. *Artivate: A Journal of Entrepreneurship in the Arts, 4*(1), 25–48.

Goldberg-Miller, S. B. D., & Xiao, Y. (2018). Arts Entrepreneurship and Cultural Policy Innovation in Beijing. *Artivate, 7*(1), 23–47.

Greenpoint Manufacturing and Design Center. (2023). https://gmdconline.org/ (accessed 1 September 2023).

Grodach, C. (2017). Urban Cultural Policy and Creative City Making. *Cities, 68,* 82–91.

Grodach, C., & Loukaitou-Sideris, A. (2007). Cultural Development Strategies and Urban Revitalization. *International Journal of Cultural Policy, 13*(4), 349–370.

Guerra, P., & Lamontagne, S. (2023). Contemporary Music Ecosystems' Transformations: Live Music, the Gig Economy, and Social Changes. *Ethnomusicology Review, 24,* 1–10.

Hewison, R. (2004). The Crisis of Cultural Leadership in Britain. *International Journal of Cultural Policy, 10*(2), 157–166.

Jeannotte, M. S. (2021). When the Gigs Are Gone: Valuing Arts, Culture, and Media in the COVID-19 Pandemic. *Social Sciences & Humanities Open, 3,* 1–7.

Johnson, S. (2018, November 13). As Tech Companies Hire More Liberal Arts Majors, More Students Are Choosing STEM Degrees. *EdSurge.* www.usnews.com/opinion/knowledgebank/articles/2018-01-19/in-this-digital-agestudents-with-liberal-arts-training-stand-out

Jung, Y., & Vakharia, N. (2019). Open Systems Theory for Arts and Cultural Organizations: Linking Structure and Performance. *The Journal of Arts Management, Law and Society, 49*(4), 257–273.

Kaiser-Schatzlein, R. (2021, January/February). Struggling Artists: Why the Creative Class Once Flourished. *New Republic, 252*(1/2), 54–57.

Kingdon, J. W. (2011). *Agendas, Alternatives, and Public Policies* (Updated 2nd ed.). Longman.

Kuhn, K. M., & Galloway, T. L. (2015). With a Little Help from My Competitors: Peer Networking Among Artisan Entrepreneurs. *Entrepreneurship Theory and Practice, 39*(3), 571–600.

Lepanjuuri, K., Wishart, R., & Cornick, P. (2018). *The Characteristics of Those in the Gig Economy.* Britain's Department for Business, Energy & Industrial Strategy.

MacDowall, L. J., Dunphy, K., & Blomkamp, E. (2015). *Making Culture Count: The Politics of Cultural Measurement.* London: Palgrave.

Markusen, A. (2014). Creative Cities: A 10-Year Research Agenda. *Journal of Urban Affairs*, *36*, 567–589. https://doi.org/10.1111/juaf.12146

Markusen, A., Wassall, G. H., DeNatale, D., & Cohen, R. (2008). Defining the Creative Economy: Industry and Occupational Approaches. *Economic Development Quarterly*, *22*(1), 24–45. https://doi.org/10.1177/0891242407311862

Maurrasse, D. J. (2001). *Beyond the Campus: How Colleges and Universities Form Partnerships with Their Communities*. New York, London: Routledge.

McNicholas, B. (2004). Arts, Culture and Business: A Relationship Transformation, a Nascent Field. *International Journal of Arts Management*, *7*(1), 57–69.

Montalto, V., Moura, C. J. T., Langedijk, S., & Saisana, M. (2019). Culture Counts: An Empirical Approach to Measure the Cultural and Creative Vitality of European Cities. *Cities*, *89*, 167–185.

Morcol, G., & Wachhaus, A. (2009). Network and Complexity Theories: A Comparison and Prospects for a Synthesis. *Administrative Theory & Praxis*, *31*(1), 44–58.

Mordechay, K., Gandara, P., & Orfield, G. (2019, April). Embracing the Effects of Demographic Change. *Educational Leadership*, 34–40.

National Endowment for the Arts. (2023). Los Angeles, CA: Cultural Quarter/Promise Zone Arts. www.arts.gov/impact/creative-placemaking/exploring-our-town/los-angeles-cultural-quarter-promise-zone-arts#:~:text=Recognizing%20the%20need%20for%20affordable%20artist%20housing%20and,group%20of%20Angelenos%20through%20internships%20and%20training%20opportunities (accessed 1 September 2023).

Nows, D. (2022). The Local Nature of Equity Crowdfunding. *University of Pennsylvania Journal of Business Law*, *24*(2), 476–515.

Ortega-Villa, L., & Ley-Garcia, J. (2018). Analysis of Cultural Indicators: A Comparison of Their Conceptual Basis and Dimensions. *Social Indicators Research*, *137*, 413–439.

Peltoniemi, M. (2015). Cultural Industries: Product-Market Characteristics, Management Challenges and Industry Dynamics. *International Journal of Management Reviews*, *17*(1), 41–68. https://doi.org/10.1111/ijmr.12036

Petridou, E., & Mintrom, M. (2021). A Research Agenda for the Study of Policy Entrepreneurs. *Policy Studies Journal*, *49*(4), 943–967.

Petriglieri, G., Ashford, S., & Wrzesniewski, A. (2019). Thriving in the Gig Economy. *Harvard Business Review*, 109–116.

Redaelli, E. (2008). Thinking about Local Cultural Policy in America: Navigating the Theoretical Confusion. *The International Journal of the Arts in Society*, *2*(4), 55–64.

Redaelli, E. (2013). Assessing a Place in Cultural Planning: A Framework for American Local Governments. *Cultural Trends*, *22*(1), 30–44.

Santos Vieira de Jesus, D. (2021). Living on the Edge: Brazilian Creative Workers in the Gig Economy During the COVID-19 Pandemic. *Psychology Research*, *11*(2), 56–62.

Stern, M., & Seifert, S. (2010). Cultural Clusters: The Implications of Cultural Asset Agglomeration for Neighborhood Revitalization. *Journal of Planning Education and Research*, *29*(3), 262–279.

Treefort. (2023). *B-Corp.* https://treefortmusicfest.com/ (accessed 2 September 2023).

Tremblay, D. G. (2008). From Casual Work to Economic Security: The Paradoxical Case of Self Employment. *Social Indicators Research, 88*(1), 115–130.

Venalainen, J. (2021). "The Future Demands We All Become Prolific Artists"— Cultural Ideals of Gig Work in Popular Management Literature. In B. Dolber, M. Rodino-Colocino, C. Kumanyika & T. Wolfson (Eds.), *The Gig Economy.* New York, London: Routledge.

Visit Austin. (2023). *Film Commission Incentives & Grants.* www.austintexas.org/film-commission/incentives-and-grants/#:~:text=Administered%20by%20the%20City%20of%20Austin%20%E2%80%93%20Economic,is%20produced%20by%20Austin-based%20company%20or%20promotes%20Austin (accessed 1 September 2023).

Weible, C. M., & Sabatier, P. A. (Eds.). (2018). *Theories of the Policy Process* (4th ed.). New York, London: Routledge.

Whitaker, A. (2023). The Rise of Hybrid Practice: Creative Institutional Design as Arts Entrepreneurship. *Artivate: A Journal of Entrepreneurship in the Arts, 11*(3).

World Economic Forum. (2022, February). *Creatives Have Experienced Significant Job Losses During COVID-19: What Needs to Be Done to Protect Employment in the Sector?* www.weforum.org/agenda/2022/02/creatives-job-losses-covid-employment/

Woronkowicz, J., & Noonan, D. S. (2019). Who Goes Freelance? The Determinants of Self-Employment for Artists. *Entrepreneurship Theory and Practice, 43*(4), 651–672.

Centering artists and creatives

Chapter 6

INTRODUCTION

Without the imagination, talent, and hard work of artists and other creatives, there would be no creative economy. While the terms artists and creatives are related and used interchangeably in the creative economy context, they have slightly different meanings. Artists can be defined as those who engage in creative expression or production, often specializing in a particular discipline such as visual, performing, or literary arts. But they may just as easily be multidisciplinary, work collaboratively across disciplines, or create new discipline areas based on emerging technologies. They may or may not have formal training. Artists use their talents and skills to solve problems and translate ideas into symbolic forms that have aesthetic characteristics and convey ideas, experiences, heritage, or social commentary (Baldin & Bille, 2021). A "creative" is a broader term encompassing those who engage in creative problem solving and thinking—one that may not be limited to traditional art forms. They may be artists, but may also or instead be producers, recording engineers, software designers, or marketing executives. Creatives use their skills for creative expression to make a living; or they may use them to solve a complex social problem (McRobbie, 2016). Creatives and artists both engage in creative activities that require knowledge, skill, and mastery. They play crucial roles reflecting cultural, societal, and political realities; and many also push against the boundaries of those realities, innovating while challenging social norms.

DOI: 10.4324/9781003147688-6

Individual artists and creatives must be centered in the community clusters and global networks of the creative economy—as without them, it wouldn't exist. Who they are and the roles they play are multifaceted, manifest in different professional arcs, and engage differently in various sectors. Creatives contribute to the economic lifeblood of society through the products they create, the participatory experiences they provide for audiences, the innovative processes they develop, and the ways they shape how people think about the problems and opportunities of the world. Their work can inform, attract, and wed people to places. They self-organize, working with other artists and non-artists to create businesses, co-working spaces, and communities. They experience unique challenges related to the production and distribution of their work, protection of their intellectual property, and pursuit of a living wage.

To support individual artists, many cities have a portfolio of arts and artist programs; discipline-specific arts organizations; facilities that feature artists' work and grant opportunities to facilitate cultural and creative expression for intrinsic and instrumental value; and staff and volunteers who work to champion and advocate for the arts at different scales, sectors, and disciplines. We do not cover all the assets that make up the creative soul of a city; rather, we focus on illustrating how economic development plays out in different ways. If you are interested in learning more about what your neighborhood, community, city, or region offers, we encourage you to find your city's arts and cultural affairs websites and their arts and cultural plans. Additionally, keep your eyes open for how the arts might show up in your libraries, schools, parks, transit, and public work locations.

Centering artists in the Creative City is a theme throughout this book. In this chapter, we continue this thread by exploring topics such as common mythologies; changing social constructions; contemporary roles of artists; and concepts about the "creative class," situated in the Creative City and creative economy frameworks. Arts economic development may focus on artists as creative workers, entrepreneurs, and collaborators (Ashley, 2015). We focus on artist-driven economic development and on the artistic and creative workers that are at the core of the creative economy. We explore the various ways artists train—formally and informally—to join and remain in the creative workforce, as well as how higher-education institutions support workforce development.

Artists, artisans, and creators draw on multiple activities and spaces to acquire their talents and skills and to build community. For example, if you do an internet search for "artist studios," you will be amazed by the plethora of options that appear in your search discovery. There are a range of opportunities that cross discipline, career stage, facility type, ownership structure, fee structure, and more. They each represent different missions and visions about how best to support the arts. Many artists also are the curators, creative entrepreneurs, and social entrepreneurs behind arts organizations, collectives, and activities that add to the richness of place and provide new opportunities to participate in the cultural and artistic life of a city. We detail examples of the types of arts-business structures that serve artists, such as incubators and co-ops. We ask questions about who is recognized and valued as an artist, related to diversity, equity, and inclusion. We could not possibly cover this ecosystem in a single chapter or even a book; rather, we provide insight into different facets of this ecosystem, with an eye toward how individual artists fit into the system. We end this chapter with a discussion of the challenges facing artists and creatives, as well as a look to the future; and we provide examples of strategies, we have observed, that aim to support artists as integral members of thriving creative ecosystems.

ARTIST MYTHOLOGIES

The cultural mythologies and stereotypes around what an artist is, who gets to be an artist, and the qualities artists reportedly embody can seriously get in the way of being a real creative person in society. Before we talk about the actual roles that artists are play in communities and the challenges they face, let's name and debunk the typecast personas of artists.

The number one myth is that *artists are geniuses born with talent and do all their great work alone*. Think of assumptions around Picasso. While many artists begin their craft at a young age, some learn, grow, and pass through different phases in their work. While some of them may have innate talent or natural proclivities, being an artist in any discipline is a skill and is learned through effort, application, and environment. Creative expression is always rooted in a cultural and historical environment; and it requires a social context to come into being and be communicated to others (Montuori & Purser, 1995). If you look at the context around any individual who has achieved great recognition for their creative achievements, you will find that they may have mentors, financial or social champions, family members or spouses, producers, managers, and educational or professional environments that contributed to their advancement.

Artists have to be poor. We've all heard of the starving artist, the one who suffers for their craft, eschews worldly comforts, and withdraws from society for the love of their work (D'Souza & Gurin, 2017). Vincent van Gogh, who died by suicide after creating paintings that are celebrated today, is the archetypal figure who typifies this storyline. This myth is closely related to another myth that *artists don't care about making money*—they dance, make music, paint, and design video games solely out of passion. Historically, industry gatekeepers have used this myth to their advantage, underpaying artists willing to work for "exposure" or asking artists to sign away their intellectual property rights (Sharp, 2023). In reality, many artists are highly entrepreneurial, want and need to be paid fair wages for their creative labor that brings benefit to others, and are often highly enmeshed and involved in the communities in which they live and work. Marketplaces like Pike Place Market in Seattle, continually operating since 1907, have artisans and boutique food producers who operate as small-business owners serving a welcoming public (see Figure 6.1).

Another myth is that *artists must have formal training* to succeed. The proliferation of university programs professionalizing career paths in the arts is one way that artists may progress in their field. But being self-taught, learning through an apprenticeship or mentorship model, or other ways of learning are also pathways to meaningful, successful careers in the creative economy. While it is undeniable that higher-education institutions offer valuable skill-building and accreditation, often what is most helpful from formal training is a stronger network that provides more opportunities for

Figure 6.1 Mr. Dan at the Pike Place Market in Seattle, Washington, where he has been selling his work since 2002.

Source: Photo by Matilda Rose Bubb

individuals through connections. Later in this chapter, we will explore other ways that higher educational institutions contribute to workforce development, which are not traditionally considered. Some assume that *artists are always highly educated*, which is why they fit into the knowledge economy; but, this is not the case. Being highly educated does not necessarily equate with being highly creative. Self-taught visual artists like James Castle, Bill Traylor, and Frieda Kahlo or musicians like David Bowie and Prince illustrate this point well.

The glamorization of artists as celebrities and wealthy stars sets expectations that this is what true success looks like and does a disservice to the acknowledgment of the successes of most artists who live life as middle-class people. Of course, there are artists, particularly commercial artists, who are able to maximize the media spotlight and achieve well-deserved fame and a great following. We do not diminish their achievements or talent. One of the authors recently attended a sold-out concert of Florence and the Machine at the Hollywood Bowl with 17,500 adoring fans in attendance. It was a magnificent experience (see Figure 6.2). However, most working musicians are not performing on a stage to thousands. Young people are fed social constructions of what it means to be an artist and the belief that real artists are separate and different from regular people. These stereotypical and grandiose conceptions may discourage some from realizing their creative ambitions, because they aren't flamboyant or don't think they are that special—so they must not really be an artist (Gaztambide-Fernandez, 2008). In this chapter, we reflect on the contemporary roles of artists we've observed in life and in literature.

CONTEMPORARY ROLE OF ARTISTS AND CREATIVES

A subset of Chapter 3 explains what it means to focus on artists and creators. It describes an occupational or labor force approach to understanding the creative economy, as opposed

Figure 6.2 Florence and the Machine performing at the Hollywood Bowl in Los Angeles, CA.

Source: Photo by Matilda Ross Bubb

to an industrial approach. We know that artists cross sectors, have a variety of different types of career profiles, and possess a higher-than-average entrepreneurial streak. We know that it's risky for many to choose an artistic career and that many are working to overcome the myths associated with an artistic life. If we assume that the creative and artistic attributes, skills, and knowledge are important to the creative economy and to the broader regional economy, then it's valuable to consider strategies and tools that help unleash and nurture this creative potential.

It's also important to recognize that it is challenging to convince policymakers to support artists for their economic contributions. For the most part, the patron model is still the most dominant; although, this has shifted considerably in the past twenty years. Rather than relying on collectors, grants, or patron benevolence, artists have turned to digital platforms and crowdfunding mechanisms to garner support directly from audience members, gain a following, and monetize their content through advertising or merchandising. In these ways, artists have changed what the creative economy looks like. Quantifying cultural tourism and the multiplier effects associated with it, which is what a lot of the early economic impact studies focused on, is a valuable perspective; but, it's an incomplete portrait. Even though the broadening and deepening of arts economic development is centuries in the making, we haven't unleashed its full power and potential, as artists are demonstrating (Ashley, 2015), from a growth or development perspective. By looking at artists as creators, makers, and doers, we can continue that quest.

As touched upon in Chapters 3 and 4, artists are part of the knowledge or information economy, which can be defined as "production and services based on knowledge-intensive activities that contribute to an accelerated pace of technical and scientific advance, as well as rapid obsolescence" (Powell & Snellman, 2004, p. 199). In this economy, intellectual and creative capabilities are more important than natural resources connected to a place or physical inputs. The creative economy is part of this overall knowledge economy. With this in mind, let's consider the multiple roles that artists play in the creative economy.

Artists are entrepreneurs, community organizers, and economic developers. Later in this chapter, we'll talk more about artists as entrepreneurs and organizers, who create opportunities for themselves when they don't see the opportunities they want to be a part of.

Artists may be producers of original visual or performing arts in one or more discipline areas. They may be working in "high" art environments like a violinist playing in a philharmonic orchestra or more "low" artists like those playing music in commercial venues. Or, they may be the same artists performing in the orchestra during the day and a bar later that night (see Figure 6.3). The concepts of high and low art are social categorizations, which have been used to divide commercial artists whose work is sold widely or sold for less, from those deemed worthy, by funding gatekeepers, to receive patronage at high dollar values (Friedman & Jones, 2011). Concepts of "quality" and "taste" have also historically been gatekeeping mechanisms to keep those who are different from the norm—which has

Figure 6.3 208 Ensemble, an innovative chamber music group made up of musicians who also play in traditional professional orchestras, perform in Freak Alley Gallery, Boise, ID.

Source: Photo by Matilda Rose Bubb

predominantly been White, western, heterosexual men—from gaining patronage in cultural hierarchies. While underrepresentation of Black, Brown, female, and non-cis White artists in museums, galleries, orchestras, leadership roles, and other cultural environments has been shifting since the advances of social movements of the 1970s, economic disparities still exist. As comic books and graffiti art have made their way into museums and galleries and popular music forms have become big business impacting societal buying and attention habits, artists have become players in the taste-machine—making the seeming divisions between commercial and fine art less distinct.

Artists may be designers of something that is produced and sold by others. Everything we touch in our material world was designed by someone (or teams of people), including the speakers on our desk, the clothes on our back, and the cars we climb into every day. Their creative vision and innovative thinking have changed the aesthetics of buildings, textile design, everyday products, and the digital environment of icons and software interfaces. People like Charles and Ray Eames changed modern furniture design, Milton Glaser influenced the look and feel of graphic design, Coco Chanel gave us the little black dress and other iconic fashion designs, and I.M. Pei designed modernist architecture such as the Louvre Pyramid.

We often focus on the aesthetic value of what artists produce; but the social value they bring can be equally or more important. They can help solve or bring attention to pressing community challenges with their work, such as environmental or social issues. Artists can be protesters or political actors. They have unique skills that translate problems and conflicts into stories, songs, performances, or objects that help audience members understand or think about those things differently. Banksy started as a cheeky graffiti artist in Bristol and London. Works he did adjacent to canals in Camden, England in 2021 during the Copenhagen Climate Summit poked at global warming issues with a nod toward the talks (Kuang, 2021). Banksy's hidden identity and continued questioning of authority have maintained his position as an activist as much as an artist (Reyburn, 2020). Artist Cannupa Hanska Luger (Mandan, Hidatsa, Arikara, Lakota) created the Mirror Shield Project to protect his family's

Standing Rock Sioux Tribe Reservation, under threat from the oil pipeline in 2016 (Luger, n.d.). This project, which provided protection and reflected the police's own image back at them during protests, has made its way into other protests across the world since. During the Black Lives Matter protests that took place in the United States in 2020, artists painted murals on the wood, covering up boarded businesses in Oakland, CA; New York, NY; and Portland, OR—memorializing those killed by police (Krales & Pavic, 2020). They brought media awareness and heightened visibility to explosive and painful issues facing the community. Other artists also use art to heighten public awareness of issues important to them. Established in 2017, the Three Sisters Collective is an "Oga Pogeh/Santa Fe based Pueblo/Indigenous women-led grassroots organization" that focuses on restoring wellness, preserving traditional practices, and bringing awareness to the epidemic of missing and murdered indigenous women. They use murals to tell stories, hiring indigenous artists to create them. Lead artist Autumn Dawn Gomez (Taos Pueblo/Comanche) worked with the Three Sisters Collective to complete Connected: A Collective Dreaming in the Indian Pueblo Cultural Center, in Albuquerque, in 2023 (Three Sisters Collective, n.d.) (see Figure 6.4).

Artists reflect the past and imagine futures outside of what others may be able to see. Rap and hip-hop transnational artists reveal experiences and histories unique to Black artists, as well as the cultures and people they represent. Groups representing visual artists, like the Guerrilla Girls, question cultural paradigms, such as gender roles and power dynamics. Musicians like Imogen Heap, Robert Henke, and Suzanne Ciani push against boundaries in technology, science, and engineering to create sounds like we've never heard before. Visual artists like Olafur Eliasson, Mel Chin, and Amy Balkin force us to reevaluate the trajectory of our planet by depicting the environmental degradation of our air, melting ice caps, or contaminated land. While most known for her groundbreaking design of the Vietnam Memorial, Maya Lin's recent work has focused on environmental issues, such as the mass extinction of species and climate change, and things we might do to reverse these seemingly inevitable changes (Cotter, 2021). In summary, artists contribute to the knowledge and creative economy

Figure 6.4 Autumn Dawn Gomez is the lead artist working with Three Sisters Collective, painting a mural at the Indian Pueblo Cultural Center, Albuquerque, NM.

Source: Photo by Matilda Rose Bubb

through their creative output, innovative imagination, cultural and social output, and aesthetic and economic contributions.

CREATIVE CLASS

Here, we would like to situate the artist within the concept of the "creative class,"—an outgrowth of Richard Florida's investigation into the shift from industrial models of production to a more knowledge-based workforce (Florida, 2002). A synthesis of ideas about economic development theory, economic geography, political economy, and social science together inspired the idea of a new way of understanding this economic, social, and workforce-based paradigm (Florida, 2014). Florida dubbed this the "creative class." The theory incorporated the philosophy of Jane Jacobs (1961), wherein human-scale people-centric planning and the aggregation of residents and businesses in a more community-centric way were paramount. This thinking of Florida's had as its primary foci on cities, issues of clustering, and the expansion of the concepts of economic development—to include the human dimensions of cities, in addition to the economic ones.

Florida embraced the idea of creativity as a driver, rather than focusing on economic prosperity as the fruit, solely, of physical labor or manufacturing. This concept of creativity as a growth engine led him to look more closely at cities as places, where this "creativity engine" would flourish. Putting a stake in the ground, Florida categorized this creative class as consisting of, "jobs in knowledge-intensive industries that involve the production of new ideas and products or that engage in creative problem-solving" (Florida, 2014). This sector of the US workforce accounts for 41 million individuals and makes up a third of all US workers, with half of its wages and salaries. Aggregating seemingly disparate categories such as law, engineering, finance, and medicine with design, media, entertainment, and architecture—not to mention what Florida calls the "super creatives", which includes actors, dancers, poets, and university professors—seems to encompass just about everyone except for politicians, industrial workers, and the service class.

However, the subsequent study of urban areas as magnets for this gargantuan sector of any population has resulted in a plethora of research, scholarly writing, and popular literature. In the United States, the US Department of Agriculture has designated a census-tract county code called the "creative class," a development that could be seen as the entrenchment of Florida's concept within the policy lexicon. Now that the "creative class" theory is embedded in the thinking about municipal economic development, cultural and city planning, community building, and urban development worldwide, a more nuanced focus on the specific ways that this concept can be implemented and leveraged is both timely and necessary.

Currently, scholars are concerned with the creative economy's sustainability, given the competitive pressures limiting urban creative diversity, necessary for sector resiliency (Florida & Mellander, 2015; Goldberg-Miller & Fregetto, 2016; Timberg, 2015). This concern is driven by the conflicting, dual nature of Creative City placemaking, whereby it requires both disruptive innovation and a respect of the authentic, vernacular culture for economic viability (Greenwald, 2012; Podmore, 1998;

Zimmerman, 2008). Without a proper understanding of the local creative class, cities may advocate for changes that threaten the very identity of these districts, triggering neighborhood change displacement and a loss of creative production diversity (Goodsell, 2013; Talen, 2006).

This is, in part, because the Creative City's dual nature lends itself to ad hoc public-private partnered boosterism, which is inherently difficult to direct toward long-term goals (Stern & Seifert, 2007; Zukin, 2009; Zukin & Braslow, 2011). At stake is the very resiliency of the local creative class. There is increased interest in applying strategic management principles toward a city's creative economy planning efforts; through these principles, a city's capacity toward creative economy adaptation and self-renewal may remain resilient in the face of continual global economy shocks (Reinmoeller & van Baardwijk, 2005). Through strategic management principles, creative cities can better understand the components of a resilient creative economic engine, including creative district typologies and the successful promotion of creative production.

ARTISTS IN THE WORKFORCE

Creatives move fluidly through the varied aspects of the creative economy. Since this field includes so many facets—and artists and creative workers may be involved in cultural production within the entertainment and arts sectors—there are many options for individuals. They may be involved with nonprofit entities, such as theater, music, dance, and visual arts organizations, as well as for-profit industries, including film, publishing, galleries, design, and fashion. Within the aspect of entertainment, sports play a role, as does tech. In each case, artists can be cultural entrepreneurs and innovators. In addition, each of these segments has distinct outputs, issues, audiences, and markets.

The overarching connection between creative working in for-profit and nonprofit entities is creativity. As discussed in Chapter 5, both sectors utilize management techniques, which an individual may learn and become adept at. Also, many of these entities are in urban centers and are often merged in the minds of the public, policymakers, and consumers. However, the link between these sectors for an individual artist or arts producer is creativity, innovation, and culture. An artist needs to be concerned with market development and regeneration, as do each of these entities (see Figure 6.5).

When an artist works with or chooses to start a nonprofit or for-profit entity, they must keep in mind that the nonprofit has a mission and needs to ensure a revenue stream, whereas the for-profit has a revenue goal and focuses on building their core brand and demonstrating corporate citizenship. There are linkages between these sectors, however. Both arts workers and leaders flow between these sectors; and in all cases, issues such as stakeholder partnerships, community relationships, and the role of policymakers factor into success. As mentioned, these entities are often found in cities; and so, artists need to understand the issues of urbanism as well as the way that creative economy workers as well as consumers may be involved in the changing demographics of a city. In this

Figure 6.5 Indigenous dancers with the Kaltonaka Dance Group (Chichimeca Mexica Azteca) perform at the nonprofit Indian Pueblo Cultural Center in Albuquerque, New Mexico as part of their weekly Cultural Dance Program.

Source: Photo by Matilda Rose Bubb

globalized economy, as there is tremendous mobility, an artist may move not only from sector to sector, but from city to city.

Artists who become managers of organizations either in the nonprofit or for-profit field face many challenges. These include financial and revenue issues, retaining top talent, ways to utilize the latest tools and technology for marketing purposes, and building and sustaining the demand for the brand. An artist who works in a company or nonprofit as well as one who has their own business need to understand how to keep the energy flowing, stay entrepreneurial, and be contemporary and agile. Quality-of-life issues are key for an individual artist or one who works in a company or a nonprofit. We want artists and creatives to be able to live where they want to and not be pushed out by rising costs, brought on by the development they attracted to an area. The culture of these arts organizations is very important. They need to view innovation as a watchword and a draw, as well as prizing creativity and valuing content as a key to differentiating the entity.

An artist may learn from working in each sector. Nonprofit organizations tend to be strong at relational skills, connecting with the donor base and constituents, building a loyal following, and being transparent and accountable to the public. For-profit entities require powerful transactional expertise and have a strong need for data, research, and technology. These entities utilize forecasting tools, strategic planning, and analysis. Thus, an artist who succeeds in one sector can easily translate this knowledge base into the other, by being a valuable member of a team in either.

The mobility of workers within the knowledge economy means that, for an arts manager, it may be hard to attract and keep the best teams. This is a high-energy field, with constant interest in products and services; and it's one that is visible within any geographic setting. An individual artist needs to develop their own brand as well, focusing on their strengths, differentiation, and core brand promise—and what they stand for (see Figure 6.6).

ARTISTS AS ENTREPRENEURS

As discussed in Chapter 5, many individual artists become what can be called "arts entrepreneurs." Relevant to individual

Figure 6.6 Artists in Georgetown paint a Black Lives Matter mural during the 2020 protests, 2020–06–27.

Source: Library of Congress

artists involved in arts administration, cultural management, and business management fields, the concept in the literature can be dated back to the early 2000s (Caves, 2000; Mulcahy, 2003; Rentschler, 2003). Arts entrepreneurship and cultural entrepreneurship can be used interchangeably. While artists, makers, craftspeople, and other members of the creative class have been entrepreneurial since time immemorial, we now know that there are some keys to success for artists wanting to make a living from their work.

Some of the hallmarks of arts entrepreneurship include not only artists making a living from their work, but also being a part of socially conscious business practices that contribute public value (Essig, 2015). The B Corp certification we discussed in Chapter 5 is one of these socially conscious business practices. Other practices include fair compensation for artists and collaborators, transparency and accountability to the public, engagement with community in meaningful ways, or committing to eco-friendly materials and waste reduction. For Beckman and Essig (2012), arts entrepreneurship has to do with "individual artist self-management and self-actualization." Artists add value to society both in terms of financial benefits and their contributions to cultural and intellectual production, which also hold great worth (Frey, 2005).

Artists, as entrepreneurs, often can be understood to have three main areas of activity: first, developing new ventures or businesses; second, finding new financial capital; and third, ideating and developing new markets (Chang & Wyszomirski, 2015). In this research, these authors develop the following definition: "arts entrepreneurship is a management process through which cultural workers seek to support their creativity and autonomy, advance their capacity for adaptability, and create artistic as well as economic and social value." According to Essig (2015), an aspect of using ingenuity in fostering success despite scarce resources—or what could be thought of as creative inspiration—is a key hallmark of the arts entrepreneur. This is what differentiates arts entrepreneurs from businesspeople, that is, the way that artists imbue innovation and creativity as a part of their business acumen.

Factors including resilience, opportunity spotting, and bricolage are aspects of the way that artists approach entrepreneurship (Goldberg-Miller & Xiao, 2018). Bricolage, which can be understood as how to find ways to realize and meet goals by doing more with less, is a hallmark of the creative sector (Baker & Nelson, 2005; Preece, 2013). Opportunity spotting is a practice whereby innovation, imagination, and respect for the unexpected is highly valued. All these aspects make creative individuals pioneers in the burgeoning field of arts entrepreneurship.

Another aspect of the focus within arts entrepreneurship is the self-employment landscape, which can be viewed as part of the study of traditional entrepreneurship (Woronkowicz & Noonan, 2017). Often located in urban areas, individual artists may take advantage of resources such as robust market opportunities, collaborative milieus, and an environment that fosters innovation and experimentation—each of which contribute to the development of the arts entrepreneur.

An additional aspect that differentiates "traditional" entrepreneurship from arts entrepreneurship, in the literature, has to do with the contrasting bottom line. In the arts-entrepreneurship case, scholars posit that a motivating factor may be something beyond the financial remuneration associated with successful enterprises; this would include personal satisfaction, aesthetic fulfillment, or a contribution to society that exceeds the purely economic motivation (Caves, 2000; Essig, 2015; Preece, 2011). Yet, as we discuss elsewhere in this chapter, artists still need to support themselves, even if they derive more than monetary benefits from their work (see Figure 6.7).

Artist entrepreneurs are distinguished by their experimentation and innovation, and the recognition that they may have the chance to offer unique solutions to business challenges, instead of using conventional means. This way, arts entrepreneurship does not have to follow the traditional business model and can rely upon unusual solutions. One interesting addition to the formal models of nonprofit and for-profit entities is the idea of social enterprise, which has gained popularity among the creative class. Social enterprise (SE) and

Figure 6.7 Jewelry business owner of Silver Cherry Studios who designs, creates, and sells her own jewelry pieces at Pike Place Market in Seattle, WA.

Source: Photo by Matilda Rose Bubb

social entrepreneurship can be applied to the arts where a market focus is not the primary drive, but includes other social and environmental purposes. Trapp (2015, n.p.) shares examples of this alignment:

> Earthen Symphony, a decorative art and design studio in Bangalore, India, provides untrained women with employment opportunities as designers, artisans, and craftsmen, as well as promotes a healthy work culture in the local community. Indego Africa is a lifestyle brand company in Uganda that works with women artisans through local cooperatives to generate income to support women and their families in the present, provide them with training to build profitable and sustainable businesses for the future, and gain access to international export markets. The avatar therapy project, led by Thomas Craig of King's College London, is a computer-based system that aims to treat people with schizophrenia who suffer with hallucinations despite drug treatment. There are even digital artists and health care providers coming together to tackle bold projects, like *PR:EPARe*, a video game developed by the Serious Games Institute designed to help teenagers deal with sexual coercion during adolescence.

Trapp (2015) also notes that impact investing has had some difficulty finding, recognizing, and including artists and arts entrepreneurs within this framework. There is ongoing work to be done about how and when different sectors work together to support these hybridization efforts for the creative economy and the creative society (Ferreira et al., 2023).

Artists such as Andy Warhol, Beyoncé, Rhianna, and Jessica Alba embody the tenets of arts entrepreneurship. Each stretched the boundaries between art and commerce, resulting in successful careers. Rhianna moved beyond musical performance to found her clothing brand, Fenty, as well as start a makeup line. Warhol broke through the traditional understanding of what constituted artwork by starting what he called the "Factory," in which he hired a group of people to fabricate his pieces. Beyoncé has created a global empire that draws millions of fans and, together with her husband Jay-Z, has built a brand that has endured for over 25 years.

Jessica Alba, through her dedication to creating products that are environmentally sustainable, now has a company worth well over $1 billion. These artists, each, created their success through innovation, tenacity, and business acumen.

EXAMPLES OF ARTS SUPPORT STRUCTURES

As we mentioned earlier in our discussion of artist myths, artists don't operate in isolation from society. To be successful, they often collaborate, create, or embed themselves in formal or informal institutions that provide training and other forms of support. Here, we discuss a few types of artist support structures.

Artist workforce development through higher-education institutions

One of the most common, but overlooked, environments to examine as a place for how artists learn the skills to become entrepreneurs or managers of nonprofits is higher-education institutions (HEIs). These anchor institutions, each rooted in a place, are a primary mechanism for artist workforce development. Chapter 3 talks broadly about how HEIs contribute to the creative economy. While we stand by our statement, in the myth section, that not all artists have to have a formal education to be creative and successful, universities, four-year colleges, community and technical schools, and art-and-design-focused academies support artists in many ways. As major employers, they hire artists as faculty to teach and train the next generation of creative workers. In addition to the traditional curriculum associated with the craft of their particular arts discipline, students often have access to career-readiness curriculum and credentialing, including arts entrepreneurship, arts management, design thinking, project management, creative placemaking, and Science-Technology-Engineering-Arts-Math (STEAM) opportunities, to name a few. As Tepper and Kuh (2011, n.p.) argue, arts degree programs "cultivate creativity" in ways that are valuable and competitive in an expanded set of fields and situations outside the traditional arts. We see art experts and students partnering with biology, geology, environmental studies, and other fields to figure out how to translate tough or complicated ideas in ways that are compelling and easier to understand. These translation skills are a competitive job market skill; and they often feature the social purpose of a university to create a better and more sustainable future. For example, one of the authors worked with graphic design, geoscience, and biology faculty to develop a Snow-Artist-in-Residence program. This program helped students develop science illustration skills that could be used to communicate how technology instrumentation matters in measuring snow as a mechanism for studying sea-level rise. In another example, environmental studies and arts students worked with local artists and alumni to develop technical assistance toolkits to share how the arts could contribute to neighborhood conversations around pollinators, water quality, and affordable artist housing and workspace.

Arts-entrepreneurship programs, often aligned with new venture creation and business curriculum, are also increasingly common in HEIs. While there isn't a singular curriculum, there is "some consensus about pedagogy," where the curriculum includes experiential learning, whether its about business development plans, competing in pitch competitions, participating in incubators or accelerators, or needing to have an internship. (Essig & Guevara, 2016, pp. 20–21). There are different interpretations and applications of cultural entrepreneurship in European higher education and arts entrepreneurship in the US higher education—where the former focuses on an additional business school education with a focus on the creative economy (Kuhlke et al., 2015) and the latter is centered on an interest by arts disciplines to provide career-readiness support (Essig, 2017). Research is increasingly clear that experiential learning is what provides a value-added college experience (Eyler, 2021) and that the arts have historically done this by default. Arts programs continue to work on broadening their reach.

As a portion of their workload, faculty are often asked to conduct research and creative activity that may lead to new ideas, products, and processes. In addition to allocating "time" as part of regular academic contract, these anchors may provide physical infrastructure resources like incubators, studio spaces, maker spaces, and co-op opportunities to support this work. For example, the University of Chicago has developed a neighborhood platform, Arts & Public Life, in Washington Park, to provide residencies for Black and Brown Artist and creative entrepreneurs, in addition to arts education for youth and artist-led programming and exhibitions. This includes a collection of activities, businesses, and organizations. In addition to an artist-in-residence program, they also host a L1 Creative Business Accelerator Fellowship, which prioritizes:

> Ready-to-scale small business owners who have already developed a customer base and product line that is relevant to or well-received by South Side consumers. Occupants of the retail space on Garfield Blvd are selected not only to signal that high quality South Side commerce is possible, but also to show that such commerce is uniquely well-suited to take root on the Arts Block—drawing energy from the other cultural and commercial activity happening on this historic corridor while contributing to the Block's vitality and growth.
>
> (Arts & Public Life, n.d.)

This initiative is a ten-month program, with funding and support by The Silver Room Foundation, with additional collaboration and resources from the UChicago Polsky Center for Entrepreneurship and Innovation. The program provides mentorship on commercial real estate, marketing and public relations, pitch decks, networking, sale and product placement, legal compliance, and financial bookkeeping, while offering spaces to work, sell, and connect.

   HEIs have large- and small-scale venues for community members to attend events and exhibitions by nationally touring artists or featuring local faculty and student work. HEIs feature public and civic art; and they often sit within or are adjacent to arts and cultural districts. These clusters provide opportunities for people to develop, share, and sell their work, or to experience different types of arts activities within a relatively confined set of spaces and places (see Figure 6.8).

   Whether it's part of a curriculum or a separate service and support structure, HEIs may also assist art students, art faculty, or artists in the community by guiding them through tech transfer, licensing/copyrighting/intellectual property, or small-business development.

Figure 6.8 Printmaking students host a free to the public event to test out printmaking processes.
Source: Photo by Matilda Rose Bubb

They provide seed funding to launch ideas or help and support faculty, staff, students, and community partners that want to apply for external funding, where the HEI gets a cut. They may also provide technology or instrumentation to faculty, staff, students, and community partners. For example, HEIs may provide "green screens" for filmmaking faculty and students or expensive printmaking and ceramics facilities and materials (Ashley & Durham, 2021).

While HEIs are key players in arts and cultural economies, we also know that city officials have a difficult time understanding how to advance strategies to capitalize on these anchor institutions in their communities (Ashley et al., 2023). Yet, our analysis of US arts and cultural plans finds that they provide limited detail on, and display a limited, conceptualization of these institutions' contributions to the city's arts scene and cultural economy—thereby missing important economic development opportunities. We encourage you to look at the HEIs, especially community colleges, in your city to learn more about how they support and invest in artist workforce development.

Cooperatives

Arts workers and entrepreneurs may face a rocky career trajectory as they cobble careers together, as discussed in Chapter 3, or in an entrepreneurial environment and system that is still learning how to navigate and support this kind of work. We focus particularly on those that are looking to have a regular middle-class existence, rather than those who are at the elite end of the spectrum. The life of an artist can be precarious with significant financial instability. Artists often must invest in their own supplies; in traveling for research, exhibitions, performances, and events; in shipping their materials, products, and innovations to different marketplaces, festivals, commercial outlets, and more; and in hiring people to support their work. They often must learn, on their own, how to market and communicate their work, as well as sell their wares, processes, products, and ideas. They are hustling to drum up new projects, clients, and funding sources without certainty of success.

One strategy for addressing these challenges is for artists to develop or participate in a co-op environment. Co-ops bring artists together to pool resources, so they can afford space, equipment, services, opportunities, and other needs. Beyond these practical items, participants may benefit from sharing knowledge, expertise, and community with others interested in similar fields and practices. The idea behind co-ops is that participants can share the risks of investment, collectively work together to make decisions in a democratic environment, and improve their artistic careers and/or passions.

Berman (2020) introduces three different categories of artist or artistic co-ops. First are "worker co-ops" where the workers are owners and have a say in what happens in the space and how it is managed, rather than being at the mercy of a manager or board. For example, "if you are a part of a set-design co-op, the people who wield the power drill are the same people who negotiate day rates and safety requirements" (Berman, 2020, n.p.). The Sound Co-op in New York is an example of a worker co-op, which was organized in 2015 in a quest to be part of a sustainable economic development system, based on cooperation rather than competition. They provide sound services for broadcast, commercial, documentary, and scripted shows, while also providing playback on music video shoots, post-production sound, and podcast set-up/recording. They describe their structure as:

> Members each own the business and work together on co-op decisions, information exchange, shared assets, and making sure we do the best job possible for our clients. We run our systems through direct workplace democracy and consensus decision-making, each member having a vote. Members work managerial and administrative positions internally and are each an integral part of the cog that makes us run smoothly and that allows for the most focus and follow through in our work. Members can also apply to be board members, and the board convenes on decisions that affect the livelihood of the cooperative.
> (Sound Co-op, n.d.)

"Studio co-ops" are a second type; and they create an opportunity to have a space without assuming the sole or primary financial requirements of that space. For example, "artists might decide to work together to purchase a physical studio space collectively" (Berman, 2020, n.p.). There is not a single organizer or landlord; rather, the group makes decisions together about how the space is used, how much they might charge, or what artistic activities they would promote, exhibit, and sell. The third kind is also a "gallery co-op," where artists show their work together; this can be a permanent situation where a group of artists own a space, or they rent it or use it for a brief time (Berman, 2020). By showing your work together and sharing a percentage of the profits, you can hopefully expand your audience of buyers and curators. It means that curators are less important or less crucial, which can be useful, given the nature and trends of these gatekeepers (Berman, 2020).

It is also possible for these co-ops to evolve over their lifespan into new forms of organizations. For example, the Manhattan Graphic Center, a co-op started in 1986 by 20 printmakers, was originally run by a group of volunteers—where they could "support the learning and practice of fine art printmaking by providing an affordable, inclusive, professional studio and exhibition space, where a community of printmakers at all stages of artistic development can create and present their work." By 2021, the volunteer model could no longer; and they appointed a management team to run the studio with the input of the members, volunteers, executive committee, and board (Manhattan Graphic Center, n.d.).

Arts incubators

Incubators are tools for economic development that often focus on new ventures or product creation. They often focus on emerging companies or entrepreneurs who need the support services that incubators provide to move to their next level of growth and productivity. The idea is that these innovators and firms "graduate" and eventually move out of the incubator, after they have matured and can succeed on their own.

We have seen arts incubators emerge, taking this idea and translating it to arts and creative activity. They also typically focus on small or emerging organizations or on individual artists. These incubators can be nonprofits, for-profits, government entities, or a hybrid of sectors. The art incubators provide a range of development services that are often subsidized or supported by membership fees. As part of their offerings, these incubators may include facilities (work space, meeting space, spaces for creating, exhibiting, or performing art), artistic equipment (e.g. kiln, film post-production equipment and technology, or computers with creative software), training on non-arts skills (bookkeeping, marketing, investing strategies, or business planning), networking (with industry leaders), and access to potential funding and financing opportunities (grants, angel investing, or fiscal sponsorship). Incubators may also require participants to participate in other aspects of their programming.

For example, the University of Texas at San Antonio Arts Incubation Research (AIR) Lab studies the economic potential of "artists as non-conventional entrepreneurs" (Americans for the Arts, 2021, n.p.) The AIR Lab, funded by the National Endowment for the Arts, implemented a national survey of arts incubators to learn more about their structure, programming, and financial situation. The survey, based in the United States, yielded some interesting results from the 147 incubators that participated:

- The responding organizations reported that the median operating budget (expenditures) for the current fiscal year was $375,000.
  - A median of $45,000 was dedicated to the arts incubator programming.
  - Respondents provided a median of $25,000 in funding (e.g., scholarships, grants) to participating organizations and/or individual artists to offset the cost of participation.
- The responding organizations reported that they served a median of 40 individuals through their arts incubator programming during the past year.
- 30% of the organizations reported that their arts incubator programming is specifically designed to serve historically underserved communities.
- 47% of the responding organizations reported that they offer their arts incubator programming for free.
  - 40% charge some participants, but not others.
  - 13% charge all participants in their incubator programming.
- The responding organizations reported that an average of 83% of their participants typically complete the entirety of the incubator program.

(Americans for the Arts, 2021, n.p.)

These survey findings are helpful, because they show such a range of activities, as well as illuminate how the incubators function. It is important to note that we do not have a lot of information about how these incubators differ from others that we find in economic development or how they are connected to economic development goals.

There are many different kinds of incubators; and they have a wide variety of attributes and characteristics. For example, the NOLA Arts Incubator focuses on collaborative learning, teaching, and artistic experimentation in urban gardens. The nonprofit works with artists and youth to "grow gardens, green spaces, and environmentally focused public art that gives back to the community." This New Orleans incubator, through the Galvez Garden, also sponsors Artist-in-Residency opportunities for "Southern artists with interests in experimenting in green architecture, environmental art installations, or hosting workshops connecting art and nature" (NOLA, n.d.).

Another example is the Canada Music Incubator, which focuses on emerging musicians and music businesses to support music infrastructure, creative economic development, and high school creative entrepreneurship programs. This national nonprofit offers different programs with different services based on the varied kinds of careers that are connected to the music industry. Their Artist Entrepreneur program supports bands, from any genre, to learn how to develop sustainable careers through mentoring from industry experts, who provide insights on touring, marketing, promotion, performance and production, talent buying, music publishing, and more (see Figure 6.9). Their Artists Manager program centers on emerging managers to help

Figure 6.9 Young the Giant lead singer Sameer Gadhia performing on tour.
Source: Photo by Matilda Rose Bubb

them learn how to grow as industry professionals who need to manage artists as well as their own management careers. The program helps them learn how to navigate these dual roles by developing business plans, learning about different revenue streams, and making connections to people across the industry (Canada Music Incubator, 2021).

South Carolina's Commission on the Arts hosts an Arts Incubator program that targets mid-career professionals, rather than emerging artists; and they prioritize those who are freelancers. Applicants learn how to develop a business plan, and if they finish the program, they are given a small honorarium of $200. They are also given access to business planning, market analysis and customer segmentation articulation, financial planning and forecasting, and a reflection opportunity to articulate artistic visions and goals (South Carolina Arts Commission, 2023). There are additional prerequisites for applying, including not being in a degree-granting program and participating in a course to lay the foundation for a productive session.

The Berlin Arts Institute has an interdisciplinary arts incubator that supports work across the art, cultural, creative, and digital industries, as well as arts tech, research, technology, and science. They target "entrepreneurially minded artists, inventors, innovators, researchers, and (prospective) entrepreneurs seeking further training in the creative environment of the arts to incubate their ideas and develop their future or already existing projects or startups" (Berlin Arts Institute, n.d.). Their approach focuses on co-working spaces primarily; and participants can also opt into additional service and professional development with coaching, programs, and curriculum (e.g. master classes, seminars, workshops, and lectures).

We highlight these few incubator snapshots to underscore the breadth and depth of coverage.

Artist-in-residence programs

Another common programmatic approach is artist-in-residence (AIR) programs. AIRs provide the opportunity for artists to remove themselves from their normal environments, as well as their everyday patterns and habits, and move temporarily to a different place or environment that allows them to create

Figure 6.10 Public artist JR collaborated with Cuban-America artist José Parlá to create *The Wrinkles of the City* in Havana, Cuba—featuring 25 senior citizens who lived through the Cuban revolution.

Source: Photo by Matilda Rose Bubb

new work, try new processes or practices, or reflect on their artistic and creative journey (Nuendorf, 2016). For example, the Independent Publishing Resource Center in Portland, Oregon, seeks to offer affordable access to space, tools, and resources for independent published media and artwork. They host a Re/Source Artist and Writer Residency program, which "is designed specifically to support artists and writers of color to develop their art practice and share with the wider community" (Independent Publishing Resource Center, n.d.). They offer access to space, equipment, and mentoring, as well as a $4000 stipend. AIRs really vary in terms of what they provide, what they request in return, and how long they last. The National Park Service has over 50 AIR programs across the country for visual artists, writers, musicians, and other creative media; this includes lodging in a national park for two to four weeks to make new work and then share it with the public, encouraging them to visit a national park (National Park Service, n.d.). The Artist Communities Alliance (ACA) is a national organization, based in the United States, that includes listings and opportunities at more than 300-member artist communities, residency programs, and institutions that support living artists in the creation of new work (ACA n.d.). They also provide research and best practices to help these types of organizations succeed.

Other artist-centered models

In addition to co-ops, incubators, and artist-in-residency programs, there are also a variety of other artist spaces and opportunities that support economic and community development. Markusen et al. (2006, p. 7) studied artists' centers, which are defined as "dedicated spaces—where artists are routinely welcome; where membership and access to programming are open to all comers; and where workspace, residencies, grants, mentorships, and exhibition and performance spaces are available on a selective, often competitive, basis." The study focused on these centers in Minnesota; it shows how they morphed from informal entities, a narrow constituency of artists, into a robust source of inclusive artistic activity that benefited artists and their neighborhoods and communities. Their research featured Centers for Composers, Literary Artists, and Playwrights (e.g. American Composers Forum, The Loft Literary Center, The Playwrights' Center, and SASE: The Write Place); Centers for Visual Artists (e.g. Highpoint Center for Printmaking, IFP Minnesota Center for Media Arts, Minnesota Center for Book Arts, Minnesota Center for Photography, Northern Clay Center, and Textile Center); Community and Affinity-based Centers (e.g. Center for Independent Artists, Homewood Studios, Interact Center for the Visual and Performing Arts, Intermedia Arts, and Juxtaposition Arts); and Smaller City Centers Bridging Artists and Community (e.g. Banfill-Locke Center for the Arts, Duluth Art Institute, Grand Marais Art Colony, New York Mills Regional Cultural Center, and Northfield Arts Guild).

We list these categories and types to show the range of these types of centers, as well as how they support those who practice art for their own enjoyment and growth and those who also draw on these to help develop their careers. These examples of artist spaces are an important part of the creative economy ecosystem; and there are many other types of spaces, programs, and initiatives that also contribute to supporting artists.

CHALLENGES

Through the lens of an artist family

We have discussed in this chapter, and others, how significantly artists contribute to the creative and overall economies. Artists' talent, creativity, and hard work, coupled with artist support structures described in this chapter, can make them successful businesspeople, workers, and creators. However, as we have also mentioned, artists face many challenges as they build careers and support themselves with their creative enterprises. In this section, we discuss several of these challenges; although, we don't pretend this is a comprehensive list. We ground this section in the experiences of a two-artist family in Toledo, OH. Rachel Richardson is a public art and cultural event coordinator, performer, and author. Her husband Yusuf Lateef is a visual artist, muralist, educator, and community engagement professional. They have an eight-year-old daughter.

First, as we discussed in Chapter 5, employment as an artist often comes with precarity, especially at the beginning of a career. There are several reasons for this. Artists often take on several part-time jobs to supplement their arts income. These jobs are often part of the gig economy, with irregular hours and inconsistent pay; and, in the US, they are unlikely to provide benefits such as health insurance or a retirement plan (Guerra & Lamontagne, 2023). Artists who do work for public or nonprofit agencies may wait months to get paid, often finding themselves, as Richardson says, "at the mercy of nonprofits' fiscal years"— which makes it almost impossible to project the family's earnings for the year. This precarity means that creatives are less likely to be able to build wealth, afford high-quality housing, or invest in training or equipment that could further their arts careers.

As they work to establish their careers, artists may encounter different forms of gatekeeping—"the act of controlling or limiting access to an institution" (Rivard, 2020). Gatekeeping can be diffused and subtle, where certain art forms or artists from certain backgrounds aren't considered worth buying from or funding. Funders often don't want to take a chance on an unknown quality—so artists must be successful before they can be successful. Sometimes, there is a single arts agency in a small- or medium-sized city that largely controls funding and public art. The kinds of art and the particular artists this agency wants to fund are the only ones that will make it through the process. Gatekeeping can also come from financial institutions. Artists often don't have access to traditional forms of financing for starting businesses, because banks don't see the businesses as a good risk. And, if they don't accumulate wealth, they also lose access to other forms of capital, such as home equity loans, that could be used to finance a career.

Artists must also be uniquely concerned with control over their own creative output. Predatory, or lopsided contracts, signed early in an artist's career may become increasingly problematic when an artist gains commercial success. A notable example of this is Taylor Swift's re-recording and re-releasing of her entire catalog prior to August 2019. At that time, her former record label, Big Machine Records, sold her song catalog to Scooter Braun, which meant that he had full control over who could play her music and how it could be used. Swift had negotiated control over the master rights to her songs when she switched to Republic Records in 2018; so, to regain full control over her entire creative output, Swift took the radical step of fully re-recording her early albums, naming each newly recorded song with its original name (Taylor's version) (Grady, 2023). This way, she is taking back her own voice (Sherman, 2023).

The development of AI, which surely will have gained further capabilities between the time we write these words and when you read them, has brought up an additional set of concerns for artists. Tom Hanks recently warned fans that his likeness had been appropriated without permission and fed through an AI to create an ad for a dental plan (Cooper, 2023). Kareem Abdul-Jabbar comments, "we can give birth to a whole generation of actors that don't exist in real life, but are made up of stolen physical characteristics of real actors" (2023, n.p.).

Public agencies, such as arts commissions, are convenors and funders of the arts. The rules they have put in place over the years, around the process, are meant to ensure fairness. In practice, they can also sometimes stifle creativity or result in the artist losing some control over the work. For example, Richardson says she might approach an institution with an idea for a mural. She might have the artist and the work ready to go. At that point, however, the agency might need to put out a public call, solicit more stakeholder input, or even choose a different artist. The independent idea becomes a project by committee. The powerful leaders of anchor institutions are ultimately making the decisions.

Public artists may encounter difficulties when the owners of the property want to make changes. Murals that have been painted with the agreement of the building owner are supposed to be legally protected from destruction; but, in practice, they can be at risk if the building ownership or tastes change (Haver, 2013). Artist Robert Wyland painted an iconic and enormous mural of humpback whales on a building in downtown Detroit in 1997. In 2021, the building's owner commissioned a temporary advertising mural banner, by local artist Phillip Simpson, that hung down over (and covered up) the whales. Many Detroiters, and Wyland, were upset by the covering of the whale mural. The company that commissioned the mural banner, however, saw it as "bringing more art" to downtown; and others saw it as a "win" for Black Detroit artists over an out-of-town artist (Robinson, 2023, n.p.). A storm in August 2023 ripped down half of the banner, reigniting the debate over which mural deserved visibility.

We have discussed some of the challenges artists face as they work to establish their creative careers; but, artists and other creatives who achieve commercial success may encounter different challenges. Fed, in part, by the myth that artists shouldn't care about money or should be poor, commercially or financially successful artists may face resentment toward their success. Visual artists, in particular, may even believe that commercial success renders them artistically unsuccessful. Creatives who are businesspeople—who own breweries, galleries, or jewelry shops where they sell their products—may be seen as selling out and may be scrutinized (or question themselves) for how they treat their employees to a higher degree than other business owners (Roberts, 2012). Banksy, the wildly successful underground graffiti artist we mentioned earlier, complained about his art being shown outside its original context in a 2013 Village Voice interview (Hamilton, 2013):

> But there's no way around it—commercial success is a mark of failure for a graffiti artist. We're not supposed to be embraced in that way. When you look at how society rewards so many of the wrong people, it's hard not to view financial reimbursement as a badge of self-serving mediocrity.

Yet, even Banksy acknowledges, in the same interview, that disdaining money is a luxury reserved for the privileged. Artists need to be able to afford instruments, supplies, transportation, apartments, day care, and vacations, just like other workers. Public artists or those who receive public funding may face particular blowback from those who don't want their tax dollars used for art or disagree with the art being funded.

Finally, artists face challenges rooted in space and place. Artists often locate in cities, because of the availability of venues, services, patrons, and ensembles. These same cities, which are full of opportunity, are also often expensive. Finding affordable places to live and work remains a perpetual challenge for artists. When they do find space and cluster there, the neighborhood often becomes so interesting that they are priced out by non-artist buyers. We discussed issues around art and gentrification extensively in Chapter 4 and do so again in Chapter 9; so, we do not go into much detail on those topics here. However, we want to point out additionally that, at least in part, because of the "lone wolf" artist myth, even when cities or nonprofits invest in artist support structures such as live-work space, those spaces may not be suitable for artists with partners or children. Artist housing is undersupplied; and family-friendly artist housing is even more undersupplied (Rosario Jackson & Kabwasa-Green, 2007). Richardson says her husband has been invited to and has participated in artist residencies; but they have yet to find one that is truly family friendly, in that it is set up for her to also do her work. The residencies are set up to accommodate an individual artist, or at best to accommodate an artist with a non-working spouse.

Despite the challenges of being a family with two working artists as parents, Richardson emphasizes that she finds it rewarding to be able to give their daughter "experiences that are unique to being in a family of artists," such as going along on an artist residency where they lived in a gallery with people painting murals on the walls and floors or singing in a citywide jazz festival. To Richardson, "experiencing the world in a larger way is as or more important" than a conventional education.

Diversity, equity, and inclusion

Many of these initiatives, programs, and tools are also helpful for addressing some of the ongoing challenges with DEI in artist workforce development, as discussed throughout the book. We know that traditional gatekeepers in arts and cultural activity have long favored White, male, heteronormative work—whether that's in terms of whose galleries and exhibitions were featured, what playwrights and plays were produced, what film directors were awarded and acknowledged for their work, or how work was compensated.

While the situation has improved, this is still an issue today in both the activities that are considered in the cultural and creative economic realm. This is important to address when thinking about how we support artist workforce development and who may or may not have equal access to support, services, and financing. We address these DEI issues throughout the book; and we offer a variety of place-based strategies in Chapter 9.

CONCLUSION: STRATEGIES TO CENTER AND AMPLIFY ARTISTS AND CREATIVES

We included this chapter in the heart of this book to remind the reader that if we didn't have artists and creatives, the rich ecosystems about which we speak would not exist. As policy makers, organizers, and leaders, we need to consider what the creative economy experience is like from the creatives' perspectives; and we need to ask and respond to what their needs are if we value their creative knowledge, expertise, and training, as part of our economic and community development efforts. We also need to get into the habit of looking at the broader arts ecosystem and imagine how artists and creatives draw on this ecosystem in indirect and direct ways that may not be readily apparent. We also stress that the concept of who gets to be determined to be an artist or creative is expanding and changing, based on social factors, personal identities, technology innovations, and creative output. We encourage questions in this arena. Can a person call themselves an artist if they have an unrelated day job and just do their creative work on the side? What role does skill, craft, and education play? Is recognition by peers or institutions essential to be validated as an artist? Is intent and self-identification enough to make one an artist or creative? While we don't proclaim answers to these questions, we would like to offer some open-ended strategies to encourage the centering of artists and creatives and their work in the creative economy.

Include artists at the decision-making table as early as possible. One of our writing partners managed a public art program for nearly twenty years. During this time, she saw that if artists were brought in early in the process—before significant architectural, engineering, or space-planning decisions were made—and were made full partners in the team design process, they could contribute significantly to innovative design approaches. This principle runs true in other environments as well. Treefort Music Festival has several touring, working artists on their management team and this changes how they welcome artists—providing amazing goodie bags for new artists, comfortable lounge spaces for performers to hang out between shows, and favorable business terms in contracts. Not all artists want to be in the board rooms; but for those who do, make room for them and invite them in as equal partners.

Echoing what we discussed in the challenges section, *think about artists and creatives as whole people who may have families, need affordable housing, and a living wage*. How can policies and infrastructure support artists' work/life balance and lives in the communities in which they want to live? Facilitate access to healthcare, retirement benefits, and other benefit plans for artists and creatives, who often work freelance or in nontraditional employment settings.

Provide fair compensation and payment when you ask them to do something. This includes a transparent contract that considers artist's rights to their intellectual property and workable payment structures. Don't ask artists to work for exposure or on spec. Treat them like the professionals they are.

Advocate for policies and legislation that protect the rights and interests of artists—including copyright protections, artist resale rights, and legislation that addresses fair wages. If artists have to leave their chosen profession because they can't get the protections they need, that is a loss to the economy and a loss to the creative ecosystem.

How might we ensure that artists and creatives have the tools, technologies, and facilities they need to do their jobs and have successful careers? *Create and maintain affordable workspaces, studios, and maker spaces* for artists and creative professionals to work collectively, check out gear, and learn from each other.

Invest in arts and entrepreneurial training and professional development programs that equip artists with the skills and knowledge to navigate the creative economy and its opportunities effectively. Engage higher-education institutions in your cultural planning processes and consult with them when planning workshops and workforce training programs.

Think about who gets the opportunities and who the opportunities are framed for. By *promoting diversity and inclusion* in the creative economy, the potential for innovation increases due to more diverse perspectives and experiences at the table. What are the gatekeeping mechanisms at play in your call to artists, invitation to participate, or criteria? How can you make sure that you are not excluding artists of color or various gender identifications by the way you are scoping the call?

Organizing conventions, workshops, or networking events may *foster collaboration and develop formal and informal connections between artists and creatives in multiple disciplines.* Introduce artists to technology geeks and real estate developers. Throw a party where everyone does three-minute presentations on their passion project and see what happens.

Support artists at emerging, mid-career, and established levels and their crossover across sectors, recognizing that they need different resources and opportunities at different stages. Ask what they need. Respond to their feedback.

Identify how the broad arts ecosystem enhances career trajectories for artists, understanding that artists draw on these different experiences, programs, and spaces for both intrinsic and instrumental reasons. Remember that ecosystems are complex adaptive systems and meaningful occurrences can come from any direction at any time. Connections that happen by chance, because your workshop is next to someone's writing studio, can be as impactful as negotiated and planned partnerships.

Support artists who are working in the activist sphere to raise awareness of the issues that are important to them. Grants, training, space, consultation, or amplification may be what they need to engage with communities in meaningful ways.

Imagine your community without painters, musicians, dancers, architects, designers, software engineers, and chefs—it would not be a place in which you'd want to live. Everyone benefits to some extent from the work of artists and creatives, whether one attends a performance, an exhibition, a lecture, or not. The availability of these opportunities and the dynamic ecosystem formed by these artists and creatives, working together in a shared environment, is vital to shaping what becomes of our neighborhoods and cities.

TAKEAWAYS
- There are many myths about what it means to be an artist; but, the reality of being a working artist in contemporary life is very different from these myths.
- It is important to understand the similarities, differences, and alignments when speaking of artists and creatives.
- There is a variety of programs, spaces, and initiatives that center artists in creative economic development; and each serves a unique purpose.
- Anchor institutions, primarily those in higher education, are an integral—but hidden—part of arts workforce development.
- There are many challenges that artists face; and these need to be addressed if we value the creative knowledge and expertise these workers have.
- There are several strategies that can be used to center artists in the creative economy.

Discussion questions:

1 How do the arts show up in your libraries, schools, parks, transit, and public works locations?
2 What are the higher-education institutions in your community? How do they support and invest in artist workforce development? Are there gaps in what they provide? And is this addressed by any other institution in your community?
3 What are the primary myths about arts? Why are these myths problematic from a policy and planning perspective?
4 What are incubators, co-ops, artist residencies? And how do each of these distinctly support artist economic development?
5 What are the primary challenges that artists face? And what solutions or strategies might help address some of these obstacles?

Activities

- Search for an example of social practice of the arts and share with your classmates or colleagues.
- Identify three examples that resonate with you from this chapter; and journal about why you think these are powerful illustrations of how to center artists in economic development.
- Debate if there is a difference between an artist city and an Arts City.
- Design your own arts social entrepreneurship idea and create a pitch for it.

REFERENCES

Abdul-Jabbar, K. (2023, October 6). Tom Hanks Warns Against Malevolent AI Coming for Your Money, Your Vote, and Your Self-Esteem. *Kareem. substack.com.* https://kareem.substack.com/p/tom-hanks-warns-against-malevolent?r=f7s8&utm_campaign=post&utm_medium=web

Americans for the Arts. (2021). *Profile of Arts Incubators.* www.americansforthearts.org/by-program/reports-and-data/research-studies-publications/2021-profile-of-art-incubators

Artists Community Alliance. (n.d.). https://artistcommunities.org

Arts and Public Life. (n.d.). *Creative Entrepreneurship.* University of Chicago. https://artsandpubliclife.org/entrepreneurship

Ashley, A. J. (2015). Beyond the Aesthetic: The Historical Pursuit of Local Arts Economic Development. *Journal of Planning History*, *14*(1), 38–61.

Ashley, A. J., & Durham, L. (2021). Universities as Arts and Cultural Anchors: Moving Beyond Bricks and Mortar to Entrepreneurship, Workforce, and Community Development Approaches. *Artivate*, *10*(2).

Ashley, A. J., Loh, C. G., Durham, L., Kim, R., & Bubb, K. (2023). Identifying Plan Perceptions: Higher Education Institutions as Arts and Cultural Anchors. *Urban Affairs Review*, *59*(5), 1496–1529. https://doi.org/10.1177/10780874221108103

Baker, T., & Nelson, R. (2005). Creating Something from Nothing: Resource Construction Through Entrepreneurial Bricolage. *Administrative Science Quarterly*, *50*(3), 329–366.

Baldin, A., & Bille, T. (2021). Who Is an Artist? Heterogeneity and Professionalism Among Visual Artists. *Journal of Cultural Economics*, *45*, 527–556.

Beckman, G. D., & Essig, L. (2012). Arts Entrepreneurship: A Conversation. *Artivate: A Journal of Entrepreneurship in the Arts*, *1*(1), 1–8

Berlin Arts Institute. (n.d.). *Arts Incubator.* https://berlinartinstitute.com/arts-incubator/

Berman, N. (2020, June 24). What Are Artist Co-ops? *Fractured Atlas*.

Canada's Music Incubator. (2021). *About CMI*. https://canadasmusicincubator.com/

Caves, R. E. (2000). *Creative Industries: Contracts Between Art and Commerce*. Cambridge, MA: Harvard University Press.

Chang, W. J., & Wyszomirski, M. (2015). What Is Arts Entrepreneurship? Tracking the Development of Its Definition in Scholarly Journals. *Artivate: A Journal of Entrepreneurship in the Arts*, *4*(2), 11–31.

Cooper, G. F. (2023, October 3). AI Deepfake Ads: Tom Hanks, Gayle King Sound Warning. *CNET*. www.cnet.com/tech/ai-deepfake-ads-tom-hanks-gayle-king-sound-warning/

Cotter, H. (2021, July 1). In Maya Lin's "Ghost Forest," the Trees Are Talking Back. *The New York Times*.

D'Souza, J., & Gurin, M. (2017). Archetypes Based on Maslow's Need Hierarchy. *Journal of the Indian Academy of Applied Psychology*, *43*(2), 183–188.

Essig, L. (2015). Means and Ends: A Theory Framework for Understanding Entrepreneurship in the US Arts and Culture Sector. *The Journal of Arts Management, Law, and Society*, *45*(4), 227–246.

Essig, L. (2017). Same or Different? The "Cultural Entrepreneurship" and "Arts Entrepreneurship" Constructs in European and US Higher Education. *Cultural Trends*, *26*(2), 125–137.

Essig, L., & Guevara, J. (2016). A Landscape of Arts Entrepreneurship in US Higher Education. *Alliance for the Arts in Research Universities*, 1–67.

Eyler, J. (2021). *The Power of Experiential Learning*. Association of American Colleges and Universities. www.aacu.org/publications-research/periodicals/power-experiential-education (accessed 29 July 2021).

Ferreira, S., Fidalgo, P., & Abreu, P. (2023). Social Enterprises in Culture and the Arts: Institutional Trajectories of Hybridisation in the Portuguese Changing Cultural Mix. *International Journal of Cultural Policy*, 1–16.

Florida, R. (2002). *The Rise of the Creative Class*. New York: Basic Books.

Florida, R. (2014). The Creative Class and Economic Development. *Economic Development Quarterly, 3*, 196–205.

Florida, R., & Mellander, C. (2015). *Segregated City*. Martin Prosperity Institute. http://martinprosperity.org/media/Segregated%20City.pdf

Frey, B. S. (2005). *What Values Should Count in the Arts? The Tension Between Economic Effects and Cultural Value* (Working Paper Series). Zurich: Center for Research in Economics, Management and the Arts (CREMA) & University of Zurich.

Friedman, W. A., & Jones, G. (2011). Creative Industries in History. *Business History Review, 85*(11), 237–244.

Gaztambide-Fernandez, R. A. (2008). "The Artist in Society" Understandings, Expectations, and Curriculum Implications. *Curriculum Inquiry, 38*(3), 233–265.

Goldberg-Miller, S. B. D., & Fregetto, E. F. (2016). Urban Creativity: An Entrepreneurial Focus. *Journal of Enterprising Culture, 24*(1), 79–99.

Goldberg-Miller, S. B. D., & Xiao, Y. (2018, Winter). Arts Entrepreneurship and Cultural Policy Innovation in Beijing. *Artivate: A Journal of Entrepreneurship in the Arts, 7*(1), 23–47.

Goodsell, T. L. (2013). Familification: Family, Neighborhood Change, and Housing Policy. *Housing Studies, 28*(6), 845–868. https://doi.org/10.1080/02673037.2013.768334

Grady, C. (2023, August 10). Why Taylor Swift Is Rerecording All Her Old Songs. *Vox*. www.vox.com/culture/22278732/taylor-swift-re-recording-1989-speak-now-enchanted-mine-master-rights-scooter-braun

Greenwald, R. (2012, September 17). *The Lifecycle of a 'Cool' Neighborhood*. www.citylab.com/design/2012/09/lifecycle-cool-neighborhood/3280/

Guerra, P., & Lamontagne, S. (2023). Contemporary Music Ecosystems' Transformations: Live Music, the Gig Economy, and Social Changes. *Ethnomusicology Review, 24*, 1–10.

Hamilton, K. (2013, October). Village Voice Exclusive: An Interview with Banksy, Street Art Cult Hero, International Man of Mystery. *Village Voice*. www.villagevoice.com/village-voice-exclusive-an-interview-with-banksy-street-art-cult-hero-international-man-of-mystery/

Haver, K. (2013). Murals and VARA Rights. *Portland Street Art Alliance*. www.pdxstreetart.org/articles-all/2016/11/24/murals-art-copyright-and-vara

Independent Publishing Resource Center. (n.d.). *BI/POC Artist & Writer Residency*. www.iprc.org/education/bi-poc-artist-writer-residency/

Jacobs, J. (1961). *The Death and Life of Great American Cities*. New York City, NY: Random House.

Krales, A. H., & Pavic, V. (2020, July 5). 33 Powerful Black Lives Matter Murals: Artists Have Turned Boarded-Up Businesses into Powerful Black Lives Matter Art. *The Verge* (theverge.com).

Kuang, C. (2021, December 9). Street-Artist Banksy Takes on Global Warming. *Fast Company*.

Kuhlke, O., Schramme, A., & Kooyman, R. (2015). *Creating Cultural Capital: Cultural Entrepreneurship in Theory, Pedagogy and Practice*. Utrecht, The Netherlands: Eburon Uitgeverij BV.

Luger, C. H. (n.d.). www.cannupahanska.com/social-engagement/mirror-shield-project

Manhattan Graphic Center. (n.d.). *About*. www.manhattangraphicscenter.org/about

Markusen, A., Johnson, A., Connelly, C., Martinez, A., Singh, P., & Treuer, G. (2006). *Artists' Centers: Evolution and Impact on Careers, Neighborhoods and Economics*. University of Minnesota.

McRobbie, A. (2016). *Be Creative: Making a Living in the New Culture Industries*. Cambridge, UK: Polity Press.

Montuori, A., & Purser, R. E. (1995). Deconstructing the Lone Genius Myth: Toward a Contextual View of Creativity. *Journal of Humanistic Psychology, 35*, 69–112.

Mulcahy, K. V. (2003). Entrepreneurship or Cultural Darwinism? Privatization and American Cultural Patronage. *The Journal of Arts Management, Law, and Society, 33*(3), 165–184.

National Park Service. (n.d.). *Be an Artist-in-Residence*. https://www.nps.gov/subjects/arts/air.htm

NOLA Artist Incubator. (n.d.). *Sustainable Collaborative Learning, Teaching and Artistic Experimentation*. https://nolaartistincubator.org/

Nuendorf, H. (2016, September 5). Art Demystified: How Do Artist Residencies Work? *Arnet*. https://news.artnet.com/art-world/art-demystified-artist-residencies-649592

Podmore, J. (1998). (Re)Reading the "Loft Living" Habitus in Montréal's Inner City. *International Journal of Urban and Regional Research, 22*(2), 283–302.

Powell, W. W., & Snellman, K. (2004). The Knowledge Economy. *Annual Review of Sociology, 30*, 199–220.

Preece, S. B. (2011). Performing Arts Entrepreneurship: Toward a Research Agenda. *Journal of Arts Management, Law, and Society, 41*, 103–120.

Preece, S. B. (2013). Social Bricolage in Arts Entrepreneurship: Building a Jazz Society from Scratch. *Artivate: A Journal of Entrepreneurship in the Arts, 3*(1), 23–34.

Reinmoeller, P., & van Baardwijk, N. (2005, July 15). The Link Between Diversity and Resilience. *MIT Sloan Management Review Post*. https://sloanreview.mit.edu/article/the-link-between-diversity-and-resilience/.

Rentschler, R. (2003). Culture and Entrepreneurship Introduction. *The Journal of Arts Management, Law, and Society, 33*(3), 163–164.

Reyburn, S. (2020, February 5). Banksy Is a Control Freak: But He Can't Control His Legacy. *The New York Times*.

Rivard, A. (2020, November 18). Tearing Down the Gates—and Gatekeepers—of the Art World. *Canadian Art*. https://canadianart.ca/essays/tearing-down-the-gates/

Roberts, J. S. (2012). Infusing Entrepreneurship Within Non-Business Disciplines: Preparing Artists and Others for Self-Employment and Entrepreneurship. *Artivate: A Journal of Entrepreneurship in the Arts, 1*(2), 53–63.

Robinson, S. (2023, August 28). Whale Mural Visible Again Downtown after Storm Damages Rocket Ad. *Axios Detroit*. www.axios.com/local/detroit/2023/08/28/whale-mural-visible-storm-rocket-downtown-detroit

Rosario Jackson, M., & Kabwasa-Green, F. (2007). *Leveraging Investments in Creativity*. Urban Institute. www.urban.org/sites/default/files/publication/31226/1001176-Artist-Space-Development-Making-the-Case.PDF

Sharp, M. A. (2023). Give Starving Artists a Piece of the IP Pie. *Journal of Intellectual Property Law*, *30*(2), 392–425.

Sherman, M. (2023, July 7). 'Speak Now (Taylor's Version)' Is Here. Here's How to Reconsider Taylor Swift's Transformative Album. *Associated Press*. https://apnews.com/article/taylor-swift-speak-now-taylors-version-a41998c4d1f08af9d89c6d314ed4c2bd#

Sound Co-op. (n.d.). *Co-op?* www.soundcoop.tv/coop

South Carolina Arts Commission. (2023). *Arts Entrepreneur Incubator*. www.southcarolinaarts.com/artist-development/artist-entrepreneur-incubator/

Stern, M. J., & Seifert, S. C. (2007). *Cultivating "Natural" Cultural Districts (Creativity & Change)* (pp. 1–16). New York: Rockefeller Institute. www.giarts.org/sites/default/files/Cultivating-Natural-Cultural-Districts.pdf

Talen, E. (2006, February 1). Design That Enables Diversity: The Complications of a Planning Ideal. *Journal of Planning Literature*, *20*(3), 233–249. http://journals.sagepub.com/doi/abs/10.1177/0885412205283104

Tepper, S. J., & Kuh, G. (2011, September 4). Let's Get Serious about Cultivating Creativity. *The Chronicle of Higher Education*.

Three Sisters Collective. (n.d.). https://threesisterscollective.org/murals/

Timberg, S. (2015). *Culture Crash: The Killing of the Creative Class*. New Haven, CT: Yale University Press.

Trapp, R. (2015). The Creative Social Enterprise: An Impact Investment. *GIA Reader*, *26*(2), 26.

Woronkowicz, J., & Noonan, D. S. (2017). Who Goes Freelance? The Determinants of Self-Employment for Artists. *Entrepreneurship Theory and Practice*. https://doi.org/1042258717728067

Zimmerman, J. (2008). From Brew Town to Cool Town: Neoliberalism and the Creative City Strategy in Milwaukee. *Cities*, *25*, 230–242. www.thecyberhood.net/documents/papers/zimmerman08.pdf

Zukin, S. (2009). Changing Landscapes of Power: Opulence and the Urge for Authenticity. *International Journal of Urban and Regional Research*, *33*(2), 1187–1201. https://doi.org/10.1111/j.1468-2427.2009.00867.x

Zukin, S., & Braslow, L. (2011). The Life Cycle of New York's Creative Districts: Reflections on the Unanticipated Consequences of Unplanned Cultural Zones. *City, Culture and Society*, *2*(3), 131–140. https://doi.org/10.1016/j

Policy and the creative economy

Chapter 7

INTRODUCTION: WHAT IS CULTURAL AND CREATIVE POLICY?

It is important to note at the outset of this chapter that, as we have discussed, there is no single, unified definition of cultural or creative in the context of policy or economy; there are, however, ongoing efforts to clarify these blurry concepts (Markusen et al., 2008; Newbigin, 2019). In the academic literature in this arena, the use of the term "cultural" is primarily understood to reference the arts as found in the traditional nonprofit or public arena, such as opera, theater, dance, fine art, or heritage preservation sectors (Throsby, 2011). The term "creative industries" was first defined in 1998 by the United Kingdom's Department for Culture, Media, and Sport to reference sectors having a strong focus on intellectual property and innovation, including film and television, publishing, music, advertising and marketing, design, software and video games, visual arts, architecture, crafts, cultural heritage, performing arts, and radio. "Creative" became a replacement term for "cultural" to expand the field beyond traditional nonprofit arts to include, or alternately represent, those individuals, organizations, occupations, and industries that entrepreneurially capitalize on the knowledge economy—to produce value or wealth through products with intellectual property (De Beukelaer & Spence, 2019; Throsby, 2011; Newbigin, 2019). Rather than use the terms interchangeably, for clarity, the authors use them either together to encompass a larger cross-sector frame of both nonprofit arts and for-profit creative industries, or singularly to reference distinct sectors, recognizing that this is an imperfect boundary separation.

When governments choose to act or dedicate resources in response to a particular problem or need, they are creating policy. Cultural or creative policy is how the government chooses to resource the arts to address a particular problem, challenge, or opportunity connected to the aesthetic, social, community health, or/and economic wellbeing of a place (Rosenstein, 2018). In other words, there are many arguments for why and how governments should intervene to support arts and culture. Traditionally, policymakers deployed cultural policy to support beautification projects (e.g. public art, see Figure 7.1), cultural heritage and preservation initiatives (e.g. historic preservation and architectural walks), and nonprofit arts programming and participation (e.g. leasing out buildings to arts and cultural nonprofits at reduced rates). Some policymakers and staff champion the cultural economy as the primary driver for allocating resources to nonprofit arts activity, because it brings in tourists who spend money that is distributed, circulated, and then magnified to other service industries. Signature public art, performing arts facilities, and other cultural amenities become part of the city's identity (see Figure 7.1).

Many government entities have adapted their cultural policy scope to include the creative economy. This means doubling down on nonprofit arts tourism, but also broadening its policy reach to new arts disciplines and for-profit industrial and occupational sectors, as well as considering how to brand and market their artistic strengths to attract and retain knowledge workers. Policymakers and arts leaders advocate for film and television tax incentives and artist-friendly property development. They incubate new or hidden industries like music. The creative economy language and related interventions pop up in branding and marketing campaigns and new programs and policies; and they are included in arts, culture, and creative plans. Each of these policy approaches that we address in this chapter exist simultaneously, forming different layers of urban cultural policy with different policy targets and purposes (Ashley, 2014; Grodach, 2017).

Figure 7.1 Chicago's *Crown Fountain,* designed by artist Jaume Plensa with Krueck and Sexton Architects, features Chicago's diverse population.

Source: Photo by Matilda Rose Bubb

Public policies do not manifest from thin air, but are informed by earlier policy legacies. The political environments, geographic location, and public attitudes of a place shape what policies are used in a city, state, or nation (Campbell, 2012). Path dependency, which we saw in Chapter 5 in the context of complexity theory, is the quality of earlier events affecting the trajectory and equilibrium of later events (Djelic & Quack, 2007). If we look at policy development as a form of path dependency, we can see how historical applications of cultural and urban policy related to arts funding, cultural preservation, heritage protection, trade, and urban redevelopment have evolved over time through their application in multiple environments across the globe—affecting the types of policies that are passed. To break out of a path-dependent trajectory, path transformation typically occurs either incrementally or suddenly if there is some type of shock or sudden change (Djelic & Quack, 2007). This shock could be technological, social, or natural. An election turnover could dramatically change policy direction. A leader in Minneapolis shared with us that, historically, there has been a department of Arts and Cultural Affairs with a staff of nine within the city government. In 2002, the newly seated Mayor, R.T. Rybak, eliminated the department due to budget issues. While the Mayor did save the public art program and a film officer's role (which was later eliminated), this was a drastic reduction in structural and policy support for the arts in Minneapolis (interview 10/28/2023). We will be talking about some other transformational shocks, such as the impact of and response to COVID-19 shutdowns on artists and arts organizations.

In the previous chapters we've already encountered several references to policies that govern cultural and creative practices, including the funding of creative districts and spaces for art exhibitions, performances, and creative-industry production; creative economic development strategies; incentives for television and film production; Creative City branding; Percent for Art programs; higher-education investment in arts-based workforce training; and various placemaking strategies. In this chapter, we discuss the policy process and place these policies in context to each other. We explore the policy tools scholars are discussing and practitioners are applying, so that readers can consider using (or not using) them for their own purposes and motivations. We share illustrations of problems or needs that cities leverage cultural policy to address; and we highlight examples of actors and policy entrepreneurs who are proposing solutions and testing policy approaches.

In 2018, Denver Arts & Venues—a city and county agency responsible for operating multiple performing arts venues, a public art program, festivals and events, and cultural grant programs—released a music strategy report. The policy document highlights jobs, revenue, and employment growth in the local music industry, while outlining how the city might grow their music scene into a Music City (2019, p. 4). Programs featuring hip-hop dance, deployed to help at-risk youth, are offered as exemplars alongside mention of cities noted to be music tourism meccas, demonstrating the potential for billions in tax revenue.

Are the policy makers behind the report, proposing civic investment in music for its intrinsic value, to solve social problems, or as an economic driver to add earned revenue to a city's bottom line? In a 2023 interview with the executive director of Denver Arts and Venues, we asked about this intersection of motivations. "On the one hand, we are civically focused and work for the city. But on the other hand, we are a business that does arts, culture, and entertainment." This multiplicity of purposes hints at the complexity of government policies and purposes; and it underscores that many arts initiatives may be efficient in being able to address more than one challenge.

When a Seattle arts leader was asked about why and when she brings new cultural policies forward, she provided an example related to solving the problem of equity:

> The basic question is, are the public benefits going to the public? And are they going with equity to the public? You bring policies forward to offset or to change the lens of opportunity. Is there a lack of opportunity? You bring policies and resources forward [meaning that new policies or programs are approved through allocated resources].
> (interview 10/26/2022)

Elsewhere in the interview, she expounded on issues related to equity, specifically identifying that she was referring to racial equity. Seattle has a commitment to racial equity and anti-racist approaches in their art selection processes, program identification, and general management. Her comments provide insight into how cultural leaders approach a civic problem and how policy options may get on political agendas.

Multiple Streams Theory (MSF) is a theoretical approach that is particularly helpful when trying to understand how policies get on political agendas. We use it to explore why and how policies are selected for their cities, looking for patterns of how policy change occurs.

We reflect on policy change and the context of contemporary cultural and creative economy policies and trends emerging from, and in use in, the policy field. We investigate and frame the ways public entities, private sector development, community organizations, and the public influence the context and landscape of policy, as it relates to the creative sectors. To do this, we share literature focusing on the evolution of cultural and creative economy policies; and we draw on practitioner interviews to see how this materializes in the everyday work that happens in practice. We use primary documents such as policy documents, websites, plans, and reports, to provide additional framing.

THEORETICAL FRAMEWORK: MULTIPLE STREAMS FRAMEWORK

One way to understand the policy process is to consider that governments at the local, regional, and national scale rationally and purposefully design, approve, and implement policy to respond to identified problems that need solving on behalf of the public they serve (Rosenstein, 2018). But is this rational approach really how it happens? Where do the policy ideas come from and how do they get on the political agenda? What are the conditions that allow for policy change to occur? To develop a shared vocabulary and understanding around how policy change may occur, we engage the use of MSF, developed in 1984 by John Wells Kingdon, a professor Emeritus of Political Science at the University of Michigan in Ann Arbor (Cairney, 2018). He is a highly respected public administration and policy scholar. In the MSF process, there are three streams: (1) policy, (2) problem, and (3) political. These three streams are parallel and operate independently; they must come together under favorable circumstances for a new policy to advance and move through an open policy window, for change to occur. While we will not be applying this framework to a singular case study, we will introduce the process, define the terms, and subsequently use them to discuss the various components and stages of the policy process.

The *policy stream* is the stockpile of ready solutions developed by policy networks, including bureaucrats, academics, and elected officials. Policy ideas waiting for a problem might include zoning regulations, grant programs, or the building of a new arts facility. The *problem stream* is made up of the difficulties policymakers are trying to solve in civic environments such as budget shortfalls, population loss, and downtown disinvestment. The *political stream* consists of the local and national political mood, colored by current events, interest groups, or administration shifts (Kingdon, 2011). The *policy entrepreneurs* are those who champion policies that advance their goals, pairing them with the emergent policy problems and political opportunities (Jones et al., 2016; Kingdon, 2011). They might be arts administrators, business owners, or nonprofit leaders. A *policy window* opens because of a problem or event in the political stream—such as an election, natural disaster, or other change in conditions—and the policy entrepreneur is able to couple the three streams together and shepherd them through the policy window to implement policy change and have a policy output (see Figure 7.2).

Cairney asserts that policy entrepreneurs are the "heroes" (2018, p. 201) of the MSF process as they tell a compelling story, provide ready solutions to problems, and adapt their political strategy based on the nature of the opportunity presented. Policy entrepreneurs have a passion for specific policy positions; and they will do what it takes with their time, money, political or social position to move their ideas into the policy environment for adoption and implementation (Kingdon, 2011; Weible & Sabatier, 2018). We are particularly interested in the way this theory centers the role of the policy entrepreneur, as a change agent, who selects and advances favored policies through relationships, political positioning, and advocacy.

We are interested in how we might use Kingdon's MSF to helps us understand why some topics receive attention on governmental agendas, while others are ignored, and why

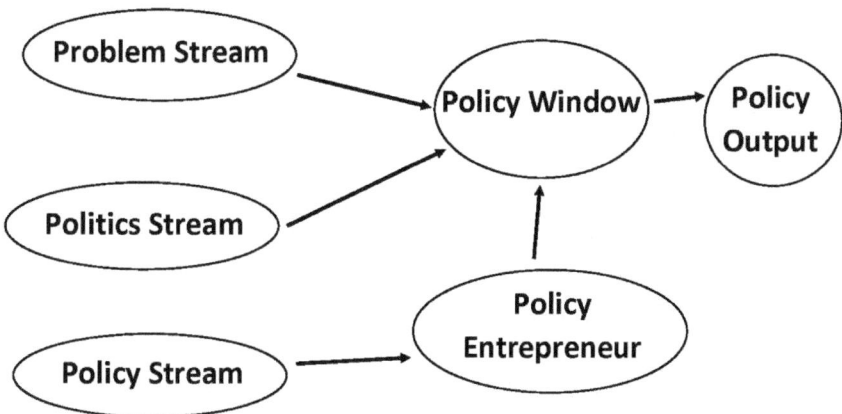

Figure 7.2 Overview of the MSF Policy Process, created by Matilda Rose Bubb.
Source: Adapted from E. Bouw

government leadership may choose one policy alternative over another in which to invest resources and time (Kingdon, 2011). Within MSF, in addition to the policy entrepreneurs, there are a variety of actors—such as policymakers, politicians, and community advocates who are part of the process of policy consideration and passage (Cairney, 2018).

The basic policy process is a sequence of stages. According to Weible and Sabatier (2018), first there is *agenda setting,* where issues or problems are identified and brought to the attention of policy makers. Next, *policy formation* occurs, where policy makers and experts review different policy solutions. This is followed by *Policy adoption,* where policymakers, such as elected officials, review and debate solutions and decide on a specific policy to approve. Then the *policy is implemented* by government agencies and relevant organizations. *Policy evaluation* follows; this is the assessment of the implementation to make sure the policy does what it was intended to do. Finally comes *Policy revision,* which is the updating of the policy, based on the course of action identified in the evaluation.

We encourage you to think about who the policy entrepreneurs are in your community; what kind of policies they are championing; and how they are able to work with partners to move through the policy process.

Since 2013, some arts policy scholars have effectively used MSF as a tool to ask questions about cultural policy entrepreneurs, policy formation, adaptation, and change. For example, Goldberg-Miller and Xiao (2018) analyzed an art museum, arts district, and a performing arts center in China to better understand and articulate the policy formation, change, and current conditions of these institutions, as a strategy for arts entrepreneurship. In another case, Burgess (2006) engaged MSF to analyze the decision dynamics of the 1990 NEA Independent Commission—formed in response to the culture wars that we talked about in Chapter 3 and calls for a greater use of this framework—to apply Kingdon's framework to other cultural policy case studies.

However, as Burgess (2006) notes, arts policy scholars have not capitalized on this useful theoretical framework. In a content analysis of peer-reviewed articles engaging MSF between 2000 and 2013, Jones et al. (2016) identified only one out of 311 articles that addressed the arts, while most articles focused on health, the environment, or governance. They also note that there is an upward trend in application of the MSF, demonstrating that the framework is the focus of robust scholarly attention, but is lacking in its application in the cultural arena. We would like to build on the work of previous authors to inform our understanding of those who are advancing creative-city and creative-economy policies, in cities across the globe, and how they work within the policy system. If we had better information about the identity, choices, motivations, and actions of the policy entrepreneurs, we could better understand why some cultural policies are selected over others, what success or failure looks like, and how the replication of policy processes may be orchestrated.

This chapter contributes to MSF theory development by identifying—through interviews and other data collection—the political problems that cultural economy policies are put forward to solve, the various policy solutions selected and promoted by cultural policy entrepreneurs, and the political realities in which these policies move through.

ACTORS AND STAKEHOLDERS IN THE CULTURAL AND CREATIVE POLICY PROCESS

In Chapter 5, we introduced the actors and their organizations who are working at varying scales and are involved in furthering creative economy agendas. Specifically the actors involved in influencing the political process around cultural and creative policy making include the arts administrators and cultural planners bringing forward the policy ideas; consultants brought in to advise in their areas of expertise, such as public art or cultural planning; academics who may be critiquing or recommending policy approaches; elected officials who have to consider resource allocations; and the public who responds to the resource allocations made (Bell & Oakley, 2015) (see Figure 7.3).

Cultural intermediaries or administrators acting as policy entrepreneurs—working with governments, redevelopment agencies, or other taxing authorities—identify policy solutions that meet their preferences, pair them with problems to solve,

Figure 7.3 Arts Entrepreneurs participate in a Garden City, Idaho panel discussion about art and community.

Source: Photo by Matilda Rose Bubb

and prepare to put them forward as cultural policy options for elected officials to consider. Once they are adopted, the administrators and their staff implement and evaluate those policies (Rosenstein, 2018). Actors in government may also author or commission reports or studies to collect data or propose policy ideas, prior to being pursued, as a way of testing the waters or gathering political and public support for a new investment direction. This is a way to prepare the political stream for coupling with a particular policy idea, by laying the groundwork for acceptance. For example, in 2012, the City of Albuquerque engaged a nonprofit organization, Creative Albuquerque, to create a report on the city's creative economy status, using three different national cultural data initiatives. The analysis also compares Albuquerque to other cities in the region or of relative size across the country. This report, which, according to its introduction, seeks to find synergies between business and arts and culture communities and revise the brand of Albuquerque to focus on its cultural and creative economy assets; it also shows the way data is collected and used to compete with other cities and marshal community agreement about a course of action.

Although policy is typically perceived as the purview of government, non-governmental actors exert considerable influence in their roles as partners and advocates. These actors include corporations, private companies, creative industries, non-governmental organizations (NGOs), intergovernmental organizations (IGOs), nonprofit organizations, philanthropies, date artists, individuals acting on behalf of organizations or coalitions, educators, and higher-education institution leaders (DeVereaux & Griffin, 2013). Actors and stakeholders rarely work alone, especially when tackling large projects. public-private partnerships or dual nonprofit partnerships enable partners to take on larger property-led arts development projects that can have transformative impacts on the communities in which they are located (Ashley, 2014). Actors involved in partnerships or the passage of creative economy policies may vary depending on whether one is in an industrialized country or a developing country, as the purposes for cultural policies are different in varying economies; small-scale craft producers, those involved in maintaining cultural heritage practices, or intermediaries, acting in the interstitial spaces between government and makers, may be these ones involved in the transfer of creative economy policy to far-flung locations (Fahmi et al., 2017).

There is not always agreement about what policies should be advanced between elected leaders and administrators running the programs. This comes back to the concept that policymaking is not necessarily a rational process, but is built on actor preferences (Goldberg-Miller, 2017). While some cultural administrators experience the centrality, value, and impact of the creative economy in their location, explaining it to elected officials, organizational leaders, philanthropists, and the public can be difficult; this is due to lack of broader understanding about the creative economy or a lack of clear data. Leaders may question how the arts impact the economics and identity of a place, resulting in a persistent marginalization or denigration of arts and culture in budgets, economic development plans, and policy considerations (Frenette, 2017). This can lead to conflict or stymied projects. In some communities, in the minds of some elected officials, the creative economy is superfluous to the real economy, reflected a cultural leader in Minneapolis. This makes it difficult to get the policies, budget, and staff to effect industry change.

> I keep saying, invest, invest. It's not about decoration and entertainment; it's not about people who are doing this as a hobby. This is about real jobs, real lives, people who want to make a living doing this as a business. And still, you don't want to invest because it's not politically expedient.
> (interview 10/28/23)

At the government level, there can be a disconnect between the agency identified to serve the creative economy, the needs creative entrepreneurs have, and the agencies with the power or budget to serve those needs. Identifying the actors who can make a difference and secure resources is often what is needed to get an initiative off the ground. For example, in the city of Denver, cultural staff discussed what they might do for the film community that is within the city's purview, such as permit a street closure in less than forty-eight hours or bag meters for free to provide parking for film crews. But these seemingly easy gestures are left undone, because it is not in the cultural agency's budget to do so or those acts would impact another agency's budget and staff time, and the other agency is not willing to take fiscal responsibility for those requests (interview 11/21/23).

In Detroit, it was not the city government leaders that had the idea to apply for the UNESCO's Creative Cities Network designation, as a City of Design. It was a new organization, formed in partnership between a private art school and business association, with a tangential relationship with the city of Detroit. Design Core Detroit, formerly known as Detroit Creative Corridor Center or DC3, formed in 2010 as a partnership between the College for Creative Studies and Business Leaders for Michigan. The problems they were facing included disinvestment in the central city, the need for physical regeneration of the city, and an under-resourced, diverse workforce. In 2015, they applied for and received recognition for Detroit as a City of Design. As policy entrepreneurs, the organizational leaders are leveraging this international brand to their advantage.

> The idea is that we can help develop talent, we can influence policy, we can encourage investment under this larger umbrella of positioning Detroit as a global thought leader in the practice of inclusive design.
> (interview 1/27/2023)

They use their organization to engage artists and designers to creatively solve problems, make changes in neighborhoods, and work with business leaders and government organizers to address public policy issues (interview 1/27/2023). This example shows how policy actors can come from outside the government and implement change.

The government is purportedly working on behalf of constituents; therefore, relevant constituents must be involved in the process of new initiatives for them to be successful. For example, in the City of New Orleans, cultural and creative community members initially fought the city's initiative to create the Mayor's Office of Cultural Economy. Some expressed that they didn't like it, because it was a new approach, and they did not understand its purposes. Others did not feel that the years of ad hoc work they had been doing was recognized by this new entity. The community needed to be brought into the process through group meetings and one-on-one consultations before they supported it—which, in the end, they did (interview 2/27/2023). To win community support, the new director of this division had to actively listen to constituent concerns, visit them in their environments to better understand their experiences, and recognize their important contributions—leading up to this new office. She had to demonstrate that she was not supplanting them, but was there to amplify and support their work (see Figure 7.4).

POLICY ADOPTION OBSTACLES AND BARRIERS

Obstacles to new policy adoption include limited financial resources, the need for persistent policy entrepreneurs who see the value in new options and advocate for innovations, administrative or political opposition, and the clear opportunity

Figure 7.4 The Mardi Gras Museum of Costumes and Culture celebrates the signature annual New Orleans Mardi Gras parade costumes.

Source: Photo by Matilda Rose Bubb

to introduce ideas into an oversaturated information policy environment (Weible & Sabatier, 2018). For example, a government cultural worker in Albuquerque mentioned that an obstacle to initiating creative economy programs was the difficulty of prioritizing resources, for political leaders, in a sensitive political environment (interview 3/10/2023). A representative in Boston noted that in cities with high land values and increased cost for housing, small creative businesses, artist studios, and housing for creative workers are becoming scarce commodities. Large-scale development and planning priorities easily displace creative economy clusters, because there is often a disconnect between the part of the city responsible for zoning and development and the part of the city advocating on behalf of small-scale creative enterprises (interview 1/27/2023).

Advancing new policies, even when they are anticipated to benefit the jurisdiction, can be difficult because of the bureaucratic structures in place. Path dependency, mentioned earlier, can be an impediment to new policies in several ways. This includes institutional inertia, where internal partners are invested in maintaining the status quo and thus resist change; budget constraints or the push to continue allocation to old programs; political resistance from leaders who are reluctant to champion new policy directions that could make them a political target; lobbying or interest groups who block or delay policies they consider counter to their interests; public perception; lack of sufficient expertise or information; risk aversion and the fear of negative consequences; and political ideology that may prevent consideration of ideas the politician believes does not fit their party's platform (O'Brien, 2014). Grodach (2012) conducted an in-depth case study of Austin, Texas, where he identified how some of their path-dependent legacies interfered with the acceptance of *CreateAustin*, a cultural plan that failed to unite the dominant commercial music industry and their community's nonprofit organizational peers. The interests of those who saw the cultural planning agenda as one focused on an amenities-driven, central city, urban, and nonprofit development clashed with those who wanted resources to go instead to sector-specific creative-industry areas such as music (Grodach, 2017). Many of these obstacles fall into the political stream, which, if not aligned with the policy and problem streams, prevents new policy from being adopted, according to MSF.

To overcome path-dependent obstacles, advocates or policymakers must collect data about possible policy change and provide a clear case of its strengths and shortcomings; engage with stakeholders who may be resistant to change, address their concerns, and garner support; develop strategies to mitigate risks associated with policy transitions; consider gradual or phased approaches to policy change to minimize perceptions of alteration of the status quo; and educate decision-makers and the public about the need for change, the benefits of the new policy, and how it has been used in other places (O'Brien, 2014).

This section provides several ways to think about the actors in the policy process, from various angles, and explains the role of policy entrepreneurs in advancing policy ideas. In Chapter 8, we will see some of these roles played out in short case study examples.

CULTURAL POLICY

Culture can be understood anthropologically as an expression of a general way of life; however, in the context we are discussing, culture is a reference to artistic practices, products, and patterns of production and consumption (Bell & Oakley, 2015; Bradford et al., 2000). In the United States, the origins of cultural policy practices applied in cities can be found in City Beautiful campaigns, as discussed in Chapter 4 (Ashley, 2015). At the federal level, the first major support of artistic and cultural workforce activity took place from 1935 to 1943, in the form of the Works Progress Administration's efforts. The Federal Art Project, Federal Music Project, Federal Writers' Project, and the Federal Theatre Project employed artists to paint murals for federal buildings, write guidebooks, make films, photographically document people in rural environments, perform in orchestras, put on plays, and collect oral histories (Ashley, 2015; Rosenstein, 2018; Rosenzweig & Melosh, 1990). Bureaucracy's pairing with creative practice was celebrated for its workforce development and questioned for the quality and content of its output and compatibility within the limitations of government patronage; and it ceased within a few years (Rosenzweig & Melosh, 1990).

In the United States, cultural policy is limited by an American belief that government involvement in the arts is to be constrained, based on concepts such as free speech—and, as an extension of that, that government should not interfere with expression (Rosenstein, 2018). Separation of church and state also plays into America's reluctance to meddle in cultural arenas (Rosenstein, 2018). It was not until the 1950s that America began developing formal national cultural policies; this was in response to the Cold War and the formation of UNESCO as an instrumental act of national competitiveness—not necessarily a desire to support local culture in America (Rosenstein, 2018).

Rather than being valued for its intrinsic benefits, in the 1950s, culture was brandished as a sword in the Cold War fight—dispatching performances abroad like the musical Oklahoma, the Julliard String Quartet, and a production of Medea at the Berlin Cultural Festival—to demonstrate America's national character and excellence (Rosenstein, 2018). And at home, in an effort to compete internationally and host diplomatic offerings, the United States built the Kennedy Center in Washington, DC (Rosenstein, 2018). The US government established formal federal arts policies with the establishment of the National Foundation on the Arts and the Humanities Act in 1965; the Historic Preservation Art in 1966; and the Public Broadcasting Act in 1967. These policies created a foundation for cultural administration structures to be created, including the National Endowment for the Arts (NEA) and Humanities (NEH), Smithsonian museums and festivals, the National Register of Historic Places, and the Corporation for Public Broadcasting (Rosenstein, 2018).

Traditional cultural policy—which remains part of the policy stream options, such as grantmaking to nonprofits or individuals as a subsidy—is supported under "merit good arguments." This means that a product or service benefits not just the person who buys it, but is good for society as a whole, including the arguments that culture is a public good, subject to market failure, and that it:

- strengthens national identity and enhances quality of life;
- provides greater public access to excellent artistic experiences for consumers of all income and class levels;
- shapes the artistic tastes of a population or reflects government leadership preferences;
- brings in tourism expenditures; and helps support the service industries (Craik, 2005).

The "culture wars," referenced in Chapter 3, sparked by conservative lawmakers responding to a few controversial NEA grants, jeopardized the existence of the National Endowment for the Arts; raised questions about the elitism of art; and brought up questions regarding the legitimacy of public funding for the arts, particularly in the face of growing government debt (Cargo, 1995). Much of the testimonial objections to the reauthorization of the NEA were based on economic concerns and questions regarding government funding of art (House floor debate of October 11, 1990, on H.R. 4825). Government-funded individual-artist grants were largely lost due to this battle; and arguments about the purpose of public funding for the arts began to change to help justify investments in arts and culture from an economic perspective, rather than a public-good benefit. There has been a decided shift in policy approaches after this time, as communities moved to considering the economic value that creative activity can bring to a city.

In contemporary times, the NEA has been involved in several national areas of policymaking. Their multifaceted impact is felt through the funding of grants, through allocations to state and local arts agencies; fostering of creative placemaking through research, grants, and partnerships with third-party funders; and targeted initiatives that address topics such as healing veterans through the arts, city design, Shakespeare in communities, and arts education partnerships (Redaelli, 2016; https: arts.gov). The NEA also provides awards such as the National Medal of Arts, National Heritage Fellowships, and the NEA Jazz Masters' Fellowships, which reward and encourage particular creative activities.

CULTURAL POLICY TO CREATIVE ECONOMY POLICY AND THE RISE OF CREATIVE CITY IDEAS

In Chapter 3, we began the discussion about the broadening of cultural policies from solely targeting nonprofit arts organizations, heritage preservation, and the promotion of artistic excellence and access to the inclusion of creative economy purposes as exemplified by Creative City models. This represents a paradigm shift in cultural governance, driven by a confluence of socioeconomic, technological, and ideological factors. This shift has catalyzed the recognition that in addition to aesthetic and social value, cultural and creative sectors have economic value as engines of economic growth, job creation, and place competitiveness (Peltoniemi, 2015). Creative economy policies that emphasize the economic and innovative potential of the cultural and creative sectors and harbor an interest in competing creatively on a global scale have increased in places around the world in the last twenty years. The authors will discuss some of the reasons for this shift and provide examples of these new policy directions.

De-industrialization and shifts away from manufacturing to the knowledge economy in the latter part of the 20th century forced many cities to look for new employment sources, as cities shrunk with the depletion of labor (Grodach et al., 2017). The knowledge economy can be defined as an economy based on activities rooted in intellectual and creative capabilities, rather than physical inputs and natural resources; and it includes the design of products, experiences, places, and services "based on knowledge-intensive activities that contribute to an accelerated pace of technological and scientific advance, as well as equally rapid obsolescence" (Powell & Snellman, 2004, p. 201; Evans, 2009; Ashley, 2015). Changing work, employment, and migration patterns have spurred the shift toward creative economy policies, as more people work remotely, engage in the gig economy, or work multiple jobs. While the ability to work from home has influenced people to move to smaller cities or more rural places, there are many factors that contribute to why cities may grow or diminish. Examples include the age of the city; the geographic region in which they are located; the affordability of housing; the cultural or recreational amenities provided; employment opportunities available; or their openness to foreign-born residents (Glaeser & Shapiro, 2001). Creative economy policies aim to leverage the talents and entrepreneurial spirits of individuals, fostering innovation and entrepreneurship that contributes to economic diversification and resilience.

In an increasingly competitive global economy, cities compete in an effort to differentiate one place from another and to attract new residents and visitors (Goldberg-Miller, 2018, 2015; Comunian, 2011). Creative City rhetoric, originating in the late 1990s, offered cities a potential solution to rebuild challenged places. The arts, culture, and creative industries are offered as potential drivers of urban economic growth and development (Grodach et al., 2017). Key aspects of creative cities, include:

- investment in cultural and creative industries to generate economic value, attract tourists, and brand places;
- investment in cultural and creative occupations to generate new products, processes, and innovations;
- urban regeneration through cultural investments such as districts, creative business clusters, or cultural facilities;

- talent attraction by creating an inclusive and open environment that appeals to entrepreneurs, artists, and young professionals; and
- placemaking efforts such as investments in public art, cultural or music festivals, or heritage preservation (Landry, 2000).

Support for a thriving cultural environment has emerged as a policy response for places to foster instrumental ends, such as attractiveness of a city, social cohesion, technology innovation, and attraction of educated transplants to urban cores (Evans, 2009). These instrumental purposes of culture broaden the value of this research beyond those interested only in culture—to those public administration scholars and community leaders who want to see their places thrive in a changing, dynamic world. Researchers are showing that the arts and creative industries have relationships to the generation of direct economic benefit to cities, regions, and nations through job creation, capital investments, tax revenues, tourism, attraction of knowledge workers, benefits of placemaking, and encouragement of consumer purchases, as well as additional intrinsic values such as beautification and social connectivity (Saha & Sen, 2016; Ashley, 2015; Grodach & Loukaitou-Sideris, 2007). The Creative City is seen as one with regenerative power, fueled by the production of creative products and services, which are concentrated and supported by multiple partners (Comunian, 2011).

Globalization of markets and digital technologies have made traditional cultural industries open to disruption, policy transfer, and change. As the digital age has democratized the creation and distribution of cultural content, boundaries between cultural producers and consumers have thinned—and provided room for innovation (Snowball et al., 2021). While creative economy strategies or programs seem new to political leaders in places where they may have not been used before, many of the strategies are adapted from other places (Markusen, 2014). New government policies, including those that may have been used elsewhere, are considered "innovations" if they are applied in a context where they have not been used before; "inventions" are original policies that have not been done before in any place. A government body may adopt a new-to-them policy due to a combination of internal determinants, policy diffusion, or transfer mechanisms led by policy entrepreneurs (Weible & Sabatier, 2018).

Ideologically, there has been a shift toward recognizing culture and creativity as assets, rather than liabilities, within the broader context of regional and national development. Governments have increasingly embraced the notion that investments in culture and creativity not only enhance the quality of life for residents and visitors, but also strengthen the overall competitiveness and sustainability of their economies. But this acceptance does not necessarily mean that governments or private interests are ready to heavily invest in these areas. The instrumental use of culture to drive revitalization, tourism, and place-based development has demonstrated how cultural and creative facilities and businesses can reshape urban centers—even if it may come with some downsides like gentrification, heightening of urban inequalities, or the reordering of what is valued in civic settings (Comunian & Mould, 2014).

CREATIVE ECONOMY POLICIES

In the last 25 years, several creative economy policies approaches have been developed to focus on Creative City objectives, to build the creative workforce, and to foster environments where economic growth within the cultural and creative sectors increases and where innovation and entrepreneurship flourishes. In this section, we've grouped these policy approaches to provide a framework for practitioners and students to better understand their purposes and when they might choose a particular approach for their city. Think of this list as part of the stockpile of ready policies in the policy stream that might be selected by a policy entrepreneur to apply to an emerging problem. Also, consider how these policies are presented to win political support.

Intellectual property rights and *copyright retention* are legal measures argued to be critical to encourage current and future innovators to continue innovating, as well as share those innovations in a way that protects their initial risks and invested resources. Governments implement and enforce this protection through copyright and trademark registration, patent laws, and efforts to combat piracy of intellectual ideas or products. Think of the disruption and loss that occurs when unique products are pirated, music is copied without revenue going back to the original artists, or a photographer's image is used without permission or payment.

Policies targeting the support of creative-industry sectors using *taxing regulations* focus on specific economic growth opportunities that a city, region, or country wants to encourage, such as film, music, fashion, or gaming. The economic power of creative sectors and creative production is emphasized in this policy approach. Strategies are aimed at supporting those industries based on individual creativity, skill, and talent that generate intellectual property and financial return. These strategies include *tax incentives* and *tax deductions* to encourage private investment in the creative industries such as film production, tax breaks for art collectors, or reduced taxes for creative startups (Grodach, 2017). For example, in 2000, only six states in the United States had financial tax incentives for the filming of television and movies in their cities; by 2010, all but six states had such incentive programs, showing the spread and popularity of this policy mechanism (Leiser, 2017).

Education and *training initiatives* recognize the creative economy as a place where workforce training and skill-building can spur economic growth by developing human capital. Investing in education and training programs in creative fields helps develop a skilled and competitive workforce and facilitates knowledge transfer (Gilmore & Comunian, 2016). Public-private partnerships with businesses and universities, specialized vocational training, or creative entrepreneurship programs are promoted for *workforce development* (Bridgstock, 2019). While insecure employment situations, under-employment, low wages, and portfolio career lifestyles—discussed in the section on the gig economy, in Chapter 5—can be a red flag to someone entering into creative employment training, there are also the success stories of those embedded in creative occupations, inside other industries, as designers, marketers, and digital content creators (Bridgstock, 2019). Higher-education institutions also play a role in cultural production and presentation, as they sponsor arts-based research, frequently have art galleries and performing arts centers, and play a role in the cultural life of the city as anchor institutions (Ashley & Durham, 2021; Gilmore & Comunian, 2016). Encouraging partnerships and collaboration between the creative industries and other sectors, such as education, technology, and manufacturing, can lead to innovative solutions, new product development, workforce training, and expanded trade opportunities.

City and cultural planning act as spatial regulators of culture in municipalities. Cultural planning practices include assessing existing infrastructure and cultural resources, conducting public engagement, and making recommendations for future resource allocation and goals (Rosenstein, 2018). It is often in the cultural planning process that policy ideas like the ones we are discussing are put forward. It is a tool to build community and political support for policies (see Figure 7.5).

Local government authorities use *zoning regulations* to determine what kind of development can occur in a city—be it residential, commercial, or manufacturing. This dictates what

Figure 7.5 A page from the *Boise City Cultural Master Plan*.
Source: Boise City Department of Arts & History

types of buildings and uses can be built (Rosenstein, 2018). Zoning is a factor tied to supporting small manufacturing and repurposed public properties to establish creative clusters, incubators, co-working spaces, and innovation hubs dedicated to building the creative sector workforce and arts-entrepreneurship opportunities (Grodach, 2017). These cultural spaces may have social or workforce development benefits like mentorship, networking opportunities, and workshops. Within these incubator hubs, governments or public-private partnerships may provide targeted access to finance for business development for creative entrepreneurs through grants, loans, venture capital, and crowdfunding to accelerate creative business growth.

Using the *arts as an amenity* to enhance a city's brand is accomplished by replacing decreasing manufacturing industries with *creative business clusters or districts*, within cities, using geographic designations or zoning regulations. This practice can foster collaboration between creative organizations and professionals and become an attractor for residents and visitors. For example, in Shanghai, China cultural-led urban regeneration was used as a tool to transform a former textile mill complex into a contemporary art district with galleries, studios, and cafes. The government designated it as a cultural and creative-industry cluster, now known as the M50 art district (Zhong, 2011). Another example is the Titanic Quarter in Belfast, Ireland, which was once an industrial shipyard area. The area was remade into a cultural tourist destination, highlighting the cultural identity of Belfast and acting as an economic hub that includes a conference center, arts and entertainment venues, and a park (Etchart, 2008).

Investment in cultural resources as *urban development* mechanisms includes the type of place-based development we addressed in Chapter 4. There is also the support of creative production and places through the *repurposing of city-owned land or buildings for creative uses* with public-private partnerships; this is a creative economy policy, as it is focused on growth in creative industries and human capital. The use of such facilities could be to house artistic production and public performances and programs; or it could be to provide affordable housing for the purposes of job creation and flagship cultural developments that add to cultural vibrancy (Comunian & Mould, 2014). These types of projects add to city branding. Depending on the scale and partners on the project, possible downsides include uneven access to cultural opportunities, lack of connection with smaller local workshops or creative producers, and resources going into private hands that may have been better used elsewhere (Comunian & Mould, 2014).

Governments and private foundations use *grants, subsidies, and funding opportunities* to support artists, cultural organizations, and creative entrepreneurs for the development of new projects or the preservation of cultural heritage aimed at encouraging tourism. Sponsoring of festivals like the Edinburgh Festival Fringe in Scotland showcases a wide range of performing and visual arts and attracts thousands of tourists to this city every August. Cultural tourism initiatives highlight what is special about a place, such as heritage, creative offerings, performances, festivals, or other cultural experiences. Diwali (or Deepavali), the Festival of Lights, showcases India's rich cultural heritage and provides visitors with a unique opportunity to immerse themselves in the vibrant and diverse traditions of the country. It is a Hindu festival that signifies the triumph of light over darkness and takes place between October and November each year in India—involving traditional customs, food, light displays, street fairs, and community engagement. This approach is about providing an appreciation of cultural heritage and more robust sites for public consumption of creative products.

Cultural diplomacy is a method of promoting a country's cultural and creative products on an international stage, through participation in international exhibitions, cultural exchanges, and artistic collaborations or through assistance with trade negotiations. Synergies between place branding and public diplomacy can be found in international programs such as the UNESCO Creative Cities network, which will be discussed in Chapter 8 (de Andrade & dos Santos, 2021).

The *funding of research and data collection* on the creative economy to better understand what is present and the dynamics at work, as we have shared in previous chapters, is a strategy employed by many to create advocacy pieces and convince others to join policy agendas. This data can be used in reports, to inform on opportunities and make informed policy decisions. This is often how policy ideas spread to new locations as well.

Policies that promote *diversity, accessibility, and inclusion* within the cultural and creative sectors ensure that people from diverse racial or socioeconomic backgrounds can participate and benefit from cultural and creative activities and opportunities. This can be extended to gender, sexual orientation or identification, or other markers that may marginalize or exclude people (Ashley et al., 2021). An example may be sponsoring projects that target specific demographic experiences or reflections. Making sure that people of diverse backgrounds are on the selection panels, boards, and committees making decisions is another way to include various voices in positions of power.

Unlike some other policy areas, it is not very common to see governments evaluating and assessing cultural or creative economic policy to determine impacts and contributions of specific interventions. This is a rich area of study and research that could use more attention.

MUSIC POLICIES AS CREATIVE POLICY EXAMPLE

Live music performance sits at the crossroads between the commercial market and art (Cummins-Russell & Rantisi, 2012). While music is identified as a creative industry, the policy arena that governs it in cities is most often regulatory and aimed at controlling alcohol, public safety, and noise levels, as well as managing restaurants more than it is about fostering a vibrant music scene (Cloonan, 2011). In addition to the place-based policies regulating music, there are also policies that govern the international production, consumption, and trade of music, dominated by multinational companies situated in cities such as Tokyo, Los Angeles, New York, and London (Brown et al., 2000).

Kane et al. (2020) conducted an in-depth case study of San Francisco's evolving regulations affecting the music scene from the 1990s to 2020, which shows the arc of policy changes that went from safety-oriented, punitive permits governing entertainment venues as a nuisance to be managed to policies, programs, and services that support performance spaces as a critical part of the local economy. This shift can be looked at as a change in the social construction of how the public and public officials view music venues and musicians—from noisemakers and vagabonds to city-branding institutions and celebrities (Goldberg-Miller, 2017).

Across the world, a robust, live, local music ecology—one that supports and grows talent and hosts physical spaces for people to rehearse, perform, consume, record, and purchase music—has been shown to contribute to a modern city's economic health and important social and cultural goals, such as encouraging public engagement, establishment of a city's identity, fostering community vibrancy, and nurturing new creative talent development (van der Hoeven & Hitters, 2019; Florida & Jackson, 2010). Austin, Texas and Nashville, Tennessee are two American cities who have claimed the Music City titles for themselves and are also recognized globally for their rich songwriting, recording, and performing environments (Baker, 2016). Local music sectors could use public-private partnerships for developing infrastructure, such as venues, rehearsal space, and studio recording facilities, and business services, such as legal, financial, and marketing assistance (Brown et al., 2000) (see Figure 7.6).

However, music venues, events, artists, and their related support infrastructure encounter many challenges and barriers to a fruitful life. Some of these include gentrification of neighborhoods, which may push music venues out due to cost or sound issues; unintended consequences of regulatory laws, such as liquor laws or building permits; lack of necessary and affordable services, such as recording studios, equipment rental, or access to right-sized venues; affordable housing for low-income artists; and lack of public transportation at night for patrons and musicians (Ballico & Carter, 2018; Zadeh, 2015).

As Shain Shapiro, the founder and CEO of Sound Diplomacy said:

> When something is wedded into the fabric of everyday life, we ignore the systems that create, sustain, and support it. The same cognitive dissonance is occurring with music and culture. When you hear a song that moves you, it's about that moment with that song, not the recording, production

Figure 7.6 Allison Miller's *Boom Tic Boom* performing at the Sapphire Room.
Source: Photo by Matilda Rose Bubb

and marketing functions that led to that moment happening. But without these systems and practices, those moments disappear; that tap runs dry.

(Shapiro, 2019)

As some cities become more prosperous and desirable to new residents, they risk pushing out the creative network of businesses and artists that contributed to making urban environments an attractive place where people want to congregate (Goldberg-Miller, 2017). Some cities, recognizing this social and economic challenge, have developed cultural and regulatory policies aimed at supporting creative industries, such as music, to nurture and grow these unique economic and cultural drivers (Cloonan, 2011, p. 406). Examples of these policies include the establishment of a music commission or consultative committee, cultivating a welcoming environment for club and bar owners, clustering related music businesses, review of alcohol licensing laws, review of noise laws, promotion of the live music scene, sponsoring of music industry forums, rent capping for musicians, provision of buildings for cultural venues, support for underage venues, preservation of historic venues as heritage sites, and support for music education in the schools (Cloonan, 2011; Homan, 2008; Sutherland, 2013; Zadeh, 2015).

The Music Policy Forum, a Washington, DC-based national organization, gathers leaders together each year to consider issues facing the sector. Their session topics include labor issues, the sustainability of existing music ecosystems, and the reimagining of what future music ecosystems could look like. They were instrumental in the Reopen Every Venue Safely initiative after the COVID-19 pandemic, which built cross-divisional conversations between venue operators, musicians, and policymakers to coordinate on best practices of how to get musicians back to work after the shutdowns. They helped inform artists on public health regulations and how to return to touring safely (Music Policy Forum, 2023). Industry-wide champions, such as the Music Policy Forum, provide valuable information to cities that don't have as much infrastructure or policy support as larger cities. In Chapter 8, we will consider some other champions that support these types of initiatives.

CONCLUSION

As this chapter demonstrates, there is a broad mix of policies employed to foster varying creative-industry sectors, their workforces, and those who want to partake of their products and services. These policies aim both at the creative industries' consumption and production sides. The scale of the policies is most often at the city level; but, regional, state, and national governments, foundations, and organizations also have an impact and an important role in passing policies, providing resources, researching and compiling data, and setting examples for what is valued and supported in the creative economy.

In this chapter, we touched on the principles of MSF as a theory to help us understand the conditions necessary for policy change to happen. The policy, problem, and political streams give us a way of thinking about the parallel tracks of information, behavior, and actors that come together after a focusing event, which creates a change in the environment—making new policy consideration possible. It is intended for this understanding to assist practitioners and students in navigating the policy process, reading the environment, and knowing how and where they might intervene to make changes in civic environments. One might research the problems a city is facing, be they related to budgetary constraints, population change (growth or decline), industry shifts, or issues spurred by urban development or suburban flight. Using the information found, you could try on different creative policy solutions you've read about in these pages to see what could be applied. Then, survey the political environment. Do you have political allies that would support your policy solutions? What is the spirit of the polis? What are the arguments that might come up against your policy solutions that you could anticipate and prepare counter arguments for? Practitioners and scholars are part of the laboratory testing; and they can help evaluate these policies to see what works, where, and why. As noted in Chapter 3, this is not a normative text trying to explain how things should be done—but an exploratory, observation-based book that is aware that there is no one right answer or solution for any problem. As you will see in the next chapters, it is through real-world examples that we learn about strategies that we may apply in our own backyards.

TAKEAWAYS
- *Cultural or creative policy* is that which the government chooses to do or not do in relation to culture or creative-industry concerns.
- *Cultural policy* originated in historical practices of arts-based urban beautification and development movements and then focused on "merit good arguments"—aiming to strengthen national and local identity, enhance quality of life, and provide access to the arts for all.
- *Creative economy policies* are informed by place-based economic development, Creative City objectives, and an interest in supporting entrepreneurial creative practices.
- *Different policy approaches* exist simultaneously, forming different layers of urban cultural policy, with different policy targets and purposes.

- *MSF* provides a lens through which we can understand how policy change occurs and can be applied when thinking about creative economy policy advances. The policy, political, and problem streams come together and, due to a focusing event, are ushered through an open policy window by an engaged policy entrepreneur.
- There are several policy actors who may be involved in the policy process, including elected officials, civil servants, planners, lobbyists, consultants, academics, bureaucrats, arts administrators, and the public.
- Policy entrepreneurs have passion for specific policy positions and will devote their time, resources, and social capital to advancing their favored policy ideas. They are critical to stewarding policy change.

Discussion questions:

1. What are the differences between the government providing a grant to a nonprofit organization to develop and showcase a performing art project (cultural policy) and government funding an arts-entrepreneurship incubator space and mentorship program for burgeoning creative business owners (creative economy policy)?
2. How might policies create sustainable economic growth that not only benefits businesses and industries, but also contributes to positive social and environmental outcomes?
3. Who are the policy entrepreneurs and actors in your community and what roles do they play? Who might be left out? Are artists at the table? Minority populations? Neighborhood advocates? Small-business owners? Elderly residents? Who else might you invite to provide input and direction on cultural and creative economy policies that your city is considering?
4. Where do you fit in as an actor? Are you a practitioner, scholar, advocate, or critic? Where might you see yourself playing a role in the policy process?
5. What policies exist in your community that impact music production or consumption?

Activities
- *Policy Simulation Game*: In this activity, participants take on different roles and work together to create and implement a cultural policy for a fictional city or community.

  Objective: To simulate the process of designing and implementing cultural policies, while considering stakeholder interests and constraints.

  Instructions:
    - Name your fictional city or community; each participant must take on a role such as Mayor, arts administrator, businessperson, artist, musician, arts advocate, fiscal conservative, and whomever else they want to identify with.
    - Identify a policy objective or challenge, such as boosting cultural tourism, promoting the music scene, fostering cultural diversity, or promoting local artists.
    - Break into discussion groups, representing different stakeholder groups, and brainstorm policy ideas for your challenge.
    - Have each group present their proposed policy to the entire group and explain the rationale, potential benefits, and any possible downsides.
    - After all have presented, discuss between the ideas, looking at the pros and cons. Negotiate which policy to pass and determine if it needs any amendments.
    - Vote on the policy.
    - Identify what you'd need to do to implement the policy.
    - Reflect on the process and share insights and experiences. Discuss the rewards and challenges of policy making.
- **Creative economy policy in your city:** Identify a creative economy policy that is in place in your city. Find out answers to questions such as: How did it come to be? Who were the policy entrepreneurs involved? Is there anyone you can interview about the policy regarding how it was selected and passed through the process? Can you interview someone who

has experienced the impact of the policy? Share your findings with the group.

REFERENCES

Ashley, A. J. (2014). Negotiating Risk in Property-Based Arts Economic Development: Exploring the Innovative But Untimely Development Partnership Between the Seattle Art Museum and Washington Mutual. *Cities*, *37*, 92–103.

Ashley, A. J. (2015). Beyond the Aesthetic: The Historical Pursuit of Local Arts Economic Development. *Journal of Planning History*, *14*(1), 38–61. https://doi.org/10.1177/1538513214541616

Ashley, A. J., & Durham, L. (2021). Universities as Arts and Cultural Anchors: Moving Beyond Bricks and Mortar to Entrepreneurship, Workforce, and Community Development Approaches. *Artivate: A Journal of Entrepreneurship in the Arts*, *10*(2), 1–41.

Ashley, A. J., Loh, C. G., Bubb, K., & Durham, L. (2021). Diversity, Equity, and Inclusion Practices in Arts and Cultural Planning. *Journal of Urban Affairs*, 1–21.

Baker, A. J. (2016). Music Scenes and Self Branding (Nashville and Austin). *Journal of Popular Music Studies*, *28*(3), 334–355.

Ballico, C., & Carter, D. (2018). A State of Constant Prodding: Live Music, Precarity and Regulation. *Cultural Trends*, *27*(3), 203–217.

Bell, D., & Oakley, K. (2015). *Cultural Policy*. London & New York: Routledge.

Bradford, G., Gary, M., & Wallach, G. (2000). *The Politics of Culture: Policy Perspectives for Individuals, Institutions, and Communities*. New York: The New York Press.

Bridgstock, R. (2019). Creative Industries and Higher Education: What Curriculum, What Evidence, What Impact? In S. Cunningham & T. Flew (Eds.), *A Research Agenda for Creative Industries*. Cheltenham & Northampton, MA: Edward Elgar Publishing.

Brown, A., O'Connor, J., & Cohen, S. (2000). Local Music Policies Within a Global Music Industry: Cultural Quarters in Manchester and Sheffield. *Geoforum*, *31*, 437–451.

Burgess, C. (2006). Multiple Streams and Policy Community Dynamics: The 1990 NEA Independent Commission. *Law and Society*, *36*(2), 104–126.

Cairney, P. (2018). Three Habits of Successful Policy Entrepreneurs. *Policy & Politics*, *46*(2), 199–215.

Campbell, A. L. (2012). Policy Makes Mass Politics. *The Annual Review of Political Science*, *15*, 333–351.

Cargo, R. A. (1995, Spring/Summer). Cultural Policy in the Era of Shrinking Government. *Policy Studies Review*, 215–224.

Cloonan, M. (2011). Researching Live Music: Some Thoughts on Policy Implications. *International Journal of Cultural Policy*, *17*(4), 405–420.

Comunian, R. (2011). Rethinking the Creative City: The Role of Complexity, Networks and Interactions in the Urban Creative Economy. *Urban Studies*, *48*(6), 1157–1179. https://doi.org/10.1177/0042098010370626

Comunian, R., & Mould, O. (2014). The Weakest Link: Creative Industries, Flagship Cultural Projects and Regeneration. *City, Culture and Society, 5*(2), 65–74.

Craik, J. (2005). Dilemmas in Policy Support for the Arts and Cultural Sector. *Australian Journal of Public Administration, 64*(4), 6–19.

Creative Albuquerque. (2012). *The State of the Creative Economy.* Published by the City of Albuquerque.

Cummins-Russell, T. A., & Rantisi, N. M. (2012). Networks and Place in Montreal's Independent Music Industry. *The Canadian Geographer, 56*(1), 80–97.

de Andrade, N., & dos Santos, S. F. (2021). Crossroads Between City Diplomacy and City Branding Towards the Future: Case Study on the Film Cities at UNESCO Creative Cities Network. *Place Branding and Public Diplomacy, 17,* 105–125.

De Beukelaer, C., & Spence, K.-M. (2019). *Global Cultural Economy.* New York and London: Routledge.

Denver Arts & Venues. (2019). *Denver Music Strategy.* www.artsandvenuesdenver.com/assets/doc/2018_DenverMusicStrategy_FullReport_3-6-19-8bdefbe36e-8bdefbe36e.pdf

DeVereaux, C., & Griffin, M. (2013). *Narrative, Identity, and the Map of Cultural Policy: Once Upon a Time in a Globalized World.* London: Routledge.

Djelic, M.-L., &and Quack, S. (2007). Overcoming Path Dependency: Path Generation in Open Systems. *Theory and Society, 36*(2), 161–186.

Etchart, J. (2008). The Titanic Quarter in Belfast: Building a New Place in a Divided City. *Nordic Irish Studies, 7,* 31–40.

Evans, G. (2009). Creative Cities, Creative Spaces and Urban Policy. *Urban Studies, 46*(5–6), 1003–1040. https://doi.org/10.1177/0042098009103853

Fahmi, F. Z., McCann, P., & Koster, S. (2017). Creative Economy Policy in Developing Countries: The Case of Indonesia. *Urban Studies, 54*(6), 1367–1384.

Florida, R., & Jackson, S. (2010). Sonic City: The Evolving Economic Geography of the Music Industry. *Journal of Planning Education and Research, 29*(3), 310–321.

Frenette, A. (2017). The Rise of Creative Placemaking: Cross-Sector Collaboration as Cultural Policy in the United States. *The Journal of Arts Management, Law, and Society, 47*(5), 333–345.

Gilmore, A., & Comunian, R. (2016). Beyond the Campus: Higher Education, Cultural Policy and the Creative Economy. *International Journal of Cultural Policy, 22*(1), 1–9.

Glaeser, E. L., & Shapiro, J. (2001). Is There a New Urbanism? The Growth of US Cities in the 1990s. *National Bureau of Economic Research.* www.nber.org/papers/w8357

Goldberg-Miller, S. B. D. (2015). Creative Toronto: Harnessing the Economic Development Power of Arts & Culture. *Artivate: A Journal of Entrepreneurship in the Arts, 4*(1), 25–48.

Goldberg-Miller, S. B. D. (2017). *Planning for a City of Culture: Creative Urbanism in Toronto and New York.* New York: Routledge, Taylor & Francis.

Goldberg-Miller, S. B. D. (2018). Keeping Creativity Downtown: Policy Learning from San Francisco, Seattle, and Vancouver for Municipal Cultural Planning in Toronto. *Journal of Arts Management, Law & Society, 48*(3), 170–190. https://doi.org/10.1080/10632921.2017.1422834

Goldberg-Miller, S. B. D., & Xiao, Y. (2018). Arts Entrepreneurship and Cultural Policy Innovation in Beijing. *Artivate*, *7*(1), 23–47.

Grodach, C. (2012). Before and After the Creative City: The Politics of Urban Cultural Policy in Austin, Texas. *Journal of Urban Affairs*, *34*(1), 81–97. https://doi.org/10.1111/j.1467-9906.2011.00574.x

Grodach, C. (2017). Urban Cultural Policy and Creative City Making. *Cities*, *68*, 82–91.

Grodach, C., & Loukaitou-Sideris, A. (2007). Cultural Development Strategies and Urban Revitalization. *International Journal of Cultural Policy*, *13*(4), 349–370. https://doi.org/10.1080/10286630701683235

Grodach, C., O'Connor, J., & Gibson, C. (2017). Manufacturing and Cultural Production: Towards a Progressive Policy Agenda for the Cultural Economy. *City, Culture and Society*, *10*, 17–25.

Homan, S. (2008). A Portrait of the Politician as a Young Pub Rocker: Live Music Venue Reform in Australia. *Popular Music*, *27*(2), 243–256.

Jones, M. D., Peterson, H. L., Pierce, J. J., Herweg, N., Bernal, A., Raney, H. L., & Zahariadis, N. (2016). A River Runs Through It: A Multiple Streams Meta-Review. *Policy Studies Journal*, *44*(1), 13–36.

Kane, J., Scholer, A., & Van Houten, B. (2020). Regulating the San Francisco Sound: How a Music Venue Crackdown Inspired Pioneering Advancements in Entertainment Regulation and Support. In C. Ballico & A. Watson (Eds.), *Music Cities: Evaluating a Global Cultural Policy Concept*. London, Switzerland: Palgrave Macmillan.

Kingdon, J. W. (2011). *Agendas, Alternatives, and Public Policies* (Updated 2nd ed.). Longman.

Landry, C. (2000). *The Creative City: A Toolkit for Urban Innovators*. London, UK: Earthscan Publications.

Leiser, S. (2017). The Diffusion of State Film Incentives: A Mixed-Methods Case Study. *Economic Development Quarterly*, *31*(3), 255–267.

Markusen, A. (2014). Creative Cities: A 10-Year Research Agenda. *Journal of Urban Affairs*, *36*, 567–589. https://doi.org/10.1111/juaf.12146

Markusen, A., Wassall, G. H., DeNatale, D., & Cohen, R. (2008). Defining the Creative Economy: Industry and Occupational Approaches. *Economic Development Quarterly*, *22*(1), 24–45. https://doi.org/10.1177/0891242407311862

Music Policy Forum. (2023). www.musicpolicyforum.org/ (accessed 29 September 2023).

Newbigin, J. (2019). The Creative Economy—Where Did It Come from and Where Is It Going? In S. Cunningham & T. Flew (Eds.), *A Research Agenda for Creative Industries*. Edward Elgar Publishing.

O'Brien, D. (2014). *Cultural Policy: Management, Value and Modernity in the Creative Industries*. New York: Routledge.

Peltoniemi, M. (2015). Cultural Industries: Product-Market Characteristics, Management Challenges and Industry Dynamics. *International Journal of Management Reviews*, *17*(1), 41–68.

Powell, W. W., & Snellman, K. (2004). The Knowledge Economy. *Annual Review of Sociology*, *30*, 199–220.

Redaelli, E. (2016). Creative Placemaking and the NEA: Unpacking a Multi-Level Governance. *Policy Studies*, *37*(4), 387–402. https://doi.org/10.1080/01442872.2016.1157857

Rosenstein, C. (2018). *Understanding Cultural Policy*. London and New York: Routledge.

Rosenzweig, R., & Melosh, B. (1990). Government and the Arts: Voices from the New Deal Era. *The Journal of American History*, 596–608.

Saha, D., & Sen, J. (2016). The Role of Place in Creative Economy: The Case of Varnasi. *International Journal of Cultural and Creative Industries*, *4*(1), 28–37.

Shapiro, S. (2019, September 11). Music Is a Vital Urban Resource. How Do We Plan for It? *World Economic Forum*. www.weforum.org/agenda/2019/09/music-is-a-vital-urban-resource-how-do-we-plan-for-it/ (accessed 25 April 2021).

Snowball, J., Tarentaal, D., & Sapsed, J. (2021). Innovation and Diversity in the Digital Cultural and Creative Industries. *Journal of Cultural Economics*, *45*, 705–733.

Sutherland, R. (2013). Why Get Involved? Finding Reasons for Municipal Interventions in the Canadian Music Industry. *International Journal of Cultural Policy*, *19*(3), 366–381.

Throsby, D. (2011). The Political Economy of Art: Ruskin and Contemporary Cultural Economics. *History of Political Economy*, *43*(2), 275–294.

Van der Hoeven, A., & Hitters, E. (2019). The Social and Cultural Values of Live Music: Sustaining Urban Live Music Ecologies. *Cities*, *90*, 263–271.

Weible, C. M., & Sabatier, P. A. (Eds.). (2018). *Theories of the Policy Process* (4th ed.). New York, London: Routledge.

Zadeh, J. (2015). No Money, No Space, No Time: How London Has Forced Out Musicians. *Vice Magazine*. www.vice.com/en/article/ryzwqb/london-is-no-longer-manageable-for-musicians (Accessed 28 April 2023).

Zhong, S. (2011). By Nature or by Nurture: The Formation of New Economy Spaces in Shanghai. *Asian Geographer*, *28*(1), 33–49.

Champions of the creative economy

Chapter 8

INTRODUCTION

When we look around for inspiration, we long to see artists pushing the boundaries of what is expected. We want them to create new forms, make music we've never heard, and write plays that make us weep or laugh hard. Similarly, we want to see cities trying new approaches to solve old problems and surprising us with their ingenuity. Those of us who work in and study cities refer to "peer" cities as ones that are similar in population or geographic size as a particular city, who may be underperforming or slightly over-performing, but are more or less the same. And then there are the "aspirational" cities—the ones that are bigger, better financed, and more adventurous than our city may ever be. But we aspire to be in their league. We aspire to be great. In these innovative and successful cities, we often find people and organizations that push the whole creative economy ecosystem to do better. This is what we want out of champions, someone or someplace to look up to, to inspire us. But champions are not just winners or those who are better resourced than we are. They are invested advocates in the game for the long haul; they believe in certain values and policy ideas and use their influence to bolster others.

DOI: 10.4324/9781003147688-8

Who are the champions of the creative economy? What are the qualities of a creative economy champion? In this chapter, we unpack some big-picture questions to make sense of how creative economy ideas and initiatives are transferred from one place to another and what makes a city want to follow creative economy policies laid out by these champions.

At the outset, we want to establish that a policy entrepreneur and a champion are not the same thing. The key differences lie in their role and focus. Policy entrepreneurs are typically individuals who are known for initiating and promoting new policy ideas to address specific problems. They are often risk-takers, willing to invest their own resources to advocate for their policy proposals and shepherd them through the policy process. They are skilled at building coalitions, partnerships, and networks to gain support for their policy ideas. This may involve collaboration with stakeholders, including government officials, interest groups, and the public. Lastly, they are persistent and determined as they navigate the policy process, working to overcome opposition to their proposal. A champion is not involved in the formal policy process, but uses their influence to advocate for values, policies, and programs that they support. They work to protect policies from potential threats, such as budget and political leadership changes. They may lobby for funding, rally public opinion, or work with stakeholders to evaluate and maintain policy effectiveness. Champions often have long-term commitments to specific causes or policies, as some of our examples will demonstrate.

In our estimation, champions of the creative economy can be individuals; organizations such as nonprofit or for-profit organizations; or entities across sectors that play an influential role in promoting and advancing creative people, creative industries, as well as related policies, programs, and initiatives. In this chapter, we will look at champions at different scales, from those who support individual creative innovators to those establishing networks for various sectors nested in international cities. We will highlight those that focus on specific sectors and those who seek to amplify sectoral or discipline crossover, as it's important to see where these different scales and scopes intersect.

We will broadly address the characteristics that make a champion and share specific examples, so that you can see these attributes in action. Creative industries encompass a very diverse set of fields—each of which has its own history, sub-disciplines, set of leaders, and unique production and consumption trajectories. While we can't fully address each sector in great depth, our intention in this chapter is to use a broad brush to provide insight on what a creative economy champion looks like and the impact they have because of their actions.

Creative economy champions have picked up policy ideas from Creative City concepts and used them to brand certain cities as cool places to live, work, and play. Some of these are international leaders who transfer their policy interests to cities across the world—these cities, in turn, use their paradigms to get residents and tourists interested in their urban centers. From our interviews with practitioner leaders, we have gleaned model examples that inspire them, which we'll pass on to you.

We use diffusion and transfer theories to frame this chapter and to explain how it is that similar policies and practices are taken up by a broad range of geographic places. Scholars and practitioners can use this information to help make informed decisions about what policies to study and advance, as well as to discuss how policies may lead to unintended consequences.

THEORETICAL FRAME: POLICY TRANSFER, DIFFUSION, LEARNING, AND CONVERGENCE

The concept of creative industries and the creative economy is fairly new as policy ideas go, having developed over the last 25 years. Concepts such as the statistical mapping of creative clusters, tracking of creative occupations and nonprofit revenue, and cultural planning are all examples of fairly new practices that have spread quickly over continents. Through this process, new networks develop and policy actors surface (Rindzeviciute et al., 2016). Globalization facilitates the exchange of policy ideas internationally, as political and economic organizations use data sharing, networking, place competitions, and marketing to promote specific practices and resource investments (Namyslak, 2014). The creative economy has become a globalized dialogue, with evidence of its policies in diverse countries, from North

America to East Asia (Oakley, 2016). Policy transfer and diffusion theories help us understand how ideas move from one place to another.

Policy transfer is a process by which knowledge and administrative processes and ideas used in one political setting are promoted, copied, and used, in perhaps an adapted form, in another similar political environment (Marsh & Sharman, 2009). The scale of these policy ideas could be small adjustments or wholesale adoption of new programs; they can be based on presented best practices scenarios or examples of failure that exemplify what not to repeat (Mattocks, 2018). *Policy diffusion* happens when choices made in one place influences leaders in another to make similar decisions, thus spreading policies around a region or country, resulting in similarities between jurisdictions (Mattocks, 2018). *Policy learning* occurs when policy leaders acquire new approaches to common problems from other political entities (Mattocks, 2018). *Policy convergence* is when—due to policy transfer, diffusion, and learning—policies in disparate geographic regions begin to look alike. There may be some differences in how the policies manifest in various places in policy convergence; but there are enough similarities to link them to similar ones in other places. We will point out examples of these concepts as they occur in the following pages (see Table 8.1).

These concepts are related and overlap in scholarly literature; but in this chapter, we are interested in the essential qualities of policy exchange and transfer of ideas from one place to another. We seek to explore how, why, and where creative economy policy concepts are manifesting and being transferred into policy streams in different geographic locations.

POLICY SPREADING MECHANISMS AND CONTRIBUTING FACTORS

The mechanisms used to spread policy include learning from experts within the policy field, through various mechanisms including:

- hiring of consultants to apply their knowledge to one's place;
- attending conferences, workshops, or trainings where the idea is introduced;

Table 8.1 Policy Definitions and Differences, created by Matilda Rose Bubb.

Concept	Definition	Key Differences
Policy diffusion	The process by which policies spread from one jurisdiction to another, often due to imitation or learning.	1. Involves the spread of policies across regions or entities. 2. Often occurs due to observation and emulation of successful policies. 3. Focuses on policy adoption.
Policy transfer	The deliberate sharing or transfer of policies and best practices from one entity to another.	1. Involves a deliberate and planned transfer of policies. 2. May involve technical assistance or consultation. 3. Focuses on policy transplantation.
Policy learning	The process of acquiring knowledge and expertise from policy experiences, often through trial and error.	1. Emphasizes learning from past policy implementation. 2. May involve feedback loops and adjustments. 3. Focuses on knowledge accumulation.
Policy convergence	The phenomenon where different entities adopt similar policies or approaches independently—to a point where policies in different areas begin to look alike.	1. Implies independent adoption of similar policies. 2. May result from shared challenges or global trends. 3. Focuses on policy similarity.

- wanting to capitalize on funding opportunities from foundations, federal agencies, or other partnerships that center on a particular idea of theory in their calls or requests for proposals and qualifications;
- participation in competitions where one place angles to rise above other locations, often by following a proscriptive set of criteria;
- coercion and normative pressure applied to encourage one place to align with other places;
- mimicry of policies in other places, even if those places are not matched in terms of population, resources, or environment; and

- reading popular or academic materials on the creative economy like this book!

(Marsh & Sharman, 2009; Weible & Sabatier, 2018)

How these mechanisms are applied from country to country and city to city vary. They can take different forms when adapted for a specific location, depending on its cultural, economic, and social context, although there are a lot of similarities in their applications. Reasons for new policy adoption may come from policy entrepreneurs, outside or within an organization, who are motivated to innovate and have the necessary resources and political acumen to overcome possible obstacles. Factors that contribute to this motivation may include problem severity, the potential for a new policy to be politically expedient, and the possibility of public support (Weible & Sabatier, 2018).

While much has been written about defining the creative economy and industries (Davies & Sigthorsson, 2013; Markusen et al., 2008), there have been limited studies focusing on the transfer or diffusion of these policy ideas from one location to another. Kong et al. (2006) trace the diffusion of creative economy ideas as they spread across Asian countries, looking at the spatial patterns and policy mutations of how these ideas radiated through Asian locations. They noted that diffusion was fueled by a desire to compete with other rising tourist locations, increased entertainment industry media attention, and high-powered consultants who proposed policy ideas modeled on normative scripts pulled from other cities (Kong et al., 2006). In 2009, Pratt conducted a study of how cultural and creative-industry policies transferred across Europe and the various manifestations they took in various places. Pratt's study is an important analysis showing the path of policy transfer and how the same policies mutate in various locations as they travel. In 2016, Rindzeviciute et al. conducted a study drawing on interviews, policy documents, and reports to trace the stages of the transfer of creative-industry policy ideas to Lithuania and report on the interviewees' perceptions of change associated with the new policy adoption. This study followed creative-industry policy into an area where it had not existed in any meaningful form before. Although Western modes of governance were adopted after the Soviet legacy ended in the 1990s, the state cultural policy system had not changed much. Creative City and industry ideas were disruptors, brought in by local creative policy entrepreneurs who wanted to see things change. This chapter brings together the work of various scholars who use these theories to explain how policy ideas spread and expand on it with original content gleaned from practitioners in cultural and creative economy fields.

WHO ARE THE CHAMPIONS?

By crossing champion definitions, drawn from organizational change management sources (Warrick, 2009) with practices in the creative economy field, we've come up with a broad definition of what it means to be a creative economy champion. Champions exhibit characteristics that engender respect and interest from their peers. They are at the forefront of innovation within their respective fields, constantly pushing boundaries and introducing novel ideas, products, or services. They are good at convincing others to buy their product, join their organization, or try out their services. Champions are willing to take risks, ask questions, and seek out like-minded partners with whom they cross-pollinate ideas—be they government, private business, or a nonprofit. Many are entrepreneurs who successfully launch startup organizations that are creative and culturally significant in their sphere of influence. Their work may be so successful that it affects societal trends. Champions for the creative economy may advocate on behalf of policies, funding, support for the arts and creative industries, and public awareness of the sectors. Mentorship of emerging talent, new cultural organizations, or growing cities is often part of their work, as they seek to strengthen the overall creative ecosystem. Preserving and promoting cultural heritage and craft traditions may be one of their activities. Another part of their mission may be contributing directly to the economy by generating jobs and revenue, as well as spurring economic growth in the communities they touch.

Champions are often recognized for their achievements and contributions, receiving awards or accolades. They may also face criticism, because everyone rarely agrees; and if one is in a highly public position and taking risks, they can be a target for people who don't agree with what they are doing. Being a creative economy champion may not just be about improving the economy; it may also be about building more sustainable cities, a commitment to social responsibility, an approach for climate change mitigation, or other justice-related areas; we will see more of this in Chapter 9.

Creative economy champions work at differing geographic scales and have a diverse set of backgrounds, expertise, and passions. We'll list these as categories, so you can imagine the span of leaders, and then we'll provide a series of real-world examples. The most obvious category is *artists and creatives* including visual artists, performing artists, literary artists, designers, film and television artists, content creators, and gaming artists who create original works of art or culture. As producers of products, services, and experiences with intellectual capital, they have much to gain from an environment favorable to their interests and deliverables. *Creative entrepreneurs* establish and manage businesses related to the creative economy, such as art galleries, advertising firms, production companies, fashion brands, or tech startups. They may be sole proprietors, have a small team, or be an international firm with offices on different continents. *Cultural institution leaders*—such as those who run museums, theaters, cultural centers, or educational institutions—may champion the creative economy through the opportunities, experiences, or workforce training they provide. *Media and entertainment industry leaders* like executives, producers, filmmakers, directors, and influencers play a role in shaping popular culture by hiring creative professionals and promoting creative content. These may be smaller independent leaders or large commercial leaders. *Design visionaries* from fashion, architecture, interior design, or the graphic world have the potential to become stars and leading advocates due to the celebrity their work inspires.

Technology innovators are designing software, tools, platforms, AI vehicles, augmented reality, virtual reality, and apps that greatly impact societal trends. *Investors and philanthropists*, which could be individuals or organizations such as foundations, provide financial support and resources to artists, cultural organizations, creative startups, and cities engaging in creative activities that they want to support. *Advocates or policymakers* are those in positions of influence, such as elected officials, civil service administrators, or lobbyists who create environments in which the creative industries operate—through policies, funding, and regulatory frameworks. *Community leaders* like heads of neighborhood association, religious clergy or rabbis, or retired volunteers who serve on boards contribute to the cultural vitality of their neighborhoods and regions. Experienced professionals who act as *mentors and educators* at the kindergarten through university level share their knowledge and skills with the next generation and nurture their talent. These categories are not mutually exclusive, as champions of the creative economy may embody various roles. What unites them is their commitment to fostering creativity, innovation, and cultural development—within the creative industries—to make a positive impact on their communities and the world at large (see Table 8.2).

MODELS AND INSPIRATION: POLICY TRANSFER

In our interviews with arts practitioners, we asked to whom or what they looked to for inspiration. Where do they find program models or policy ideas? Many turn to other cities to see what they are doing. An Albuquerque cultural official shared that, during the pandemic, they were looking to see how other cities responded to artists' needs and were particularly struck with San Francisco's move to guarantee a monthly income for artists impacted by the COVID-19 shutdowns (interview 3/10/23). San Francisco Mayor London Breed announced in March 2021 that the city would guarantee monthly payments of $1,000 for approximately 130 artists based in the city for six months (Johnson & Dominguez, 2021). The program was developed, in partnership with the Yerba Buena Center for the Arts, with the goal of reactivating the economy and supporting a struggling sector.

> From the first day the pandemic arrived in San Francisco, we knew that this health crisis would impact artists, and artists of color in particular," Breed said in a statement. "Our artists make San Francisco special and bring so much life and energy to our city. The arts are critical to our local economy and are an essential part of our long-term recovery. If we help the arts recover, the arts will help San Francisco recover.
> (Johnson & Dominguez, 2021)

Table 8.2 Creative Champion Behavior by the various roles, created by Matilda Rose Bubb.

Role	Champion Behavior
Artists and creatives	1. Creating innovative and influential art or content. 2. Inspiring others through creative expression. 3. Collaborating with peers and cross-disciplinary teams.
Creative entrepreneurs	1. Launching and scaling creative startups and businesses. 2. Investing in and supporting emerging talent and ideas. 3. Fostering innovation in a creative industry or sector.
Cultural institution leaders	1. Curating or hosting exhibitions and programs that promote creativity. 2. Providing spaces and resources for artists and creatives. 3. Connecting with diverse communities to expand reach.
Media and entertainment leaders	1. Producing and distributing creative content globally. 2. Championing diversity and inclusion in media arts. 3. Leveraging technology for new storytelling formats.
Design visionaries	1. Pushing the boundaries of design and aesthetics. 2. Solving complex problems through innovative design. 3. Adopting new technology in design applications.
Technology innovators	1. Developing and advancing digital tools and platforms. 2. Enabling new forms of creative expression through tech. 3. Supporting tech-driven creative ventures and startups.
Investors and philanthropists	1. Providing funding and resources to creative projects. 2. Establishing grants and endowments for the arts. 3. Leveraging their resources through partnerships.
Advocates or policymakers	1. Crafting policies that support the creative industries. 2. Advocating for arts, heritage preservation, and creative industries. 3. Promoting cultural diversity and equity through policies.
Mentors and educators	1. Mentoring emerging talent in creative fields. 2. Providing training and workforce development for creatives. 3. Fostering a culture of lifelong learning and growth.

To qualify, artists had to live in one of the 13 chosen San Francisco zip codes, be 18 years or older, meet an income limit, demonstrate that they actively engaged with the community through an art form, and have been affected by the pandemic.

A universal basic income (UBI) is a policy concept to provide a baseline universal income to all members of a community, without the need for work. The concept originated in 1796, when an English radical put forward the idea. UBI has resurfaced internationally over the years, due to various populists' movements and has been applied or piloted in a few places, such as Alaska, Quatinga Velho, Brazil, and Finland (Misztal, 2018). In the cases we are discussing, it is not a *universal* application of basic income, but basic income provided to a specific group for a specific time-frame—an adaptation of the UBI policy idea. The concept of basic income benefits was not new to San Francisco; but, it was new for them to apply it to artists.

In September of 2020, San Francisco piloted a program to provide basic incomes to 150 Black and Pacific Islander women during pregnancy and after giving birth; and nearby Oakland had recently launched a basic income program for 600 low-income families of color to receive $500 a month (McLean, 2021). After San Francisco launched its program for artists, the policy was picked up in Minnesota by a nonprofit called Springboard for the Arts, who distributed $500 monthly paychecks to 25 local artists for 18 months (Bishara, 2022). Following that, Creatives Rebuild New York started the largest basic income program for artists, with $125 million in funding from multiple philanthropic partners, including Andrew W. Mellon Foundation, Ford Foundation, the Stavros Niarchos Foundation, and others (Bishara, 2022). This program gave $1,000 to $2,400 to local artists over 18 months.

While Albuquerque did not end up doing its own basic income program, they did start an emergency no-strings-attached Artist Relief Fund to help artists cover losses incurred due to COVID-19 and to encourage them to continue their creative practices during the shutdown (interview 3/1/2023). This is an excellent example of policy transfer. A policy idea, UBI, that was being used to address public health, racial equity, and income inequality problems was transferred into municipal arts policy;

it was then picked up nationally and expanded by cultural nonprofit and foundation programs. The dollar amounts, criteria, length of the grants, and who and how many they served changes with the different applications; but, the underlying values of providing a basic income without a work requirement or product as well as the administrative mechanism of a monthly stipend were constant policy elements.

MODELS AND INSPIRATION: POLICY LEARNING

When the city of New Orleans launched the Mayor's Office of Cultural Economy, they took a delegation of city council members, mayor's office staff, musicians, and cultural leaders to visit Seattle and King County, Washington. The New Orleans representatives wanted to know how Seattle managed its cultural nighttime economy, the role of government in the creative economy arena, and how the government worked with creative private sector industries (interview 2/27/2023). This type of outreach is called policy learning. While there, they met with several influential leaders; toured sites within the city; and discussed funding sources, policies, and programs with Seattle and King County's elected officials and administrative staff. They left very impressed with Seattle and King County's ability to obtain funding from the state and federal levels for their cultural programs (see Figure 8.1). The trip helped unite the delegation around the goals and objectives of the new cultural economy office and gave them some aspirational programs to consider (interview 2/27/2023).

MODELS AND INSPIRATION: CITY, STATE, COMMERCIAL CREATIVE-INDUSTRY PARTNERSHIPS

Several leaders in our interviews mentioned Georgia and, in particular, the city of Atlanta, as an inspiration for the way they have developed their film industry. An administrator with Denver Arts & Venues called out the growth of film studios there, specifically mentioning Tyler Perry, who built a 330-acre film studio in Atlanta on the grounds of the former Fort McPherson army base, and Marvel Studios, which films many of their productions in and around Atlanta due to the incentives. She also mentioned that significant creative economy development, like this, does not happen if the state is not supportive

Figure 8.1 *Sonic Bloom* by Dan Corson and the *Seattle Space Needle*.
Source: Photo by Matilda Rose Bubb

and involved (interview 11/21/2013). The state of Georgia implemented its Entertainment and Industry Investment Act in 2005, which provides transferable tax credits for film, video, and digital projects in the state. In 2008, they increased the tax credit value and made other changes to make the incentives more attractive to the film industry (Bradbury, 2019). According to the Georgia Film Office, film and television productions spent $4.1 billion in Georgia during fiscal year 2023, hosting 390 productions. Atlanta is home to over 200 studios. The newest addition to Atlanta's film scene is BlueStar Studios, a $180 million film and TV production studio that will be a 53-acre campus, built on the grounds of a former military base, Fort Gillem (Caranicas, 2022).

We found positive and negative externalities in relation to the growth of the film industry in Atlanta (Zahirovic-Herbert & Gibler, 2023). The benefits include explosive economic growth around the film industry, including jobs in production, set design, catering, transportation, and support services. It has attracted new cultural infrastructure, such as studios and soundstages. Tourism has increased, as people want to see where their favorite film or TV series is produced, like *Stranger Things* or *The Walking Dead*. Cultural exchange has occurred, as Atlanta attracts global talent from various backgrounds, which fosters a more diverse community. The presence of the industry in Atlanta has led to the development of a younger skilled workforce, as more people have entered the film industry and talent pipeline in the areas of acting, filmmaking, and post-production.

The detractors include a big cost of living increase, as the demand for housing has gone up and home prices have increased accordingly. Greater traffic congestion, due to road closures for film shoots, leads to frustration among the local population. There is some environmental impact due to the increased energy consumption, waste generation, and disruption of local natural habitats for filming. There is great competition for resources—locations, talent, equipment, space, and catering—which can lead to increased costs for everyone. Lastly, there is an increase in gig workers, because film jobs are primarily project based, which can result in job instability for many. This creative economy champion illustration offers examples of partnership between the state and local government; between the government and the private sector commercial film industry; and with creative workers employed by the film studios. It also offers us a window into the benefits and pitfalls of success that must be considered and managed by all those within the ecosystem, as we discussed in Chapter 5.

RECOGNITION OF HIGHLY CREATIVE INDIVIDUALS

From the models and inspirations given to us by our practitioner interviews, we turn to another form of championing. Awards and recognition are mechanisms that organizations use to identify leaders and promote the qualities or activities they want to see in the world. The MacArthur Foundation's Fellows Program is one of the most prestigious individual award programs. Annually, it provides unrestricted, sizable financial fellowships (in 2023, the no-strings-attached amount is $800,000 per fellow, according to their website) to 20 to 30 individuals, who are nominated by peers and have demonstrated originality and dedication to their creative pursuits, as well as a capacity for self-direction (macfound.org accessed 9/20/2023).

The fellowship is intended to encourage people of outstanding talent to focus on their creative, intellectual, and professional work without having to think about making a living. The recipients range in discipline areas, including writers, sociologists, teachers, entrepreneurs, visual artists, performers, economists, and others. By recognizing diverse forms of creativity, including the arts, sciences, and social justice, they broaden our cultural assumptions about what it means to be a creative, innovative person. They may or may not have an academic affiliation and are not required to perform a service or deliver a product at the end of their grant tenure. The award fosters innovation, because the financial freedom allows recipients to take creative risks, resulting in new discoveries, artistic achievements, and projects that have a significant impact on their respective communities. The group of fellows becomes a community itself, building a network between interdisciplinary individuals who might collaborate, share expertise, and exchange ideas. The program then serves as an inspiration for other individuals or foundations to recognize and reward creative individuals. It sets a precedent for valuing creativity as a driver of positive change, societal wellbeing, and economic growth.

The MacArthur Foundation is a champion for prioritizing recognition and providing cash awards to highly creative people, incentivizing other people to continue to take creative risks with their work. The recipients become champions, by virtue of their award, as the honor catapults them into the "genius" category. They obtain a certain amount of freedom to pursue their dream creative projects, because of the foundation's financial investment in them. They, thus, further rise in their creative fields and become even more inspirational to others (see Figure 8.2).

There are other awards or prizes that recognize and invest in highly creative individuals. Private foundations, such as the Rockefeller Foundation and the Andrew W. Mellon Foundation, offer grants and fellowships to support the arts, humanities, and creative endeavors. While most of the Nobel Prizes are

Figure 8.2 Martha Gonzalez, musician, scholar, and artist/activist, and 2022 MacArthur Fellow, Claremont, CA.

Source: John D. and Catherine T. MacArthur Foundation <https://creativecommons.org/licenses/by/4.0>, via Wikimedia Commons

awarded for scientific achievements, there is an annual coveted prize for literature. Guggenheim Fellowships are awarded to artists, scholars, and scientists who demonstrate exceptional creative ability in their work. Pulitzer Prizes honor excellence in journalism, literature, and the arts. The National Endowment for the Arts offers fellowships in various arts disciplines, supporting artists in the United States. The Fulbright Program offers grants and creative-research exchange programs between the United States and other countries. The European Research Council offers grants to outstanding researchers, in the arts and humanities, to pursue groundbreaking research. At the state and local government levels in the United States, grants, fellowships, and awards are often provided to reward or bring recognition to creative individuals.

Figure 8.3 Internationally renowned cellist Dave Eggar teaches a workshop at *Surel's Place* in Garden City, Idaho.

Source: Photo by Matilda Rose Bubb

LOCAL LEVEL CREATIVE ECONOMY CHAMPIONS

Here, we pivot to look at different geographic scales and how organizations function as champions at the local, national, and international levels. In cities, there are organizations that champion the training and creative practices of artists.

Arts-related educational institutions can be seen as champions, as they employ artists of multiple disciplines, train upcoming artists, and provide facilities for the public engagement with visual art, theater, design, and music (Breznitz & Noonan, 2018). HEIs can have an outsized impact on the creative opportunities in a place and provide a pipeline of trained workers equipped to step into the employment opportunities in ad agencies, film companies, sound recording studios, and music venue operations.

Small flagship institutions can be creative economy champions. In Garden City, Idaho, an organization called

Surel's Place, founded in 2012 in the home of artist Surel Mitchell who died of cancer the year before, provides artist residency opportunities for artists of all disciplines from across the country, as well as exhibitions, workshops, readings, performances, and panel discussions. This house, and the programs it serves, have become the center point of an exploding local cultural scene, acting as a fiscal agent for other creatives, partnering with music festivals, mural programs, and arts education initiatives (see Figure 8.3). Development and gentrification have also moved into the neighborhood, following the cultural advances, just as we describe in Chapter 4. It will be interesting to see, in the coming years, how culture and development reside together in this changing landscape.

NATIONAL-LEVEL CREATIVE ECONOMY CHAMPIONS

To be a creative economy champion at the national level means to advocate for, support, and promote the creative economy within that country and with international partners through trade, cultural exchanges, and partnerships. Promoting and celebrating the cultural industries and recognizing that they contribute to economic activity, job creation, and cultural enrichment is a critical aspect of being a national champion. This may manifest through:

- National networks supporting creative industries; policy advocacy, including funding, tax incentives, and intellectual property protection safeguards; and workforce development initiatives.
- Cross-sector collaboration facilitation between the creative industries and other sectors, such as manufacturing or tourism.
- Recognizing and investing in cultural heritage preservation and intangible cultural practices to safeguard cultural expressions, particularly of indigenous peoples.
- The encouragement of innovation and entrepreneurship, access and inclusion, and sustainability and environmental responsibility may be areas of focus.
- Conducting research and preparing reports and studies with the resulting data—that is then shared with constituents, for them to use as advocacy tools.

- Most importantly, national champions provide leadership, strategic thinking, and resources to help others shape their policies and programs.

A study of the literature, focusing on why those leading national economies are interested in creative-industry policies, identified eight groups of purposes. There are fighting unemployment, adding to the GDP, participating in foreign export trade, fostering social inclusion, adding to social and cultural development, increasing quality of life, fighting youth unemployment, and other miscellaneous indicators of improved socioeconomic impact (Daubaraite & Startiene, 2015). We offer a few national-level organization examples here; and we invite future research to provide a more comprehensive comparative analysis of these national-level champions.

Established in 2002, Creative Cities Network of Canada (CCNC) is a national nonprofit organization, consisting of members that are municipalities and indigenous governments, organizations, and individuals—united in their value of using culture and Creative City policy initiatives as development tools. Their core offerings are cultural planning toolkits, Creative City summit meetings, a library of policy research, and a bi-monthly newsletter. Their annual Creative City Summit takes place in a different city each year, highlighting the place-specific amenities of conference locations, while offering sessions on nationally applicable topics, such as cultural planning, public art strategies, inclusivity approaches, data collection technologies, and heritage celebrations.

Similarly, Americans for the Arts (AFTA), founded in 1960, is a nonprofit arts advocacy member organization that aims to support a network of municipalities, organizations, and individuals through best practice models, policy recommendations, gatherings, and other resources. They have networks and councils made up of member group representatives in discipline-specific areas, such as arts education, public art, local arts, and emerging leaders. One of the book authors served as a volunteer on AFTA's Public Art Network council for five years. Through this position, she got to know leaders from other cities across the country, participated in the drafting of public art best practices for arts administrators, and designed how the organization would serve administrators in the field.

The British Council, which is independent from the UK government but receives government grants, promotes cultural relationships between UK and other countries, as one of its purposes. They conduct creative economy research, use the creative economy as a cultural diplomacy tool, facilitate trade in cultural products, promote policies, and champion arts entrepreneurs through festival production. One of the programs they advance is a Creative Bootcamp, a partnership program they initiate with countries such as Argentina, Iraq, and Kuwait to deliver in-person workshops, for creative and cultural entrepreneurs, on leadership and business skills.

INTERNATIONAL GOVERNMENT ORGANIZATIONS AND POLICY CONVERGENCE

Stepping up to the international geographic scale, international government organizations (IGO)—who have varying origin stories, agendas, and areas of influence—have picked up cultural and creative economy initiatives as vehicles to demonstrate their expertise and convince others to join their policy and programmatic bandwagons (Cunningham & Swift, 2019). Having coalesced around the burgeoning interest in cultural and creative industries, they diffuse support for creative economy policy options, to cities small and large, across the globe (Vlassis & De Beukelaer, 2019). By providing data, policy models, attractive marketing approaches, international recognition, and ready networks, national and international creative economy champions also promote policy convergence.

There are several international organizations which, among other initiatives, actively study, measure, and present reports or other information on creative sectors. Although not a comprehensive list, these include, as examples:

- *United Nations Conference on Trade and Development* (UNCTAD) monitors, collects data on, and reports on creative economy trends such as trade and exports; offers policy recommendations; and advocates the value of creative economy sectors in developing countries (UNCTAD, 2022).

- *United Nations Educational, Scientific and Cultural Organizations* (UNESCO) promotes cultural preservation and diversity in creative industries through frameworks, studies, reports, and programs on cultural and creative goods trade, cultural heritage, and the Creative Cities Network (United Nations/UNDP/UNESCO, 2013).
- *World Intellectual Property Organization* (WIPO) focuses on intellectual property rights in creative sectors through copyright-related data, patents, trademarks, and other information related to creative sectors (WIPO, 2017).
- *European Union* promotes and supports cultural and creative industries throughout the member countries with funding, research, and initiatives to activate creative sectors (https://culture.ec.europa.eu/ accessed on 8/27/2023).
- *World Trade Organization* (WTO) examines trade aspects of creative industries, looking to improve international trade policies that affect the global exchange of creative goods and services (www.wto.org/index.htm accessed on 8/27/2023).
- *Creative Economy Programme* (CEP) is based at the British Council and promotes the creative economy worldwide, by collaborating with various international partners to provide research, reports, and share information on these sectors (https://creativeconomy.britishcouncil.org/ accessed on 8/27/3023).
- *International Federation of Arts Councils and Culture Agencies* (IFACCA) is a global network of arts councils and cultural agencies, which conducts research, shares recommended practices, and advocates for arts and culture inclusion in the government (https://ifacca.org/themes/financing-culture/cultural-economy/ accessed on 8/27/2023).
- *Organization for Economic Cooperation and Development* (OECD) studies the social and economic impacts of creative industries and then produces reports and policy recommendations for governments to develop strategies that foster creative sector growth (www.oecd.org/ accessed on 8/27/2023).
- *International Confederation of Societies of Authors and Composers* (CISAC) addresses the rights of creators in

various sectors, including literature, music, and the visual arts, with the goal of protecting their rights and interests and ensuring fair use of their work (www.cisac.org/ accessed on 8/27/2023).

Again, we invite practitioners and students to conduct their own comparative research on these and other international organizations involved in creative economy policies and promotion. Due to these organizations' stature, international reach, and resources, the information they disseminate is perceived as vital to understanding what is happening in these sectors and participation in their programs is recognized by others as meaningful (Vlassis & De Beukelaer, 2019).

The rise of the Creative City paradigm, as discussed in previous chapters, gave IGOs ready, attractive urban development policy options that they could use to promote their objectives to local governments, through their programs (Mulero & Rius-Ulldemolins, 2017). These policy ideas, thought to attract benefits like job creation and business development, are synthesized and represented in a global framework by those who are in global positions of authority like IGOs (Gathen et al., 2021). They advocate for development options through widely shared reports, programs, and presentations and spur greater awareness and interest in the use of creative economy data collection, measurement, and promotion (Vlassis & De Beukelaer, 2019).

IGOs conduct studies, collect data, and use their expertise and influence to create and present reports, programs, and policy options for the purpose of influencing what policies may or may not be considered by national and local governments (Namyslak, 2014; Alasuutari, 2016). For instance, in 2022, UNCTAD produced a report called the Creative Economy Outlook 2022. It offers documentation that the creative economy is one of the world's fastest growing sectors. The document contains information on the rising value of trade exports in creative goods and services (a particular area of interest to their organization). It profiles Indonesia, Mexico, and South Africa's economic contributions to the creative sectors and presents survey results from international partners, global trends, emerging technologies, and new directions for the field. The reports or policy options that each one advances is linked to their own independent agendas, such as using education, science, and culture to maintain and foster peace, in UNESCO's case, or facilitating trade and the export of manufactured goods, in the UNCTAD's case (Vlassis & De Beukelaer, 2019).

There are other methods used, such as competitions, awards, and conferences where international organizations apply cultural and creative frames to advance their agendas and influence local policy practices across geographic boundaries. In Chapter 4, we mentioned that the European Commission developed a strategy to host an annual competition for the title of European Capital of Culture. The coveted designation aims to function as a marketing tool to attract tourism in Europe, as heritage education for residents and visitors, and as an urban development prompt that aligns municipalities with the European Union's policy goals (Namyslak, 2014). There have been more than 60 cities, across the European Union, that have achieved this designation. In 2023, selected cities Veszprem, Hungary; Elefsina, Greece; and Timisoara, Romania received $1.5 million in funding, which they are expected to apply to their efforts to amplify the cultural tourist destinations in their city. The Eurocities network promotes inclusion of cities in their organization, if they follow European Union policies. The participants engaged by these programs are political and policy leaders, administrators, business owners, and artists working at the national and local levels to distinguish their place from others (Collins, 2020).

Some researchers point out that the creative economy rhetoric has traveled extensively because it is a method of spreading neoliberal policy ideas, including competitiveness between cities, marketization and selling of the arts, and the minimizing of public space—which are increasingly attractive options in profit-focused, deregulated economies (Cunningham & Swift, 2019; Oakley, 2016). Rather than supporting artists and creative workers, some argue that creative economy policies may be resulting in urban development projects that spawn gentrification and artist displacement (Rich & Tsitsos, 2016). A study of Cuenca, Ecuador, a UNESCO World Heritage Site since 2015, identified how the UNESCO designation and historic urban commodification has attracted "lifestyle migrants," from North America, who have pushed out local occupants due to increasing rents from rising housing demands (Hayes, 2020, p. 3061). According to Hayes, UNESCO's heritage designation policies do not take into consideration "transnational gentrification" and historical colonial exploitation that end up hurting the small craft producers and local indigenous communities (2020, p. 3073).

Critics express concern that the prestige of designation prioritizes elite tourism and economic development over conservation of authentic living environments (Meskell, 2019). While this arrow is primarily slung at the World Heritage List that UNESCO maintains, it can also be applied to the Creative Cities designations. By promoting certain assets, are other worthy assets or competing values being ignored or denied? Other drawbacks of participation in the network include frustration with the bureaucratic administration of the network, which can be an obstacle to the intended goals (Gathen et al., 2021). Perhaps in response to some of the criticism, UNESCO has made efforts to promote what it is calling a Sustainable Travel Pledge, created in 2019—to foster environmental stewardship, support local communities, and protect the communities it is promoting through cultural tourism. The tenants of this pledge are:

1. Community engagement
2. Energy conservation
3. Water conservation
4. Waste reduction
5. Single-use plastic reduction

According to Ecotourism World, the pledge has been adopted by 4,200 hotels and travel companies who are committing to their tenants. This is part of their overall Sustainable Tourism Program. While not directly addressing gentrification, the program makes an effort to decrease exploitation of local communities (www.unesco.org, accessed 9/25/2023). It is important for policy advocates and deciders to consider the potentially negative impacts of creative economy policies.

UNESCO'S CREATIVE CITIES NETWORK

Founded in 1945, after World War II, to act as an international body to promote peace and rebuild shattered cities, UNESCO has

Figure 8.4 The Guggenheim in Bilbao, a UNESCO City of Design since 2014.
Source: PA, CC BY-SA 4.0 Photo by MykReeve, 2000 <https://creativecommons.org/licenses/by-sa/4.0>, via Wikimedia Commons

a multi-pronged agenda, part of which is focused on culture and heritage preservation and support of creativity to address global issues such as climate change, poverty, and the digital divide (UNESCO.org, accessed 2/20/2023).

UNESCO's Creative Cities Network aims to promote cooperation among cities worldwide. According to their website, the selection process to become part of the select network includes submitting a letter of interest, outlining the city's commitment to fostering a specific aspect of creativity and its reasoning and desire to become part of the network. UNESCO and expert or peer evaluators review and assess expressions of interest, using criteria including quality of existing creative sector infrastructure, quality and diversity of the city's creative initiatives, and its potential to contribute to the network. They make recommendations to an international jury of experts in various creative fields, who make the final decision on which cities are included in the Creative Cities Network. Once cities are selected, they receive an official invitation to join the Creative Cities Network, acknowledging the city's efforts to promote creativity in a specific area and recognizing its potential to collaborate with other member cities. If a city accepts the invitation, it becomes an official member of the UNESCO Creative Cities Network and agrees to uphold the principles of the network, collaborate with other member cities, and actively contribute to the network's goals (see Figure 8.4). The process is competitive and specific to each creative field (Mulero & Rius-Ulldemolins, 2017).

UNESCO's influence upon municipalities around the world is broad. The organization prioritizes cultural diversity and the role it plays in fostering creativity and innovation through programs that promote cultural heritage preservation, creative cities, and craft (Mulero & Rius-Ulldemolins, 2017). They leverage their designation branding (in heritage or as a Creative City) to encourage tourism, resource investment for culture and creative industries, and enhance network development. They offer education, capacity building, policy development, and training through conferences and access to staff expertise. UNESCO conducts data collection on various aspects of the creative economy and uses this information to identify trends and shape the conversation around the identified issues (Gathen et al., 2021).

In 2004, UNESCO initiated its Creative Cities Network, consisting of cities selected through a competitive process and recognized for excellence in one of seven artistic disciplines—literature, film, music, crafts and folk art, design, media arts, and gastronomy (Creative Cities Network UNESCO, 2023). The stated goal of the program is "to promote cooperation with and among cities that have identified creativity as a strategic factor for sustainable urban development" (https://en.unesco.org/creative-cities/home accessed 7/26/2023). The network is seen as a tool for collaboration between isolated international cities that share similar characteristics or sector interests (Rosi, 2014). As of 2023, close to 300 cities have obtained recognition within this program, which has a specific urban development intent that promotes local cultural resources—while considering socio-cultural diversity, advocating international networking, and advancing professionalized creative sectors (Mulero & Rius-Ulldemolins, 2017).

For example, a planning professional responded to a Request for Proposals (RFP) put out by Design Core, an organization that pursued the UNESCO designation of City of Design for Detroit—a city that declared bankruptcy in 2013, resulting in a severe economic downturn. Her company got the contract to create a plan that would outline how Detroit could use this designation as a catalytic inclusive economic development tool for the city. The planner looked to Detroit's design development history in automobile manufacturing, for inspiration, and created strategies to parlay that into future programs that would foreground young minority designers. They received the designation in 2015. Design Core manages the programs of the designation. The Detroit Department of Planning was the city partner to the application. Together, they examined other cities that had received the designation, such as Cape Town and Mexico City, to see what distinguished them and how those cities were using the designation (policy transfer), before setting out to make a case and a plan for Detroit, which would be the only City of Design designated in the United States.

The planner reflected that the biggest challenge was "getting people to understand that the creative space and design can be a catalyst for economic development," as it was outside of traditional economic development practices (interview 1/27/2023). This was a new concept to local bureaucrats, but not new across the world. Leaders in Design Core Detroit became policy entrepreneurs, using policy options provided by UNESCO's Creative City Network, to try to solve the problems of economic hardship and employment gaps for young minority designers.

Acquiring the international UNESCO City of Design designation in 2015 was central to some civic leaders in the reimagining of this declining, post-industrial city as a global thought leader in inclusive, human-centered design. The policy platform, economic and urban development strategies, and robust partner network of over 30 other international design-designated cities already in the Creative Cities Network—all provide models and inspiration for Detroit design advocates to use in their campaign to remake Detroit as an inclusive design center. A leader of Design Core Detroit, the stewarding organization for Detroit's City of Design program, remarked:

> There is no award with it; there's no money; there's nothing that comes with it. It's meant to be a call to action. How do you leverage design in all its forms and aspects—the assets, the opportunities, etc., to drive sustainable and equitable development in your region? If you agreed to be a UNESCO city within the Creative Cities Network in any discipline area, then what you're essentially signing on to is that you're committed to the United Nations 17 sustainability goals.
> (Interview with Design Core Detroit leader 1/26/2023)

As an IGO, UNESCO does not have financial or political coercive power to advance their agenda, but they offer global municipalities something else: ready-made policy platforms, data, access to expertise, a network of peers, and clout they earn by competing with other cities (Vlassis & De Beukelaer, 2019). The leveraging of the Creative Cities Network participation is an example of how worldwide cultural and creative economy policy initiatives and programs have emerged and spread across nations and into cities (Collins, 2020).

Cities apply for recognition for different reasons. Some seek the brand recognition of the international designation to compete with other cities in attracting visitors, skilled and educated laborers, and investors (Gathen et al., 2021). Bilbao, a City of Design since 2014, leads with the promotion of their design-oriented urban policies; the Frank Gehry designed Guggenheim Museum Bilbao and other architectural showcases; and participation in fashion, videogames, and crafts (UNESCO Creative City Network member description, accessed 9/25/2023). Others want to be a part of the collaborative network to share ideas and learn from international colleagues (Rosi, 2014). Hatay, located in the southern region of Turkey, is a city of gastronomy. They aspire to form collaborations with chefs and students of gastronomy-related fields, from other Creative Cities, through an initiative called the Hatay Food project and the Food Academy (UNESCO Creative City Network member description, accessed 9/25/2023). Some see it as a mechanism to further develop an existing or emerging creative sector through increased resource allocations that they hope to get from their government budgets or partnering agencies (Namyslak, 2014). Perth, a small city of less than 160,000 residents became a member in 2021 in the category of Crafts and Folk Art. To capitalize on their designation, they are implementing a series of festivals and events to promote collaboration with other international partners. They are providing low-cost space for artisans and craftspeople to make and sell their work. And they are using the stories of their craftspeople to create a narrative about their town's heritage, with the hopes of attracting people to visit (UNESCO Creative City Network member description, accessed 9/25/2023).

In a case study focusing on San Antonio, Texas, the city was able to demonstrate that UNESCO's selection of them as a gastronomy Creative City resulted in outcomes of increased entrepreneurship, newly developed and targeted local policy initiatives, an increase in sustainable food organizational support, and economic benefits (Alimohammadirokni et al., 2021). Using marketing tools, city leaders use the designation as a competitive leverage when promoting their city to would-be tourists who have their choice of destinations.

In 2017, in Kansas City, residents applied for the UNESCO Creative City Network Music City designation, based on the city's history of originating American swing and jazz artists—with the goal of elevating local appreciation of music as an intangible heritage; the residents also aimed to advocate for saving places where historically important people lived and performed as tangible local heritage. In an interview conducted with one of the Kansas City Creative Music City founders, who applied and subsequently created a nonprofit to manage the activities under the Music City designation, he reflected that he saw the international recognition—to promote cultural tourism, neighborhood preservation, economic development, and the music sector—through a creative economy lens (interview 1/17/2023). In July 2022, he attended a UNESCO Creative Cities conference in Brazil to present on their policy progress and recovery in the music industry from COVID-19 shutdowns. He found allyship with other international cities with the Music City designation, such as Hannover, and experienced policy learning as they shared the various ways their music industries are structured, promoted, and nurtured.

Our interviewee, who acted as the policy entrepreneur behind getting the UNESCO designation, is a professor from Kansas

City with a love of jazz and background in urban planning. The UNESCO Creative Cities program connects to his interest in neighborhood preservation, history, music, and urban development; and he incorporates the work of the nonprofit stewardship of Kansas City as a Music City, as part of his research and teaching (interview 1/17/2023). Another founding partner of the Kansas City designation is an African American woman with a background in heritage tourism, specifically focusing on Black American's experience in Kansas City (see Figure 8.5). She was interested in the tourism aspect of the network and the emphasis on cultural diversity (interview 1/17/2023). These two individuals had different reasons for pursuing the designation, but found common ground in working together to partner on the application.

Figure 8.5 Ahmad Alaadeen (1934–2010) was an American jazz saxophonist, educator, and fixture in the Kansas City music scene for over six decades.

Source: Copyright holder, Ahmad Alaadeen; Copyrighted free use, via Wikimedia Commons

While they have realized some of their aspirations with the organization and made some important contacts through the network, keeping the momentum in the local community has proven to be hard. They don't have continuous political or community support—financially or regarding the workload necessary—to advance initiatives. In a political environment, electoral change can greatly impact the momentum of success of programs. In Kansas City, the mayor who signed the letter to approve the city's membership into the UNESCO Creative Cities' Network left office and a new mayor came in. The new mayor, according to our informant, is more interested in sports than culture and sees the UNESCO designation as the last mayor's priority, not his. He and his administration are therefore disinclined to invest resources in it. This makes it difficult to fully realize the potential of the position in the network.

Asked about his dream scenario, our interviewee reflected that he would like to see a musician elected to city council, as he saw in Mannheim, Germany, another Music City in the Creative Cities network. If there was embedded political leadership that "got it," then that would hopefully prompt the city to invest more in the creative economy and cultural producers. He would also like to see better integration of the music scene, which he perceives as fragmented by genre. Getting musicians to work together on policy issues, with interested city officials, is what he hopes being a Music City will bring to Kansas City.

WHY CHAMPIONS OF THE CREATIVE ECONOMY ARE IMPORTANT

In this chapter, we've explored what it means to be a champion in the creative economy at multiple scales. We've been inspired by some of the models that leaders in the country look to for policy ideas. These champions play a crucial role in promoting and advancing the creative economy for several important reasons. They provide high-level advocacy and public awareness about the value and potential of the creative economy. They advocate policies that support the growth and development of the creative industries, ensuring that decision-makers and the public recognize their significance. Creative economy champions, while not actively passing policies themselves, support policymakers with information that helps them develop and implement policies that can foster the growth of creative industries. The resulting economic growth creates jobs, attracts investment, and employs youth.

Many creative endeavors are deeply rooted in local culture, traditions, and heritage. Champions play a vital role in supporting cultural diversity and preservation through the valuing of craft and equity in creative industries. As creative people are at the forefront of innovation and entrepreneurship, champions contribute to the mentoring, training, and success of these individuals and the ideas they bring to market. From many of the examples we've shared, you can see that international collaboration and cultural exchange is part of the network that creative economy champions foster. Community building—at the local, national, and international levels—is also part of this activity. The social impacts that creative endeavors can have by addressing social justice, inclusivity, and environmental issues are profound. They can be tools for positive change and public awareness. Lastly, a thriving creative economy contributes to a higher quality of life by providing access to cultural experiences, entertainment, heritage resources, and artistic expression. Champions recognize the importance of these aspects in enhancing the wellbeing of individuals and communities.

In Chapter 9, you will find more inspirational models that will help you identify possibilities you could entertain in your hometown.

TAKEAWAYS

From this chapter, we want to highlight the following takeaways:

- Creative economy champions exist at all levels of engagement in the creative economy ecosystem. They share several characteristics that define them as champions, including being at the forefront of innovation, willing to take risks, partnering with others, leading with their policies and programs, and often being recognized for their achievements.
- Creative economy champions can be categorized, which helps us see the many environments from which they spring.

These categories include, but are not limited to, artists and creatives, creative entrepreneurs, cultural institution leaders, media and entertainment leaders, technology innovators, design visionaries, investors and philanthropists, advocates or policymakers, community leaders, and mentors or educators.
- Leaders look to each other, and to other cities, for program and policy models and inspiration, which leads to policy transfer, diffusion, learning, and convergence.
- There are several influential international organizations that actively study, measure, and present reports on the creative economy, championing this field globally to their constituents.
- UNESCO and the Creative Cities Network are leaders in the global dispersion of creative economy ideas and concepts through their programs, networks, and shared models.

Discussion questions:
1 In your community, who would you identify as a creative economy champion and why? What tools do you see this person using?
2 When you look at the characteristics of a champion, do you see any that you practice or that you aspire to?
3 What models or inspirations do you look to in the creative fields?
4 Why have ideas on creative economy urban development and policymaking spread so broadly over the past twenty years?
5 Can strategies that originate in one place be transferred easily to another that has different conditions, such as population, geography, or industries? How are models or tools adapted for different locations?

Activities
- Conduct research to identify additional national champions representing various countries. What do they advocate for? How do they engage with other countries?
- Look up the UNESCO Creative Cities Network on their website (unesco.org). Review the various cities in the

network and their creative fields. Now, think about your city and answer these questions: If you were to prepare an application for your city to join the network, which creative field would you select? And what would be your argument for why UNESCO should admit your city?

- Look up the MacArthur Fellows on their website (macfound.org/programs/fellows). Watch some of the short videos about the fellows, what they do, and why they were selected. Now unpack *why* their achievements are considered highly creative and *how* they got where they are. And, present answers to these questions: Which sectors are they in? Do they have collaborators? Do they have community partners? What is their educational background? What passion inspired them? What risks did they take? Who supports them?

REFERENCES

Alasuutari, P. (2016). *The Synchronization of National Policies: Ethnography of the Global Tribe of Moderns*. New York, London: Routledge.

Alimohammadirokni, M., Emadlou, A., & Yuan, J. (2021). The Strategic Resources of a Gastronomy Creative City: The Case of San Antonio, Texas. *Journal of Gastronomy and Tourism*, 5(4), 237–252.

Bishara, H. (2022, May 12). A Universal Basic Income for Artists? US Cities Are Trying It. *Frieze New York*. www.ft.com/content/03574a31-27fa-4402-baac-8a512d8a98cd (accessed 19 September 2023).

Bradbury, J. C. (2019). *Can Movie Production Incentives Grow the Economy? Evidence from Georgia and North Carolina*. http://doi.org/10.2139/ssrn.3432035

Breznitz, S. M., & Noonan, D. S. (2018). Planting the Seed to Grow Local Creative Industries: The Impacts of Cultural Districts and Arts Schools on Economic Development. *Environment and Planning A: Economy and Space*, 50(5), 1047–1070.

Caranicas, P. (2022). BlueStar Studio, a $180 Million Film and TV Production Center, to Open in Atlanta. *Variety*. https://variety.com/2022/artisans/filming-locations/bluestar-studios-a-180-million-film-and-tv-production-center-to-open-in-atlanta-peachtree-group-1235414641/ (accessed 19 September 2023).

Collins, P. (2020). "And the Winner Is . . . Galway: A Cultural Anatomy of a Winning Designate." *International Journal of Cultural Policy*, 26(5), 633–648.

Cunningham, S., & Swift, A. (2019). Creative Industries Around the World. In S. Cunningham & T. Flew (Eds.), *A Research Agenda for Creative Industries* (pp. 146–163). Cheltenham & Northampton, MA: Edward Elgar Publishing.

Daubaraite, U., & Startiene, G. (2015). Creative Industries Impact on National Economy in Regard to Subsectors. *Procedia—Social and Behavioral Sciences*, 213, 129–134.

Davies, R., & Sigthorsson, G. (2013). *Introducing the Creative Industries: From Theory to Practice*. Los Angeles, London, New Delhi, Singapore, Washington, DC: SAGE.

Gathen, C., Skoglund, W., & Laven, D. (2021). The UNESCO Creative Cities Network: A Case Study of City Branding. In C. Bevilacqua, F. Calabrò & L. Della Spina (Eds.), *New Metropolitan Perspectives. NMP 2020. Smart Innovation, Systems and Technologies* (Vol. 178). Cham: Springer.

Hayes, M. (2020). The Coloniality of UNESCO's Heritage Urban Landscapes: Heritage Process and Transnational Gentrification in Cuenca, Ecuador. *Urban Studies*, *57*(15), 3060–3077.

Johnson, L. M., & Dominguez, C. (2021, March 27). San Francisco Is Guaranteeing Monthly Income for Artists Impacted by the Covid-19 Pandemic. *CNN*. www.cnn.com/2021/03/27/us/san-francisco-is-guaranteeing-pay-for-artists-trnd/index.html (accessed 19 September 23).

Kong, L., Gibson, C., Khoo, L.-M., & Semple, A.-L. (2006). Knowledges of the Creative Economy: Towards a Relational Geography of Diffusion and Adaptation in Asia. *Asia Pacific Viewpoint*, *47*(2), 173–194.

Markusen, A., Wassall, G. H., DeNatale, D., & Cohen, R. (2008). Defining the Creative Economy: Industry and Occupational Approaches. *Economic Development Quarterly*, *22*(1), 24–45. https://doi.org/10.1177/0891242407311862

Marsh, D., & Sharman, J. C. (2009). Policy Diffusion and Policy Transfer. *Policy Studies*, *30*(3), 269–288.

Mattocks, K. (2018). "Just Describing Is Not Enough": Policy Learning, Transfer, and the Limits of Best Practices. *The Journal of Arts Management, Law and Society*, *48*(2), 85–97.

McLean, T. (2021, March 25). SF Launched a Guaranteed Income Program for Artists. Here's Who Qualifies. *SFGATE*. www.sfgate.com/bayarea/article/SF-guaranteed-income-program-for-artists-16053841.php (accessed 19 September 2023).

Meskell, L. (2019, March). What's the Point of UNESCO? Founded to Safeguard the World's Heritage, UNESCO's Status Often Threatens What It Seeks to Protect. *History Today*, 12–15.

Misztal, P. (2018). Universal Basic Income. Theory and Practice. *Managerial Economics*, *19*(1), 103–116.

Mulero, M., & Rius-Ulldemolins, J. (2017). From Creative City to Generative Governance of the Cultural Policy System: The Case of Barcelona's Candidature as UNESCO City of Literature. *City, Culture and Society*, *10*, 1–10.

Namyslak, B. (2014). Cooperation and Forming Networks of Creative Cities: Polish Experiences. *European Planning Studies*, *22*(11), 2411–2427.

Oakley, K. (2016). Whose Creative Economy? Inequality and the Need for International Approaches. *Les Enjeux De L'Information Ed de La Communication*, *2*, 163–171.

Pratt, A. C. (2009, Springer). Policy Transfer and the Field of the Cultural and Creative Industries: What Can Be Learned from Europe? *Creative Economies, Creative Cities. The GeoJournal Library*, *98*, 9–23.

Rich, M. A., & Tsitsos, W. (2016). Avoiding the "SoHo Effect" in Baltimore: Neighborhood Revitalization and Arts and Entertainment Districts. *International Journal of Urban and Regional Research, 10,* 736–756.

Rindzeviciute, E., Svensson, J., & Tomson, K. (2016). The International Transfer of Creative Industries as a Policy Idea. *International Journal of Cultural Policy, 22*(4), 594–610.

Rosi, M. (2014). Branding or Sharing? *City, Culture and Society, 5*(2), 107–110.

United Nations Conference on Trade and Development (UNCTAD). (2022). *Creative Economy Outlook.* Geneva: The United Nations.

United Nations/UNDP/UNESCO. (2013). *Creative Economy Special Edition: Widening Local Development Pathways.* New York, NY and Paris, France: United Nations Development Programme.

Vlassis, A., & De Beukelaer, C. (2019). The Creative Economy as a Versatile Policy Script: Exploring the Role of Competing Intergovernmental Organizations. *Media, Culture & Society, 41*(4), 502–519.

Warrick, D. D. (2009). Developing Organization Change Champions: A High Payoff Investment! *OD Practitioner, 41*(1), 14–19.

Weible, C. M., & Sabatier, P. A. (Eds.). (2018). *Theories of the Policy Process* (4th ed.). New York, London: Routledge, Taylor and Francis Group

WIPO. (2017). *How to Make a Living in the Creative Industries.* www.wipo.int/edocs/pubdocs/en/wipo_pub_cr_2017_1.pdf (accessed 27 August 2023).

Zahirovic-Herbert, V., & Gibler, K. M. (2023). Residential Marketing Duration: Film Studios as Neighborhood Sales Accelerators. *Journal of Real Estate Research.* https://doi.org/10.1080/08965803.2023.2214469

Examples of equitable creative economic development

Chapter 9

INTRODUCTION

In this chapter, we talk about how to make the creative economy more diverse, equitable, inclusive, and accessible (DEIA). First, we share why DEIA is important from an economic development perspective, in addition to moral and ethical reasons. Second, we explore how arts and culture practitioners talk about DEIA and support it, including areas for growth. Finally, we focus on place-based creative economic development strategies as a mechanism for addressing and championing this topic. It is important to note that we do not provide an exhaustive list of illustrations; rather, we offer examples designed to spark your own interest and approaches.

HOW IS DEIA CONNECTED TO ECONOMIC DEVELOPMENT?

Public, private, and nonprofit sectors champion the importance of diversity, equity, inclusion, and access in economic development. Their argument is that integrating DEIA into economic development contributes to healthier and resilient economics (DeLisi, 2021, n.p.). A focus on DEIA, from process through implementation, creates the space to understand roadblocks to economic opportunity; these can then be addressed through targeted programs. We see this beginning to happen in general economic development activity with varied approaches. For example, the Greater Minneapolis-St. Paul Regional Economic Framework provides a plan for inclusive growth; and the Charlotte Regional Business Alliance prioritizes resources for economic mobility for unemployed and underemployed individuals who disproportionately affect Black and Latinx people (DeLisi, 2021, n.p.).

The Chief Diversity, Equity, and Inclusion Officer (CDO) at the Department of Commerce for the US federal government, Junish Arora (2023), wrote:

> When you weld the ethical and moral, as well as social, cultural, and business case arguments for DEIA, I think you get a powerful, multivalent management tool that is the proverbial right thing to do and the pragmatic smart thing to do. The research for DEIA is multifold: increased performance and productivity; enhanced creativity and innovation; improved morale and engagement; higher retention and lower attrition; access to top talent and a broader, deeper talent pool; and alignment with changing demographics and cultural value systems.

Arora's comments point to a variety of different ways that DEIA-focused economic development is a benefit to economic development from workforce development and production innovation to industrial growth and worker wellbeing.

There are many different interpretations of what and who is included when talking about DEIA. In the US federal policy, protected classes include age, ancestry, color, disability, ethnicity, gender, gender identity or expression, genetic information, HIV/AIDS status, military status, national origin, pregnancy, race, religion, sex, sexual orientation, veteran status, or any other bases under the law. States and municipalities may also include bases such as socioeconomic status, marginalized areas and neighborhoods, rural or isolated communities, Title

1 schools, different types of ableisms, and tribal communities. It is also important to note that we are writing this book at a time where there is significant conflict and disagreement over protection and recognition of particular groups. A new culture war is emerging, where different values are vying for political power and different levels of government (Alfonseca, 2023).

HOW IS DEIA CONNECTED TO CREATIVE ECONOMIC DEVELOPMENT?

When focusing on DEIA in arts and creative economic development, some similar motivations from above also resonate with the arts. Americans for the Arts (n.d.), a national nonprofit advocacy organization, shares:

> We envision a country where artistic and cultural creativity is embraced as a human-based, primary driving force towards impact, empowerment, and economic and social justice in lives across the country. We believe that creative and artistic solutions are central to building more equitable economies that provide opportunity for all people to reach their individual potential.

The organization articulates that we should not only consider arts and creative approaches to getting a more equitable economy, but that DEIA in the arts is an important component of economic development.

We see an increase in the connection between arts and culture and DEIA, which has been catalyzed by the Black Lives Matter movement and the murder of Black people, in their communities, by select police members. Many arts organizations have expressed commitment to the ideals of DEIA; and some have made tangible, if incomplete, progress in implementing DEIA policies (Greater Philadelphia Cultural Alliance, 2020; PolicyLink, 2023).

However, there is still sizable room for progress; and an equity focus would greatly strengthen research in arts and economic development to address questions of impact, opportunity costs, and access at different geographic scales (Markusen & Gadwa, 2010, p. 381). Municipal arts and cultural plans—a strategy for developing a comprehensive approach to arts and culture—are largely vague about what diversity means in their city's specific context (Alvarez, 2005; Ashley et al., 2021). Plans do not emphasize DEIA to the extent they should (Markusen, 2014). As our previous research has indicated, municipal arts and cultural plans often describe their city's diversity as an important asset; yet, many do not include demographic analyses or qualitative descriptions about what that diversity means in the city's specific context and population (Ashley et al., 2021). Most plans do not discuss the equitable allocation of public arts and culture investment. Plans are largely silent as to whether and how the planning process was made to be inclusive.

It is common to see DEIA as a focus of the motivations and rationales behind arts and cultural planning and creative economic development (more specifically). It is less common to see a diverse process for economic development planning, and even rarer to see a focus on programs and policies that support DEIA-related economic development. This orientation leaves little room to discuss the ways in which an economic development rationale shuts some people out, in terms of both the process and what arts and cultural planning can do to advance social justice (Stevenson, 2004, 2005).

There are also long-standing critiques over the exclusionary practices of mainstream arts institutions and organizations (Coffee, 2008; Massing, 2019) and the divisions between arts engagement and socioeconomic class (Stevenson & Magee, 2017), particularly those arts institutions and organizations that have deep resources and support traditional hegemonic art practices. Arts and cultural policymaking, of which municipal arts and cultural planning is one stream, is also criticized for its placemaking practices, as we have mentioned in Chapter 4; this may contribute to gentrification and displacement (Murdoch et al., 2016) or take on a new place identity at the expense of previous histories (Lloyd, 2002). As Scott (2006, p. 15) notes: "Cities today may well harbor unprecedented creative capabilities; but, they are also places where striking social, cultural, and economic inequalities prevail. And there can be no truly final achievement of the Creative City where these stubborn problems remain." These are important areas to keep in mind when thinking about public investment of resources into creative economic development.

APPROACHES TO RESEARCH AND EXTERNAL SHOCKS

Many cities during the COVID-19 pandemic saw how hard the arts and creative economies were hurt; and this was even more so for those in marginalized communities. An arts leader in Philadelphia shared that the pandemic "laid bare the inequities in [their] city's creative economy," and that moving forward, the city's economic development policy should focus on prioritizing resources to help individual artists and small-to medium-sized organizations in the underserved areas of Philadelphia and to help build networks and opportunities—so we can include them in enhancing the vibrancy of the city's economy, rather than silo them (Forman, 2021).

Seattle's Office of Arts and Culture, in collaboration with the Evans Student Consulting Lab at the University of Washington, wrote the report "Assessing the Creative Economy of Seattle through a Race and Equity Lens." The authors argued that, while Seattle has a thriving creative economy, there are severe disparities. The report (Islas et al., 2019, pp. 6–7) found the following areas were of relevance for creatives of color:

- *Structural barriers*: Creatives of color bear the same burden of structural inequities that many people of color in Seattle face. Racism, displacement, and access to housing, among others, are larger barriers to entry in the creative economy.
- *Underrepresentation*: Artists and creatives of color are underrepresented across the creative economy. The underrepresentation is in creative occupations, predominantly. White leadership at major arts institutions, as well as lack of visibility in art itself, can all inhibit participation in the creative economy for people of color.
- *Affordability and wages*: Many creatives, and especially creatives of color, cannot afford to live in Seattle and participate in the local creative economy. Without a living wage, creatives do not have the financial resources, capacity, or time to devote to their discipline.
- *Employment and the gig economy*: Creatives tend to have more unconventional forms of employment to sustain their creative practice—often holding multiple jobs to make ends meet and functioning within the gig economy. It's no surprise

that they often lack the infrastructure and support they need, such as benefits and income stability.
- *Lack of opportunity*: Creatives of color have less access to opportunity to participate fully and sustainably in the creative economy. Lack of funding and financial resources, lack of professional networks, development and mentorship, and lack of arts education are major barriers to thriving in an artistic practice.
- *Undervaluing art created by people of color*: Creatives of color must operate within the White dominant culture of Seattle, where an emphasis on "fine art" has served as a barrier to art that is created and centered on people of color. This often looks like lower wages for creatives of color, less physical spaces and platforms for creatives of color to showcase their work, and disparities in funding and grants.
- *Career pathways*: As creative occupations do not always have traditional pathways, participation in the creative economy is often not considered a viable career option. Without arts education, paid internships, and a cultural value on arts careers, it can be challenging for individuals to participate in the creative economy.

This report recommends a variety of approaches to address these challenges, including systems for gig work, workshops to help with skill development and opportunities, internship and grant programs that support these workers, and creative residences at the city to match skills with projects across different divisions (Islas et al., 2019). While we don't know if any of these programs have been implemented and if they have been successful, they provide a way to start to imagine what support might look like after the issues have been diagnosed.

In another example, the City of Vancouver provides a strategic framework to align resources and actions. This framework, *Culture|Shift* (previously known as the Creative City Strategy), is Vancouver's arts and culture plan for 2020–2029. It calls out five primary objects:

- Support for art and culture
- Champion creators
- Build on commitments to reconciliation and eEquity

- Introduce bold moves to advance community-led cultural infrastructure
- Position Vancouver as a thriving hub for music

(City of Vancouver, 2023)

As the plan notes, the traditional, unceded territories of the xʷməθkʷəy'əm (Musqueam), Sḵwx̱wú7mesh (Squamish), and səlilwətaʔɬ (Tsleil-Waututh) are what makes Vancouver's cultural landscape unique. The authors write,

> Diverse people from across the world have imbued Vancouver's cultural landscape with the qualities, landmarks, and stories that make our city recognizable and distinct. Culture|Shift acknowledges that this landscape is critical to our shared economic prosperity, social cohesion, and sense of environmental responsibility.
>
> (City of Vancouver, 2023)

This highlights how a plan may comprehensively prioritize First Nations into its economic development planning frameworks and implementation practices. For example, there is a city-nation formal relationship, as well as First Nations representation on the cultural-plan advisory board. There are also programs and resources directed to the work, including grant programs. For example, there is a grant for "engaging creative Musqueam community members, elders, and knowledge keepers around equity access, and reconciliation for Musqueam peoples."

Arts and cultural planning may engage in innovative approaches to inclusion, such as mandating DEIA statements from arts and cultural granting recipients, requiring a diverse makeup of arts and cultural boards and including DEIA training (Ashley et al., 2021), promoting cultural asset mapping with a DEIA focus, using arts and cultural investment for economic development and community economic development (Stern & Seifert, 2008), emphasizing place-keeping over placemaking (Bedoya, 2013), surveying formal and informal arts activity across different sectors (Alvarez, 2005), or specializing in cultural equity planning (PolicyLink, 2019). This book aims to connect these efforts to creative economic development.

As mentioned in Chapter 4, arts and cultural planning and policy has a history of eliding, erasing, or editing aspects of local culture to make it attractive to visitors and investors—especially indigenous cultures that predate the city formation (Alvarez, 2005; Bedoya, 2013; Lefebvre, 2018a, 2018b; Kahne, 2015; Moss, 2012; Zitcer, 2020). Public arts and cultural activities may represent a "third space" (physical or not), where "hybrid identifications are possible and where cultural transformations can happen" (Antener, 2019, para. 1; Bhabha, 2006; Soja, 1996) when thinking about the alignment or connection with DEIA.

In the following pages, we talk about specific place-based examples where DEIA is incorporated to address some of these long-standing critiques. If this feels like a big challenge, we suggest starting by talking to arts and cultural planners or urban planners, because they are likely to have a good sense of how to create a demographic base, how to structure an inclusive process, and how to ensure that strategies and related resources are directed efficiently as part of the city's economic development strategy (Berke et al., 2006).

DOING PLACE-BASED CREATIVE ECONOMIC DEVELOPMENT

In Chapter 4, we discussed place-based creative economic development strategies, including different funding strategies, arts districts, placemaking, artist live-work spaces, and pro-arts zoning and building code changes. In this section, we'll provide many real-world examples of these strategies. We also talked about how place-based creative economic development can create issues around gentrification and equity; we'll provide examples that illustrate some of the conflicts around creative economic development. We hope these examples, taken together, give you a good sense of how creative economic development plays out in the real world and inspire you to look for ways to innovate where you live and work.

Creative-friendly building and zoning codes

In other chapters, we've discussed how critical creative economy is to the broader economy and how much it enriches cities—both culturally/artistically and economically. We've also discussed how artists and other creative entrepreneurs need and use space in unique ways, sometimes leading them to take over nontraditional spaces for living and working. Finally, we've mentioned how creative economic activity can enliven and revitalize downtowns and other neighborhoods. But this activity and newly created sense of place can lead to interest and investment from others, which can ultimately price out artists. In this section, we discuss examples of ways in which government and nonprofit actors are working to encourage and support creative enterprise, without making creatives victims of their own success.

On December 2, 2016, a fire broke out during a concert at the Ghost Ship, an Oakland, CA warehouse that had been converted, without permits, into an artist live-work space. The building was stuffed with furniture, pianos, and artwork; had no fire alarms or sprinklers; and insufficient stairways and fire exits. Thirty-six people died in the fire, devastating the Oakland arts community. The Ghost Ship fire highlighted the risks of carving out space for the arts in nontraditional spaces (see Figure 9.1). It also highlighted the incentives to do so in high cost-of-living areas.

In the wake of the fire, fire and building departments in other cities, including Baltimore and Boston, started cracking down on unpermitted artist live-work spaces—especially spaces that

Figure 9.1 Ruins of the Ghost Ship artist space, Oakland, California.
Source: Photo courtesy of Google Earth

might be used for larger gatherings (Shea, 2016, Rich, 2019). Just days after the Ghost Ship fire, the City of Denver fire department made unannounced inspections of two arts spaces in the RiNo district—Rhinoceropolis and Glob—and shut them both down. Both spaces had passed inspections previously; but this time, the fire department was unwilling to look the other way (Carney, 2021). Yet, city leaders know that doing everything by the book can be prohibitively expensive for artists; and this may drive them out of the city altogether. Attempting to strike a balance, in 2017, Denver City Council passed an ordinance authorizing the Safe Occupancy Program, a two-and-half-year grace period for creatives and others living in unpermitted spaces to come forward and work with the city to bring their buildings up to code (City and County of Denver Community Planning & Development, 2017). There was also grant funding available to help with building costs. However, out of the many inquiries the city received, only a handful of projects moved forward (Carney, 2021). In Boston, Mayor Marty Walsh directed inspectors to work with property owners to bring creative live-work spaces up to code. Although in neither case was there a permanent solution that would keep artists and visitors safe at low cost, both attempts were steps in the right direction. Cities need to acknowledge that these unpermitted spaces exist, offer technical assistance, find financial assistance to help building owners and tenants get to code compliance, and consider building code revisions that make artist live-work spaces more affordable and feasible, without compromising safety. As cities benefit from creative people living and working there, city leaders should be creative about keeping them there.

Other cities have worked to change planning and zoning regulations to support and incentivize arts and cultural uses. Santa Monica, California, introduced arts and entertainment-oriented zoning that allows "greater flexibility for restaurants that provide entertainment," expands the types of venues eligible for alcohol permits, allows outdoor rooftop entertainment uses, and gives the Community Development Director increased discretion to approve "unique business proposals" that aren't clearly defined in the zoning code (City of Santa Monica, 2023). These zoning changes signal (and provide) friendliness and flexibility toward creative uses, especially live music and other entertainment.

The City of Sydney, Australia, had already embraced progressive-minded mixed-use planning; but, its definition of mixed-use tended to favor commercial and residential uses—not the types of spaces that creative organizations and artists need. In 2015, Sydney launched a project called Creative Spaces and the Built Environment. The idea was to get a grasp on what types of spaces creative groups really need, convening public forums and workshops where artists, planners, architects, and surveyors came together to explore potential solutions to the lack of sufficient space. The effort resulted in a paper called *New Ideas for Old Buildings*; and its findings are now helping the city improve its policies that affect creative industries—for instance, how to regulate temporary performance spaces (City of Sydney, 2023). The key takeaway here? To create better policy and involve arts and culture issues in the branches of government, like planning, where they're not always present (World Cities Culture Forum, 2017).

Artist live-work spaces

As we have discussed earlier, artists often resort to nontraditional or even unpermitted spaces when they can't find appropriate and affordable housing and workspace to create (which may involve noise, dust, and/or odors) and store equipment (which may be large). Dedicated affordable artist housing solves this problem. We describe a few examples of such projects around the US.

In 2014, the City of Dearborn, Michigan, moved government operations from its historic 1922 City Hall building to a newer building. The city sold the building to Artspace, a nonprofit developer of affordable artist housing. With help from the East Dearborn and West Dearborn DDAs, the new live-work space opened in 2016. It cost $16.5 million and was funded through a combination of low-income tax credits, donations, and equity investment (Bethancourt, 2016). The building now houses 53 housing units, a gallery and work space, and an Arts and Technology Lab (Adams, 2019). This creative adaptive reuse project repurposed a beautiful historic building, provided affordable spaces for artists and other creatives to live and work, and enlivened the area. Artspace has done over 60 similar projects across the country, including in high-cost areas like Seattle and New York City (see Figure 9.2).

Figure 9.2 City Hall *Artspace Lofts* in Dearborn, Michigan.
Source: Photo by Carolyn G. Loh

The City of Boston, MA, has an Artist Live-Work Program dedicated to "developing and preserving artist space in Boston." The program works in two ways. First, the city works with developers to increase the supply of artist housing. This housing must be permanently available for artists, be located in areas that wouldn't normally have traditional housing, and offer either live-work spaces or work spaces for rent or purchase. Second, the city oversees an artist certification process that ensures that this valuable housing goes to working artists. Some of the housing also has income restrictions; so, the city also certifies compliance with those requirements. The program's website reiterates the value of having artists living and working within the city. It points out that "artists make Boston a more livable city" and that "artists also function as small businesses by providing creative economy jobs and services for Boston residents" (Boston Planning and Development Agency, 2023).

One more example from the Boston area is The Foundry, a publicly owned gallery, black-box theater, and STEAM work space in Cambridge, MA. The space in The Foundry is available to creators on a sliding rental scale with no documentation of eligibility. The opening of The Foundry, a former factory whose adaptive reuse was funded by the City of Cambridge for $45 million, followed controversial closures of Cambridge's EMF artist space and Green Street Studio—both victims of redevelopment (Mason, 2022). The Foundry attempts to fill some of the gaps left by those closures. The building itself was given to the city by a developer, in exchange for approval on a rezoning in another part of the city. The Cambridge Redevelopment Authority currently holds a 50-year lease on the property.

These examples show that it is possible for cities—working with state-level agencies, nonprofits, and for-profit partners—to create safe, affordable artist spaces that would otherwise be underprovided by the real estate market. The examples also show that it can be expensive and take many years to realize such projects; so, they need strong commitments from city leaders to be successful. But given the monetary and intangible value of creative workers to cities, it is certainly possible to make a case for the investment of money and time it takes.

Arts and cultural districts

Arts and cultural districts are formally or informally recognized corridors or neighborhoods that have a significant cluster of arts and/or cultural activity and uses. According to the advocacy group Americans for the Arts, cultural districts are: well-recognized, labeled areas of a city, in which a high concentration of cultural facilities and programs serve as the main anchor of attraction. They help strengthen local economies, create an enhanced sense of place, and deepen local cultural capacity (Americans for the Arts, 2023).

Some arts and cultural districts have a formal structure, with a governing board and delineated boundaries. Others are "naturally occurring" arts and cultural districts that have grown, as artists found work, living, gallery, or performance spaces near each other, until they reached a critical mass. We'll provide three examples of different kinds of arts and cultural districts.

The Tin District in West Dallas is an example of a naturally occurring arts and cultural district, given the organic nature of emergence and because it changes in response to artists' needs. Located in a cluster of warehouses, centered around Fabrication Street, the Tin District embodies the boundary-pushing vibe of the most successful arts and cultural districts. Graffiti covers many of the buildings; and over half of the 100 artists in the area are people of color, women, or both (Solis, 2023). The Wild West Mural Fest, in the district, celebrates spray paint murals (Tin District, 2023).

Patrons come to look at and buy art, but also to learn. Although the Tin District is currently generally affordable, which is a key reason it houses such a diverse group of artists, its success is attracting developers interested in capitalizing on the area's energy. Local artists worry that the Tin District's character and accessibility could eventually be compromised (Solis, 2023) (see Figure 9.3).

The Warehouse Arts Management Organization (WAMO) is a nonprofit that manages a district of artist spaces in Tucson, AZ. It manages four buildings with studio and gallery spaces. WAMO "is the group looking out for the entire Tucson Historic Warehouse Arts District—its history and its future. The mission of this artist-led nonprofit is to preserve, protect, promote, and program [the district]" (WAMO, 2023). At the same time that WAMO is supporting its artists, it is preserving its historic early 20th-century warehouse buildings. The spaces include artist workspaces, galleries, offices, and performance spaces (see Figures 9.4 and 9.5). The goal of the nonprofit management structure is to make the district cohesive, promote it, and ensure that a variety of arts disciplines are represented there (WAMO Tucson, 2023).

Figure 9.3 Warehouses with spray paint murals in the Tin District, Dallas.
Source: Google Earth

Figure 9.4 WAMO makerspace.
Source: Photo by Ken McAllister

Figure 9.5 WAMO main building sign and noticeboard.
Source: Photo by Ken McAllister

Even though it is supported by a nonprofit, the district is still considered a naturally occurring arts and cultural district (National Endowment for the Arts, 2023). Artists started moving into the neighborhood in the 1980s, after the warehouses were no longer needed for their original purpose. Many of the artists came from lower-income Tucson neighborhoods; and The Arizona Department of Transportation (ADOT) purchased many of the buildings, with the intention of tearing them down to build a new freeway. However, it now looks like the freeway will never be built. The nonprofit WAMO was organized in 2004, after a strategic planning process. Recently, with other partners, including an artists' council, the Tucson-Pima Arts Council collected data about all the artists using spaces in the district and created an exhaustive map—to help guide visitors and make the artists and their work more visible (National Endowment for the Arts, 2023). This naturally occurring arts district has more formal support from organizations that aim to keep the area affordable and help its artists be successful.

A National Endowment for the Arts-funded research initiative, The Place, Arts and Cultural Systems (PACS) Lab, investigates how arts and cultural districts (ACDs) support diversity, equity, and inclusion, using a national survey and case studies in the Intermountain West and Midwest. The project is designed to understand barriers to and best practices for making those districts inclusive, equitable, and drivers of economic and social innovation. PACS will both learn from and serve ACD organizations and neighbors—by creating a typology and national public database of ACD characteristics; using the database to analyze patterns of DEIA practice; identifying good practices for different district types, geographies, and capacities; and developing and sharing a flexible ACD toolkit for communities with a range of resources and needs.[1]

Special zoning districts: artist overlay zones

An overlay zone is a tool used to designate a bounded area that has additional zoning and land development regulations, in addition to an underlying base zone. Overlays are used to nurture a particular kind of activity and use. Common uses include historic preservation overlays that regulate certain design standards to conform with historic preservation guidelines or environmental protection overlays that place additional restrictions on development near environmentally sensitive areas (City of Austin, 2013). We also see it used in relation to arts and cultural districts, as well as in areas where creative activity is clustered.

Cambridge, MA experienced conflict and tension in Central Square over the displacement of artists, due to unsafe living and working conditions (MacDonald, 2018). In 2018, hundreds of musicians were evicted from studio spaces and artist lofts, living and working in the EMF building. The EMF building had an important industrial history; it later hosted such nationally known performers as Arctic Monkeys, Bearstronaut, Juliana Hatfield, The Lemonheads, Letters to Cleo, The Melvins, Scorpion, and Peter Wolf (Levy, 2019). The city created a task force to identify public policy options for prioritizing artist retention and recruitment strategies. They considered an arts zoning overlay district that would reward developers who build and maintain artistic spaces as well as other policy mechanisms, including a business improvement district. Evicted tenants successfully applied for a "Protected Land Petition" to the Cambridge Historical Commission to designate the EMF building as a historic landmark; but this has minimal impact on who uses the building and largely centers on the building exterior (Beland, 2018). While the overlay district was never implemented, it does show an example of how it can be considered. The Foundry, mentioned earlier in this chapter, was a response to this artist displacement that was fully implemented.

Artist land trusts

The San Francisco Bay Area has long embraced the tech industry, which is responsible for the region's thriving economy. But that—in combination with the fact that 75,000 people have moved to San Francisco in the past decade, while only 15,000 new housing units have been added—has led to astronomical real estate prices. In 2013, a group of investors interested in preserving the city's culture launched the Community Arts Stabilization Trust (CAST)—essentially a real estate holding company—to help address the dearth of affordable space. Investors in CAST receive tax breaks for their contributions; CAST then uses the money to buy property and renovate it. Then, the trust leases it to arts organizations at below-market rates, using a rent-to-own model to help stimulate long-term affordability (Cast-SF.org, 2023).

CAST has so far acquired four arts buildings in the Tenderloin District in San Francisco. CAST's goals are to keep the properties it owns permanently affordable for artists, arts, and cultural organizations and to preserve the culture of the neighborhood, especially queer spaces (Abello, 2020) (see Figure 9.6). As we've mentioned, arts and cultural neighborhoods, either created organically by artists or seeded by public creative place-based economic development actions, when successful, often price out the artists who were essentially responsible for that success. Community land trusts, of which artist land trusts are one type, aim to create islands of permanent affordability within rapidly changing cities.

Black farmers in Georgia developed the community land trust model in the late 1960s to give "communities the space and security to develop neighborhoods according to their needs, rather than the demands of the market" (Lim, 2020). Land is held in common by the trust and decisions are made by the nonprofit's board of trustees. Members can own and bequeath their residences or other structures. Like other, non-arts-focused community land trusts, artist land trusts enter into the real estate market on behalf of artists and exercise control over the properties they own to keep them affordable.

Figure 9.6 *80 Turk St.* in San Francisco, is owned by CAST.
Source: Photo by Scott Fin, courtesy of CounterPulse

CAST is considered a successful example of an artist land trust; but even CAST operates at a very small scale in the context of a city the size of San Francisco. There are three big takeaways from CAST's strategy. First, it takes a long time. Second, it necessitates significant capital. And third, it requires looking at properties that aren't already on the market, since it's so competitive. To achieve its goals, CAST needed to partner with private developers and property owners who are sympathetic to the issue—and not driven purely by profit. In many cities, such partners will be hard to come by.

Nevertheless, the artist land trust approach is gaining momentum, especially in other expensive cities in the San Francisco Bay Area. The Northern California Land Trust, which owns and rents out affordable housing units, is turning its efforts to space for artists. Their Artist Space Trust aims to create permanent affordable housing for artists, to ensure that they can continue to live and work in the area despite rising real estate costs (Northern California Land Trust, 2023). In Oakland, CA, the Oakland Community Land Trust (OakCLT), which owns mostly single-family rental properties, acquired a multi-unit artist live-work space, currently rented by a mix of musicians and visual artists. OakCLT's ownership will ensure that rent remains affordable, in perpetuity, for artists (Lefebvre, 2018a; City of Oakland, 2018). The artist land trust approach recognizes that artists are valuable to the character and economies of these neighborhoods, but also that they often do not have high-enough incomes to weather rent increases in gentrifying areas. Artist land trusts are an approach to partially solving the paradox of gentrification in artist neighborhoods.

Creating good neighbors

Artists seek out warehouse districts and commercial areas, in part, because some of their activities cause noise, dust, and odors that can put them in conflict with other uses. As interesting artist neighborhoods attract new residents, these conflicts can put creative enterprises at risk. London provides one example of an approach to handling these conflicts.

Before they were famous, musicians like The Who, The Rolling Stones, and Adele got their start in London's small, independent music venues. But in recent years, many of these clubs have closed down—and new ones weren't taking their place. Part of the problem? Rents are rising, licenses for these types of businesses are hard to obtain, and noise complaints are plentiful (Doward, 2015). In 2015, the city set up a Music Venue Task Force composed of artists and government officials from multiple departments to consider the issue and come up with a plan to stop the decline. Their research showed that the city had lost 35% of its venues (City of London, 2017). The city developed a Rescue Plan, which involved naming a Night Tsar—an official in charge of advocating for nightlife interests—and changing building codes to ensure new residential development is soundproofed to mitigate against noise. In 2016, the city saw no net loss in music venues. The report concludes that London's efforts were successful—the city gave hard evidence about the problem, created a strong media strategy to advocate for why nightlife is important to the health and vitality of the city, and formed a task force with representation from all stakeholders involved. Unfortunately, the story doesn't end there. The impacts of the COVID-19 pandemic, supply chain issues, and loss of tourism due to Brexit have taken a sharp toll on the live music industry, causing some to question the effectiveness of the Night Tsar (Iqbal, 2020). However, the goals of the Rescue Plan, to maintain live music venues even in the face of gentrification, are sound and the methodology—making new residential units deal with existing venues rather than try to get them shut down—is worth emulating.

CONFLICT, RESISTANCE, AND RESOLUTIONS IN PLACE-BASED CREATIVE ECONOMIC DEVELOPMENT

At the beginning of this chapter, we discussed the conflicts that can occur when artists use spaces in nontraditional ways. The tragedy of the Ghost Ship fire is an extreme example of artists resisting both conventional rules, in the form of building codes, and the tight Bay Area housing market, by inhabiting and converting a substandard space for their needs. In this section, we'll highlight some examples of attempts by artists to retain their place in neighborhoods in the face of gentrification pressure, as well as municipal policies that attempt to enable artists to stay in their neighborhoods. While the conflicts and resistance strategies that we discuss here are specific to the creative sector, many of these issues and strategies are present

Table 9.1 Equitable place-based creative economic development strategies

Strategy	Definition	Specifics
Creative-friendly building and zoning codes	Planning, zoning, and building regulations to support and incentivize arts and cultural uses.	Grace periods for fire code compliance
		Grant funding for code compliance
		Technical assistance
		Consider applying residential building codes rather than commercial building codes for live-work (not performance) spaces
		Expanded live-work zoning
		Arts and entertainment zoning
		Integrate arts and culture into comprehensive planning
		Change building codes to ensure new residential development is soundproofed to mitigate against noise
Affordable artist live-work spaces	Appropriate and affordable housing and workspace that allows artists the room to create.	Deed-restricted affordability
		Working artist certification program
		Managed by public or nonprofit agency
Arts and cultural districts	Formally or informally recognized corridors or neighborhoods that have a significant cluster of arts and/or cultural activity and uses.	
Artist overlay zones	Tool used to designate a bounded area that has additional zoning and land development regulations, in addition to an underlying base zone.	

in broader discussions around gentrification and displacement. We should also point out that, given the broadness of who make up the "creative class," some of these conflicts are essentially intramural—with one set of more highly compensated creatives (such as tech workers) supplanting lower-paid artists. Finally, it's important to note that although in some cases artists cluster in neighborhoods that weren't traditionally residential, they may also be the ones to first supplant lower-income residents of a neighborhood.

The complex relationship between artists and gentrification

It's a familiar story, one we've already told in this book: artists move into a warehouse district or lower-income neighborhood. In this story, the artists are usually White. Any people already living in the neighborhood are likely people of color. Over time, the artists' presence and the economic activity they generate signals to other (White) investors and potential residents that, while still "gritty," this neighborhood is now safe enough for them. Rents rise and, first, the lower-income non-artists are priced out. Eventually, the artists' rent gets too high for them to sustain themselves and they leave for the next disinvested neighborhood with available space. But, is that all there is to the story?

Certainly, artists and other creatives are associated with increased economic activity—after all, that is the premise of our entire book. And certainly, we can point to artists who see disinvested neighborhoods as blank canvases, ignorant of the people who already live there, their history, and needs. An example of this sometimes tone-deafness is when, in 2015, artist London Kaye hung crochet depictions of movie characters on a building in Bushwick, a Brooklyn neighborhood with a large Latino population. Her installation, put up without consulting building residents, sparked controversy over gentrification. Will Giron, a local activist, pointed out that Kaye would not have "yarn-bombed" a higher-income or White neighborhood, but that she clearly felt that Bushwick was open territory for her art; and the people there wouldn't complain (or wouldn't feel they had a right to) (Moscowitz, 2017).

However, artists alone aren't the cause of rising rents; government policies and real estate development play a significant role. The roots of this issue can be traced to suburbanization after World War II, which created a White middle class. Subsequent suburban residents brought suburban aesthetics to cities when they returned. Meanwhile, the art market grew, becoming more tied to capitalism. Not just an organic process, gentrification occurs in several stages, including government intervention—as seen in grants, tax breaks, and rezonings that encourage art-led gentrification. Artists are often associated with gentrification, due to their early role; but, decades may pass between when artists move into a neighborhood and when developers discover and transform it (Nicholson, 2018). Conversely, developers may purchase buildings in lower-income areas, and then lease them to high-end galleries. In such cases, the neighborhood becomes "artsy" without artists ever living or working there. For example, in the mid-2010s, New York City's Chinatown lost many of its rent-controlled apartments as buildings turned over. It also lost many of its lower-income and Asian residents. In place of Chinese-owned businesses, high-end retail and art galleries opened (Wong, 2019). Yet, this process skipped the part of the story where artists move into the area on their own. As a marker of how little control artists have over the larger development forces at work, some neighborhoods are bypassing the artist phase as they transition from disinvested to gentrified. Art may be used to beautify gentrifying areas—even graffiti may be commissioned to signify the "artsy-ness" of the area; but artists are no longer needed to be the pioneers (Moscowitz, 2017).

Conflict: the case of Boyle Heights

Boyle Heights, a neighborhood in Los Angeles, has become a battleground for the local community and artists, as gentrification threatens to displace long-standing residents (Wagley, 2018). The arts development plan in Boyle Heights started with a $36 million project, in 2015, to replace the Sixth Street Bridge (O'Brien et al., 2019). This bridge, which opened in 2022, connects the new arts district in Boyle Heights with the arts district in downtown Los Angeles. Boyle Heights residents had seen the trajectory of development in the arts district and wanted to stop the same arts-driven gentrification from happening in their neighborhood.

The conflict centers around galleries and studios that are contributing to the transformation of Boyle Heights into an arts district, which, in turn, raises property values and rents, displacing low-income residents. Artists and newcomers have been drawn to the neighborhood's cultural diversity and affordable living, further intensifying the tension. PSSST, one of the galleries at the heart of the controversy, aimed to create a queer-centered, experimental art space; but, it faced criticism and protests from anti-gentrification groups, who accused it of contributing to the neighborhood's displacement (O'Brien et al., 2019). This caused a split in the queer art community in Los Angeles, because some people wanted to support queer artists; but in this case, doing that could harm the poor and working-class people who lived in Boyle Heights. The gallery closed within a year. The conflict put members of different marginalized communities in opposition to one another, raising questions about who benefits from this access to art and how race and class make it more complicated for queer artists.

The debate also raises questions, in general, about the role of artists and institutions in gentrification, with some arguing that artists must carefully consider how their work impacts communities. Community organizations, such as Union de Vecinos and the Los Angeles Tenants Union, organized to resist gentrification and displacement, by forming alliances like the Boyle Heights Alliance Against Art-Washing and Displacement (BHAAAD). Although some of the galleries at the center of the controversy have moved or closed, the dialogue between artists and the community continues, with activists pushing for accountability and resistance to displacement. Ultimately, the conflict in Boyle Heights reflects the broader issues of gentrification and the changing landscape of neighborhoods in the face of redevelopment and revitalization efforts—posing challenges to both artists and residents (Fragoza, 2016).

The tactics BHAAAD and other groups used against the galleries, from traditional protests to social media and rhetorical art projects (O'Brien, 2019), can be considered "guerrilla urbanist interventions" (GUIs), which are creative and confrontational actions taken by locals who are against gentrification (Sarmiento, 2021). Sarmiento divides these actions into three main categories. The first is defense, where GUIs use disruptive actions to challenge how the community is involved in planning and development. They create spaces where people can speak out in protest. They also use disruption; GUIs don't just protest, but also try to kick certain people out of the neighborhood. Finally, they use building. Even though GUIs are small and temporary, they reveal the complicated politics and money behind gentrification, which often hides behind things like art, culture, and community organizations. This makes people think about their alliances and question the interests of certain people and processes in the neighborhood. The uncertainty among the queer community about which side of the conflict was the right one reflects the success of this strategy.

Anti-gentrification resistance and solidarity

Anti-gentrification activists propose that artists take part in housing activism, engage with local and marginalized communities, and avoid promoting gentrification through their work. Suggestions include advocating for rent control and affordable housing. Collaboration with local resistance movements can be a concrete step toward combating gentrification, as well as bridging the gap between artists and communities affected by it. Here, we present some examples of resistance to the common story we tell at the beginning of this chapter.

Art Against Displacement (AAD), a coalition of artists and arts professionals in New York City's Chinatown and Lower East Side, is supporting the Small Business Jobs Survival Act (SBJSA), which aims to provide commercial lease protections for small businesses across the city. A rally, in June 2018, in favor of the SBJSA highlighted the challenges faced by artists and small businesses due to rising rents and rampant development in Manhattan. The coalition has also supported lawsuits against luxury developments in the Lower East Side, arguing that these developments threaten affordable housing, strain local infrastructure, and contribute to community displacement. AAD emphasizes that its work is in collaboration with long-standing grassroots organizations—such as the National Mobilization Against Sweatshops and the Chinese Staff and Workers Association—to address displacement issues (Thackara, 2019). Art community members like Heather Hubbs, the director of the New Art Dealers Alliance (NADA), are joining these efforts to support small businesses and communities impacted by gentrification and development. They see their involvement as setting an example for future generations to care about their communities. While the SBJSA has not yet passed (as of 2023), supporters are still hopeful, given its broad-based support, that it will (Ryan, 2023).

A 2017 art exhibit in Charlotte, North Carolina, used real estate promotional materials and images of dilapidated houses to explore the effects of gentrification in the city's oldest historic Black community, the Cherry Neighborhood. The exhibit, by artist Janelle Dunlap, aimed to highlight the social and urban colonization happening, as gentrification threatens to displace longtime residents. Dunlap wants to raise awareness among newcomers in the area about how they often play a role in displacing entire communities, just by moving into neighborhoods. The artist challenges the notion that historic neighborhoods, before gentrification, are inherently undesirable—emphasizing that they were thriving communities with upper-class Black business owners. Charlotte, like many other cities, is facing rising property taxes and displacement, as luxury developments and commercial projects alter the urban landscape. Gentrification has become a complex and rich subject for artists, often reflecting both the transformation of areas into desirable locations and the displacement of artists themselves due to rising rents.

TAKEAWAYS
- DEIA should be central to creative economy discussions; and it's important to understand what those terms mean, how to measure them, and how they can be addressed.
- It's more common for people and organizations to talk about the importance of DEIA; and it's less common to see it in a substantive process around the creative economy or in the strategies and interventions associated with it.
- DEIA can be addressed through people-centered interventions or place-based ones; and this chapter focuses on place-based tools and strategies.
- There is an array of tools and strategies to consider for equitable development in the creative economy; and some of those are found in arts and cultural districts, zoning and artist overlay districts, affordable housing and/or work spaces, land trusts, and more.
- No singular agency or organization is responsible for this work. It's common to see many different private, public,

nonprofit, and civic sectors who try to address it; and it's common to see different types of collaborations and partnerships built to accomplish this complex work.

Discussion questions:

1. How do you define diversity, equity, inclusion, and access? Provide a strategy on how to address diversity in the creative economy.
2. What aspect of DEIA is most important to focus on from a policy standpoint?
3. What case or example did you find most compelling and why?
4. Do you think artists should be a protected class? Why or why not?
5. Why is DEIA important from an economic development standpoint?
6. How is community asset mapping different from equity-based asset mapping for arts and culture?

Activities

- Design a public process for incorporating DEIA into a creative economy plan.
- Interview a local arts organization or municipal arts agency about how they approach DEIA in their work.
- Find a podcast or a blog about DEIA in arts and culture; and share with a colleague why you think it is interesting, infuriating, or helpful in understanding the creative economy.
- Develop an assessment mechanism for evaluating a DEIA creative economy program that is authentic to your community.

Note

1 For the toolkit, see www.boisestate.edu/schoolofthearts/pacs-lab/.

REFERENCES

Abello, O. P. (2020, December 8). Permanently Affordable Real Estate for Arts and Culture Matters. *Nextcity.org*. https://nextcity.org/urbanist-news/permanently-affordable-real-estate-for-arts-and-culture-matters

Adams, B. (2019, September 26). Checking in at East Dearborn's City Hall ArtSpace Lofts. *Metromode*. www.secondwavemedia.com/metromode/features/Monica-Cavacece-Feliciano.aspx

Alfonseca, K. (2023, July 7). Culture Wars: How Identity Became the Center of Politics in America. *ABC News*. https://abcnews.go.com/US/culture-wars-identity-center-politics-america/story?id=100768380

Alvarez, M. (2005). There's Nothing Informal About It. In *Participatory Arts Within the Cultural Ecology of Silicon Valley*. San José: Cultural Initiatives Silicon Valley.

Americans for the Arts. (2023). *National Cultural Districts Exchange Toolkit*. www.americansforthearts.org/by-program/reports-and-data/toolkits/national-cultural-districts-exchange-toolkit

Americans for the Arts. Creative Economy. (n.d.). *Americans for the Arts*. www.americansforthearts.org/by-topic/creative-economy

Antener, J. (2019). *Third Space. When Cultures Mix and Merge. A Web Series*. Retrieved March 29, 2021, from https://thirdspace-webseries.com

Arora, J. A. (2023, January 25). *Diversity as a Win-Win. US Department of Commerce*. www.commerce.gov/news/blog/2023/01/diversity-win-win

Ashley, A. J., Loh, C. G., Bubb, K., & Durham, L. (2021). Diversity, Equity, and Inclusion Practices in Arts and Cultural Planning. *Journal of Urban Affairs*, 44(4–5), 727–747. https://doi.org/10.1080/07352166.2020.1834405

Bedoya, R. (2013). *Placemaking and the Politics of Belonging and Dis-belonging*. www.giarts.org/article/placemaking-and-politics-belonging-and-dis-belonging

Beland, A. (2018, August 7). *Former Tenants Want to Designate Former EMF Building as Historic Landmark*. www.wgbh.org/news/local/2018-08-07/former-tenants-want-to-designate-former-emf-building-as-historic-landmark

Berke, P., Godschalk, D. R., Kaiser, E. J., & Rodriguez, D. (2006). *Urban Land Use Planning*. Urbana-Champaign, IL: University of Illinois Press.

Bethancourt, D. (2016, September 21). Dearborn's Old City Hall Reopens as Artist Lofts: "Extraordinary". *Detroit Free Press*. www.freep.com/story/news/local/michigan/wayne/2016/09/21/dearborns-old-city-hall-reopens-artist-lofts-extraordinary/90803518/

Bhabha, H. (2006). Cultural Diversity and Cultural Differences. In B. Ashcroft, G. Griffiths & H. Tiffin (Eds.), *The Post-Colonial Studies Reader* (pp. 155–157). London: Routledge.

Boston Planning and Development Agency. (2023). *Artist Live/Work Program: Developing and Preserving Artist Space in Boston*. www.bostonplans.org/housing/artist-live-work-program/artist-live-work-housing-overview

Carney, S. J. P. (2021, January 26). DIY vs Beast Mode Capitalism. *Art in America*. www.artnews.com/art-in-america/features/meow-wolf-denver-expansion-diy-art-scene-1234582197/

City and County of Denver Community Planning & Development. (2017). *Compliance Plan and Conditional Certificate of Occupancy*. www.denvergov.org/content/dam/denvergov/Portals/696/documents/Denver_Building_Code/2016_Code_Policies/Safe_Occupancy_Policy.pdf

City of Austin. (2013). *From the Planning Advisory Service of the American Planning Association: Completed for Imagine Austin Creative Economy Priority Program*. www.google.com/url?sa=t&rct=j&q=&esrc=s&source=web&cd=&ved=2ahUKEwis4e_PqcaBAxViLzQIHS5_D0IQFnoECBcQAQ&url=https%3A%2F%2Faustintexas.

gov%2Fsites%2Fdefault%2Ffiles%2Ffiles%2FPlanning%2FCodeNEXT%2FCreativeEconomy_AmPlanningAssoc_ResearchCompilation.doc&usg=AOvVaw3-pfSzL07It-s2NSI2UKWx&opi=89978449

City of London. (2017). *Think Night: London's Neighbourhoods from 6pm to 6am.* www.london.gov.uk/programmes-strategies/arts-and-culture/music/saving-londons-music-venues?source=vanityurl

City of Oakland. (2018). *Belonging in Oakland: A Cultural Development Plan.* https://www.ebcf.org/initiatives/belonging-in-oakland-a-just-city-cultural-fund/

City of Santa Monica. (2023). *Council Approves Zoning Changes to Invigorate Arts and Entertainment Activities and Promote New Business Opportunities within the Third Street Promenade Area and Santa Monica Place.* www.santamonica.gov/press/2023/07/27/council-approves-zoning-changes-to-invigorate-arts-and-entertainment-activities-and-promote-new-business-opportunities-within-the-third-street-promenade-area-and-santa-monica-place

City of Sydney. (2023). *Public Spaces.* www.cityofsydney.nsw.gov.au/built-environment/public-spaces

City of Vancouver. (2023). *Culture/Shift: Blanketing the City in Arts and Culture.* https://vancouver.ca/parks-recreation-culture/culture-shift.aspx

Coffee, K. (2008). Cultural Inclusion, Exclusion and the Formative Roles of Museums. *Museum Management and Curatorship, 23*(3), 261–279.

DeLisi, T. (2021, Spring). DEI in Economic Development. *Chamber Executive.* https://magazine.acce.org/index.php?src=directory&view=stories&srctype=detail&back=stories&refno=102

Doward, J. (2015). Final Encore for UK's Live Music Venues as Noise Rules Lead to Closures. *The Guardian.* www.theguardian.com/music/2015/sep/05/sheffield-boardwalk-uk-live-music-venues-shut-developers

Forman, M. (2021, March 31). COVID-19 Laid Bare Inequities in Our City's Creative Economy. Here's How Philly Can Fix It. *WHYY.* https://whyy.org/articles/covid-19-laid-bare-inequities-in-our-citys-creative-economy-heres-how-philly-can-fix-it/

Fragoza, C. (2016). Art and Complicity: How the Fight Against Gentrification in Boyle Heights Questions the Role of Artists. *KCET.* www.kcet.org/shows/artbound/art-and-complicity-how-the-fight-against-gentrification-in-boyle-heights-questions-the-role-of-artists

Greater Philadelphia Cultural Alliance. (2020). *Annual Report.* www.philaculture.org/sites/default/files/GPCA008_AnnualReport_FNLWeb.pdf

Iqbal, N. (2020, August 2). London Night Tsar Faces Down Calls to Quit: "I Will Be Judged for What I Do". *The Guardian.* www.theguardian.com/news/2020/aug/02/london-night-tsar-faces-down-calls-to-quit-i-will-be-judged-for-what-i-do

Islas, A. M., Moser, C., Tipathy, S., & Vital, L. T. (2019). Assessing the Creative Economy of Seattle through a Race & Equity Lens. *City of Seattle Arts and Culture.* www.seattle.gov/documents/Departments/Arts/Downloads/Reports/Creative%20Economy%20-%20Final%20Report%20-%20June%202019.pdf

Kahne, J. (2015). Does Placemaking Cause Gentrification? It's Complicated. *Project for Public Spaces.* www.pps.org/article/gentrification

Lefebvre, S. (2018a). Art Studios Saved as Oakland Community Land Trust Acquires First Live-Work Building. *KQED*. www.kqed.org/arts/13839406/art-studios-saved-as-oakland-community-land-trust-acquires-first-live-work-building

Lefebvre, S. (2018b, September 17). Oakland Introduces Expanded Art Grants Program, Announces 2018 Awardees. *KQED*. www.kqed.org/arts/13840996/oakland-introduces-expanded-art-grants-program-announces-2018-awardees

Levy, M. (2019, December 6). *EMF Building Wins Landmarking Designation, Not Preventing Its Renovation into Office Space*. www.cambridgeday.com/2019/12/06/emf-building-wins-landmarking-designation-not-preventing-its-renovation-into-office-space/

Lim, A. (2020, July). We Shall Not Be Moved: Collective Ownership Gives Power Back to Poor Farmers. *Harper's Magazine*. https://harpers.org/archive/2020/07/we-shall-not-be-moved-collective-ownership-black-farmers/

Lloyd, R. (2002). Neo—Bohemia: Art and Neighborhood Redevelopment in Chicago. *Journal of Urban Affairs*, *24*(5), 517–532.

MacDonald, D. (2018, May 31). 'It's Such a Bummer.' In Cambridge, Musicians are Forced Out of EMF Practice Space. *Boston Globe*. https://www.bostonglobe.com/metro/2018/05/31/such-bummer-cambridge-musicians-are-forced-out-emf/Ti259MdrSIwMDv3fZFqMvO/story.html

Markusen, A. (2014). Creative Cities: A 10-Year Research Agenda. *Journal of Urban Affairs*, *36*(2), 567–589. https://doi.org/10.1111/juaf.12146

Markusen, A., & Gadwa, A. (2010). Arts and Culture in Urban or Regional Planning: A Review and Research Agenda. *Journal of Planning Education and Research*, *29*(3), 379–391. https://doi.org/10.1177/0739456X09354380

Mason, A. (2022). Cambridge Stakes Over $45 Million on a Sleek New Community Arts Space. *WBUR*. www.wbur.org/news/2022/11/04/cambridge-the-foundry

Massing, M. (2019, December 14). How the Superrich Took Over the Museum World. *The New York Times* [editorial].

Moscowitz, P. (2017). What Role Do Artists Play in Gentrification? *Artsy*. www.artsy.net/article/artsy-editorial-role-artists-play-gentrification

Moss, I. D. (2012, May 9). Creative Placemaking Has an Outcomes Problem. *Create Equity*. https://createquity.com/2012/05/creative-placemaking-has-an-outcomes-problem/

Murdoch III, J., Grodach, C., & Foster, N. (2016). The Importance of Neighborhood Context in Arts-Led Development: Community Anchor or Creative Class Magnet? *Journal of Planning Education and Research*, *36*(1), 32–48.

National Endowment for the Arts. (2023). *Tucson, AZ; Warehouse District: How Can a GIS Mapping Project Help to Create a Sense of Community in a Former Industrial Area?* www.arts.gov/impact/creative-placemaking/exploring-our-town/tucson-az-warehouse-arts-district

Nicholson, C. (2018, August 20). What Is the Artist's Role in Gentrification? *Incandescere Blog*. www.incandescere.com/post/what-is-the-artists-role-in-gentrification

Northern California Land Trust. (2023). *Artist Space Trust*. https://nclt.org/incubation/artist-space-trust/

O'Brien, K., Vilchis, L., & Maritescu, C. (2019). Boyle Heights and the Fight Against Gentrification as State Violence. *American Quarterly*, *71*(2), 389–396.

PolicyLink. (2023). *Building a Cultural Equity Plan*. www.policylink.org/our-work/community/arts-culture/plan

Rich, M. A. (2019). "Artists Are a Tool for Gentrification": Maintaining Artists and Creative Production in Arts Districts. *International Journal of Cultural Policy*, *25*(6), 727–742.

Ryan, A. (2023, February 15). Opinion: To Save Small Stores, Commercial Rent Stabilization Is Not Enough. *The Village Sun*. https://thevillagesun.com/opinion-to-save-small-stores-commercial-rent-stabilization-is-not-enough

Sarmiento, C. S. (2021). Defend, Disrupt, and Build: Guerrilla Urbanist Interventions and Fighting Gentrification in the Barrio. *Journal of Community Psychology*, *49*(8), 3178–3193.

Scott, A. J. (2006). Creative Cities: Conceptual Issues and Policy Questions. *Journal of Urban Affairs*, *28*(1), 1–17.

Shea, A. (2016, December 9). After Oakland Tragedy, Boston Area Artists Talk Need for Safe Live/Work Spaces. *WBUR*. www.wbur.org/news/2016/12/09/oakland-fire-boston-artists-spaces

Soja, E. (1996). *Thirdspace: Journeys to LA and Other Real and Imagined Places*. Oxford, UK: Blackwell.

Solis, D. (2023). How a West Dallas Warehouse Zone Keeps Artists at Work, Especially Artists of Color, Women. *KERA News*. www.keranews.org/arts-culture/2023-04-18/how-a-west-dallas-warehouse-zone-keeps-artists-at-work-especially-artists-of-color-women

Stern, M. J., & Seifert, S. C. (2008). From Creative Economy to Creative Society. Culture and Community Revitalization: A. Collaboration, 6, 1–15

Stevenson, D. (2004). "Civic Gold" Rush: Cultural Planning and the Politics of the Third Way. *International Journal of Cultural Policy*, *10*(1), 119–131. https://doi.org/10.1080/1028663042000212364

Stevenson, D. (2005). Cultural Planning in Australia: Texts and Contexts. *The Journal of Arts Management, Law, and Society*, *35*(1), 36–48. https://doi.org/10.3200/JAML.35.1.36-48

Stevenson, D., & Magee, L. (2017). Art and Space: Creative Infrastructure and Cultural Capital in Sydney, Australia. *Journal of Sociology*, *53*(4), 839–861.

Thackara, T. (2019, July 8). Artist-Led Groups Battle to Stem Gentrification in New York. *The Art Newspaper*. www.theartnewspaper.com/2019/07/08/artist-led-groups-battle-to-stem-gentrification-in-new-york

The Tin District. (2023). *We Are the Tin District*. www.tindistrict.com/about

Wagley, C. (2018, June 8). Good-Bye to All That: Boyle Heights, Hotbed of Gentrification Protests, Sees Galleries Depart. *ArtNews*. www.artnews.com/art-news/market/good-bye-boyle-heights-hotbed-gentrification-protests-sees-galleries-depart-10432/

Warehouse Arts Management Organization. (2023). *About WAMO*. www.wamotucson.org/about-wamo-1

Wong, D. (2019). Shop Talk and Everyday Sites of Resistance to Gentrification in Manhattan's Chinatown. *Women's Studies Quarterly, 47*(1 & 2), 132–148.

World Cities Culture Forum. (2017). *Making Space for Culture: Handbook for City Leaders.* www.worldcitiescultureforum.com/news/how-can-cities-make-space-for-culture

Zitcer, A. (2020). Making up Creative Placemaking. *Journal of Planning Education and Research, 40*(3), 278–288. www.pps.org/article/gentrification

Moving forward in the creative economy

Chapter 10

INTRODUCTION

Thank you for taking time to read our book, in which we have provided an introductory foundation on the creative economy. You may have read it linearly; selected chapters that drew your interest; or identified excerpts that accompanied interesting images, charts, and graphs. There is no wrong way to have read this book. What we hope is that you learned a bit, felt inspired, found your own critiques, and thought about how all this might inform what you do in your personal, civic, or professional life.

In conclusion, we aim to help you digest what you've read and figure out what to do next with what you've learned whether that's tomorrow, a year from now, or further out. First, we remind you of our motivations for this book, so that you can understand why we wrote the way we did about the creative economy. Second, we summarize what we've shared in each chapter. Third, we list nine themes that cut across the entire manuscript. These themes are good reminders for you as you seek to explain, critique, study, and plan for the creative economy. Fourth and lastly, we provide some guidance about how to activate what you've learned in ways that align with your interests, positions, and ambitions.

DOI: 10.4324/9781003147688-10

MOTIVATION

We wrote this book because there is not a singular, accessible manuscript that holistically and comprehensively describes the creative economy from different scales, scopes, and angles. While we are US scholars and practitioners and our book primarily explores American examples, we also sought to incorporate international and global examples from a multifaceted set of practices and scholarships. We argue that it is vitally important to see how this growing field manifests in different contexts, championed by different interests, and critiqued by thoughtful people and organizations that want the field to do better.

We often see scholarly literature that focuses on one aspect of the creative economy or that targets a scholarly or practitioner body. We also see fabulously inspiring stories in the popular media, dead-on critiques of creative economy practice, and scholarships that encourage us to think critically about what we put forward. While these are useful and significant as a cohesive set of literature, we aim to write for both academic and practitioner audiences, as one may participate in both environments. This is why we formed the team that we did to write this book. Our writing team consists of scholars from different backgrounds and sets of expertise, as well as practitioners who understand the pragmatic realities of trying to do this work, on an everyday basis, inside a political and policy system.

There is a practitioner and academic divide in the creative economy environment. While this tension is not absolute, it does remain prevalent. Practitioners in the creative economy are generally under-resourced; are working in reactive, highly political and siloed environments; and are often unaware of the deep observation and analysis, going on in the academic world, around their practices. When they do have time to read books or journal articles, practitioners sometimes feel that scholars sit in their own ivory towers observing, researching, creating, and testing theories and concepts that are not grounded in the messy reality and tensions of practice. To practitioners, it can look like academics critique practice without suggesting concrete action that is doable in current conditions. But, at the same time, there is also great inspiration, insight, and deep learning to be found in academic research that has the potential to inform and improve what is being done in practice.

As we have emphasized throughout this text, innovation is spread through analyzing models, talking to colleagues, and learning from peers. There needs to be more robust two-way conversations between practitioners and academics. It can be hard to get higher-education institutions to take part in research that matters to community partners and related industries. This is particularly true for the new creative economy, as opposed to long-standing industrial and community collaborations around STEM. Universities, colleges, and technical schools do not always have reward systems that support community research and public scholarship, which can make it hard for scholars to do the work even if they have the interest to do so. Scholars sometimes feel that practitioners are not interested in evidence-based work or that they are not interested in the theories and concepts that can help improve policy and political systems. Scholars critique existing systems in the hopes of making them better; and they have a hard time when those recommendations are not considered or employed.

Cultural administrators live with the fear that funding, staff, or other program resources are at risk of being cut at any time due to politicization or public outcry; so, they tend to focus on the advocacy and promotion angle of what they are doing, rather than risk looking at the failures, where things don't work, or at how programs could be improved. But that constant advocacy, with no room for critical discourse, stunts the growth and development of the field. We all must be willing to ask hard questions, learn from failure, and be willing to change course, no matter the risks.

We aim to try and bridge the divide in this book. We did so by briefly talking about theories and concepts, and then applying them to real-world examples. We talked to leading arts and culture administrators and arts entrepreneurs in cities across the United States to draw on their insights and inspirations; we then backed up what we heard with what we found in the literature. We used those real-world examples to help us think about how theory and concepts can be improved. We hope that this would help people understand different environments in ways that can improve their own work and civic lives. It speaks to our hope that people will step out of their own lane, so that they can learn from others.

Finally, we are motivated by artists, arts organizations, arts champions, and arts scholars. Art is incredibly powerful. We've seen this in our research over the past 15 years; and it's incredible to see not only how these groups can hustle, but also the ways that they can help address community challenges and help us think differently and powerfully about the comprehensive role of the creative economy in our everyday lives. This immense value was particularly amplified by how artists, arts organizations, and creative businesses worked to navigate the challenges of the global COVID-19 pandemic. We want to infuse this energy, passion, and resilience into our book through the examples we've illustrated. It is important to note that we've only scratched the surface here, and that examples of the creative economy are omnipresent and palpable. You just need to know how to look for them.

WHAT WE COVERED

We've taken you on an introductory journey through the creative economy. In Chapter 1, we outlined the multi-dimensional nature of the field with a focus on theoretical frameworks that can inform and guide the work. In Chapter 2, we introduced key economic principles, providing a foundation and context for understanding the creative economy. In Chapter 3, we delivered a creative economy framework to provide grounding in its characteristics, including its workforce delineation; sector boundaries; local, regional, national, and international definitions; and global market forces. In Chapter 4, we shared how the creative economy intersects with place-based activity and employment clusters, paying attention to positive attributes and the dark side of creating amenity portfolios. In Chapter 5, we discussed creative ecosystems and the dynamic actors and organizations networked within these complex adaptive systems. In Chapter 6, we centered artists and creatives—debunking myths, identifying ways they are trained, and exploring how they create organizations to serve their needs. In Chapter 7, we framed out the variety of ways actors influence the context and landscape of the creative sector through policy. In Chapter 8, we considered the champions of the creative economy from the context of who is studying, presenting, and measuring the creative sector with a focus on models and inspirations, policy boosters, creative entrepreneurs, and international leaders. In Chapter 9, we provided a series of place-based strategies and tools that are deployed to emphasize equitable development. Now, in Chapter 10, we turn to the broader themes from the book, as well as how to draw on what you've learned here to move forward in your civic and professional life.

NINE THEMES FROM THE BOOK

At the end of each chapter, you'll notice that we listed takeaways or big-picture points and definitions that we wanted you to understand from the readings. Here, we've also zoomed out to the 10,000-foot level to provide that for the entire manuscript. In essence, if you never look at our book again, these are the themes that we want you to remember—and to do something about.

Theme 1. The creative economy is a new field, and you are part of its emergence

We are at a profound moment in creative economy development and creative economic development. The arts and economic development were once largely seen as separate entities, or they were combined in very superficial and limited ways. Now, the creative economy is more inclusive in terms of the disciplines, industries, occupations, and placemaking tenets that it embraces. What once focused primarily on elite nonprofit arts industries in the high arts now embodies different public, private, nonprofit actors, institutions, and organizations. We see film, food, music, gaming, design, television, heritage, artisanal work, and other disciplines in the for-profit creative industries brought into the framework. We want different organizations and partnerships to collaborate to advocate for support of the creative economy at different scales; and we see structural shifts in how sectors fund and support these activities.
While this broadening does have connections to changing expectations around what governments should do, and how they should intervene, it also welcomes people and activities

that were overlooked before. You are now an important part of its emergence; and we are eager for you to share its growth and development, understand its value and contributions, and work to correct and plan for its weaknesses and limitations. Welcome to the creative economy!

Theme 2. The creative economy embodies creative collisions

The creative economy is an ecosystem, networked in some ways better than others. The field is not just for economic developers or arts advocates. Rather, it's a place that excels when it is largely integrative. For example, arts organizations can partner with urban, community, and regional planners to develop zoning and building codes that are friendly to the types of creative economic activity that is essential for cities to be dynamic places to live and work. In another example, tech entrepreneurs can work with music festival organizers to create opportunities to attract knowledge workers and can use new software systems to support cyber security with people buying tickets online. Artists can join forces with others who struggle to afford housing to form a community land trust that keeps a neighborhood accessible to all.

These integrative or collaborative moments draw on different motivations, skills, and goodwill. When these moments happen, they represent creative collisions. These creative collisions are positive when they can lead to new products, processes, and ideas related to public goods and economic development growth areas. They can also be problematic when partners have vast differences in power and resources or when one member of the partnership steamrolls its agenda over others.

Theme 3. The creative economy is evolving

The creative economy is an evolving field. The fuzziness of concepts and ideas will continue as new external and internal forces create new conditions that call for adaptations and redevelopment. For example, artificial intelligence (AI) is one of those areas that will call for radical changes in how we think about the creative economy. Policymakers, creative entrepreneurs, and everyday artists and arts organizations will be at the center of the challenges and opportunities that AI brings. In another example, the internet age has led to the rise of content creators and influencers; and it is yet unclear how this will reshape the way that we count creative industries, how we examine their connection to the creative economy, the way we think about artistic creation, and how we put in place policies and interventions to address their emergence.

Theme 4. The arts and the creative economy should be partners in our pressing challenges

We are facing serious issues locally, nationally, and globally. Global warming, economic disparity, social and demographic inequality, and political division are felt in every part of the world. These are entrenched problems that have the potential to lead to catastrophic outcomes for many if not all. The arts and creative economic development have an important role here to help us understand these issues, communicate their meaning, be resilient in the face of them, and continue to address them.

Theme 5. Equity should be at the center of the creative economy

We reflect on the challenges when framing the creative economy as pure economic growth. In reality, we need to focus on the idea of development, for whom, and under what conditions. Currently, diversity, equity, inclusion, and accessibility are still largely on the fringe of creative economy conversations. They should be at the center, given that the arts have the potential to be used primarily to serve the haves rather than the have nots. Further, many creative economic development initiatives involve public funding, which means they should benefit the public in general, not just higher-income people or people who live in certain neighborhoods.

Theme 6. Flexibility matters

It is deeply important to be flexible and, dare we say, creative in terms of how you approach the creative economy. There isn't a singular one-size fits all approach. Rather, we focus on sharing models and ideas to get your imagination going on what is possible. We are not prescriptive or normative; rather, we propose that it is vital to be context specific and authentic to your community, city, or region. At the same time, you should not limit yourself to what people in your area have already tried before; it is a good idea to look further to see other policies and strategies that might work in your area. We also hope you can see how policy concepts from various areas like health, climate change, and economic development are cross-pollinating with arts and culture policies to create new policies and cross-sector applications. These lateral or horizontal innovations are expanding the scope of what arts and culture can do in the world and what these other fields can do because of the power of the arts.

Theme 7: We need to center artists and creative workers

While it is important to understand industries and business structures, it is vital that we prioritize how to think about artists, creative workers, and creative entrepreneurs. It is the creators, makers, and doers that are the soul of the creative economy. We need to continue to learn more about how they work and what drives them, so that we can better support the ways in which they express innovation and creativity. By understanding them better, we are in a better position to unleash their potential and harness their intellectual and creative might. One example from the book is cities working to better understand artists' space needs and amend building codes to better balance safety and costs in live-work spaces.

Theme 8: The lone wolf model has no place here

The stories that we provide often center not on a singular person or organization; rather, they center on collaborations, partnerships, and mutual working relationships. For example, funding for creative economic development initiatives often involves multiple levels of government, nonprofits, and, sometimes, private sector actors.

Theme 9: Aligning theory and practice is of value

We have diligently and purposefully tried to connect and align theory to practice. We argue that the strongest practitioners and scholars are able to draw on both. We don't know what the careers or creative opportunities of the future will be.

With technology advances and environmental challenges, our research, jobs, and creative lives may look very different in the future than they look now. It is through concerted dialogue and sharing of purposes and new findings that we will make the most of what theory, empirical research, and practice have to offer.

With these takeaways in mind, we now move to planning and implementation work for the creative economy.

STRATEGY, ACTION, AND IMPLEMENTATION: MOVING FORWARD

When we wrote this book, we identified three ways forward that are connected to practice. These areas center around applied research; partnership and stakeholder development; and centering diversity, equity, inclusion, and access in the work.

Applied research by coalitions of academics and practitioners

There is still so much that we do not know about the creative economy; and this knowledge is important for us to develop. This is work that can come from the academy or from practice—but ideally in collaboration with one another. Drawing on both quantitative and qualitative methodologies is important, so that we can inform planning and strategy. While these needs will vary depending upon the context of a specific place, we do see some research areas that are ripe for investigation. First, we think more studies on occupations and workers is important for understanding the lifecycle of creative workers, why they live where they do, what they need in order to continue to move forward with their careers, and how to make sure we are making the most of their creative talents. Second, we need more information about how to incorporate diversity, equity, inclusion, and access into practice. We see that communities often talk about the importance of this work, but less often do they address it through implementation and related resources. Third, we think it is of value to study how the arts align with other sectoral and organizational priorities. This integration is central for positioning the arts as part of a series of strategies to address pressing challenges and other economic development strategies.

As we were doing this research, we also had many conversations about critiques of creative economy scholarship, where White, patriarchal, and colonized systems are driving the research agendas and related methodologies. We believe applied research needs to address this and consider new co-owned and co-constructed research that may draw on different methodologies and perspectives to inform how we think about the creative economy. This embodied and vernacular knowledge is an important component for moving forward.

Generally speaking, the field also has limited policy and program evaluation for creative economy interventions. These assessments should take into account the needs of a particular community and the context of that particular place. These evaluations can help us better dive into what initiatives work, why, and under what conditions. Part of this is also understanding unintended consequences, failure, and being accepting of the risk and pilot testing that comes with new programs and policies designed to amplify the work of the creative economy.

Developing stakeholder alliances, partnerships, and collaborations

One of the findings over the combined decades of our work is the reality that so much of the creative economy work involves collaborations, partnerships, and alliances. This is largely connected to the ideas of building capacity, cobbling together resources, and finding alignment across differing missions. Many of these collaborations center around the idea that a creative economic intervention can serve multiple purposes; it's efficient to make the most of these related values and missions. These partnerships can be formalized public-private partnerships, informal dual nonprofit partnerships, mutually agreed upon collaborations, and informal connections.

Economic development that prioritizes more than growth

One of the central places for action in our book is the idea that we should not be purely focusing on growth or the money that comes from these creative economic systems. Rather, it is important to recognize that community development is central to the work. Here, the creative economy values both the intrinsic and instrumental values of the arts as well as the full variety of people who interact with the creative economy (everyone!). Mental, social, and environmental health must be considered alongside economic health; and the evidence is compelling in how the arts can support these areas.

REFLECTION

In this final section, we ask you to embark on a journey of reflection around the ideas embedded within this book. We encourage you to find your favorite place to write, a quiet place to think, or a friend to share your ideas with about this book.

We ask you to consider the following prompts:

- Which ideas, projects, or partnerships inspire you or frustrate you? Why?
- What do you wish you knew more about? How could this book be strengthened by this information?
- How does our book help you understand your community in new ways when thinking about the creative economy?
- How does the material in the book shape the way you think about your career, civic, or personal ambitions? Can you see putting this knowledge into action? If so, how? If not, why?
- What did we not talk about that you wish we did? Write and tell us or research it yourself and send us a copy of your article or book.
- What #hashtag would you use to describe your experience with the book and your place in the creative economy?

Thank you again for taking the time to read our book. We hope it has helped you create your own foundational knowledge about the creative economy.

Index

Note: Page numbers in *italics* indicate a figure and page numbers in **bold** indicate a table on the corresponding page.

208 Ensemble *160*
798 Beijing Arts District *25*, 81, *82*

activism 143–145, 161–163, 191, 292–294; *see also* Black Lives Matter; environmentalism
Africa (sub-Saharan) 72–73, 171, 254
AI (artificial intelligence) 37–38, 119, 142, 185, 240, 306
Ailey, Alvin 95
AIR (Arts Incubation Research) Lab 178–179
Alaadeen, Ahmad *262*
Alba, Jessica 171–172
Albuquerque **118**, 128, *129*, 145, 210; COVID-19 241–243; Creative Albuquerque 206–207; Indian Pueblo Cultural Center 162, *163*, *166*; Kei & Molly Textiles 113–115, *114*, 128, *129*, 143, *145*
Alliance of Motion Picture and Television Producers 37
Amazon Publishing 70, 71
Americans for the Arts (AFTA) 62, 73, 116, 251–252, 271
Anchorage 67
Andrew W. Mellon Foundation 247
architecture 83, 84, 85–86, 92–93, 95–96, 100, 161
art, as amenity 56, 89, 220
art, public *17*, 33, 87–89, 106, 109, *182*, 186, 189, 216, 251–252
Art Against Displacement (AAD) 293
Art Basel 101
"artful life" 8, 47
artificial intelligence *see* AI
Artist Communities Alliance (ACA) 183
artist-in-residence (AIR) 181–183
artists: career challenges 140–145, 176, 184–188, 218; as center of creative economy 188–191; centers 183; and creative class 163–172; definition of 154; as entrepreneurs 115, 129–131, 146, 167–172; myths about 155–158; neighborhoods 90–91, 187, 276–288, **289**, 290–294; support structures 172–183; as workers 165–167

Arts in Transit 22
aspirational city 233
Atlanta 244–246
Austin 74–75, 124, 211, 223
avatar therapy project 171

Baltimore 64, *64*, 96
Banksy 88, 161, 186–187
B Corp Certification 137–138, 147, 168
Be An ArtsHero 142
Belfast 220
Berlin 91
Berlin Arts Institute 181
Beyoncé 171
Bilbao *257*, 260
Black Lives Matter 162, *168*, 271
Boise *17*, 47, *48*, 49–50, *50*, 101, 124–125, *131*, 138, *160*, *219*
Bollywood 72
Bonnaroo 101
Boom Tic Boom *224*
boosterism, civic 94, 95, 165
Boston **118**, 210, 278; Artist Live-Work Program 280; Cambridge 185, 280; Create Boston 42–43; Cultural Space Fund 31; Faneuil Hall Marketplace 96, *97*
boundary definition 120
Boyle Heights Neighborhood 91, 291–293
branding, city 27, 83, 108, 198, 221, 258
brewery, craft 40–41
bricolage 169
British Council 252, 253
Bronx Museum of Art 121
Brooklyn Navy Yard 39, 81
Burnham, Daniel 91
business model, creative 147; for-profit 133–134, 146; nonprofit 132–133; public sector 134–135

California 54; Alameda 39; Boyle Heights 91, 291–293; Hollywood 81–82, *158*; Los Angeles 37–38, 69–70, 82, 91, 124; Oakland 28, 162, 243, 277, *277*, 287; Sacramento **118**; San Diego 38–39; San Francisco 222, 241–243, 285–287, *286*; Santa Monica 278

Canada Music Incubator 180–181
Chanel, Coco 161
Charlotte (North Carolina) 270, 294
Chicago 48, *93*; 1906 city plan 91–92; Arts & Public Life 173–174; *Cloud Gate* ("The Bean," Kapoor) 87, *88*, 89; *Crown Fountain* (Plensa) *199*; Lollapalooza 101; University of 173–174; World's Columbian Exposition (1893) 92–93, *93*
City Beautiful Movement 92, 102, 108, 109, 212
Cloud Gate (Kapoor) 87, *88*, 89
codes, building 67, 108, 276–278, **289**, 306, 308; *see also* zoning
Cold War 212–213
Colo, Papo 121
Colombia 55
Colorado 52, 56–57, 141; *see also* Denver
complexity theory 120, 121, 126, 145–146, 199
consumption: local 3, 11; virtual 3, 10, *11*
content creator 11, *12*, 70–71, 76, 307
contracting out 20–21, 24–26, 32–33, 130, 133
cooperatives 67, *68*, 171, 176–178
Copenhagen *125*
Copenhagen Climate Summit 161
copyright 43, 174, 190, 217–218, 253; *see also* property, intellectual
COVID-19: closures 36–37, 141–142, 241; and creative economy 130, 138, 141–142, 241–244, 273, 288, 304; and digital engagement 28–29; economic impact of 52, 138, 141–142, 241; and marginalized communities 243, 273; reopening after 225, 261
creative: class 42–43, 64–65, 91, 96, 163–165, 170, 289; definition of 153; industries 55, 59–63, *61*, 72, 132, 134, 197; occupations 63–71, 218, 274; *see also* economy, creative
Creative Cities Network of Canada 251
Creative City 4, 6–7, 27, 29, 56, 64, 75, 122, 126, 143, 235, 254; concept 214–217; dual nature of 164–165; *see also* UCCN (UNESCO Creative Cities Network)
Creative Economy Programme (CEP) 253
Creative Women's Collective (Boise) 125
crowdfunding 130, 138–139, 159, 220
Crown Fountain (Plensa) *199*
cryptocurrency 130
Cuenca (Ecuador) 255–256
Cultural Vitality Index (CVI) 74, 116–117, **118**
culture wars 43, 204, 213

Dallas 281–282, *282*
Darwin (Australia) 75
DBA (downtown business associations) 107, 122

DDA (downtown development authority) 102, 107, 279
Dearborn (Michigan) 279, *280*
DEIA (diversity, equity, inclusion, and accessibility) 2, 142–145, 147, 201, 222, **242**, 294–295, 307; and arts 15, 161, 188; and arts and cultural districts 284; barriers to 15, 72, 105, 161, 188, 273–274; and Creative Cities 258, 262, 275–276; and economic development 61, 105–106, 190, 269–272; and economic disparities 71–72, 161, 273–276; *see also* trauma, community
deindustrialization *see* industrial restructuring
Denver 28, **118**, 200, 208; art districts 51–52, *52*, 67, *68*, 82, 83–84; Arts & Venues 84, **118**, 134–135, 200–201, 244; Community Planning and Development 135; music strategy report 200–201; Office of Economic Development and International Trade (COEDIT) 52; Performing Arts Complex 80; Safe Occupancy Program 28, 278
Detroit *86*, *93*, **118**, 186; as a City of Design 208–209, 258–260
development, economic 17, **123**; and arts and culture 11, 43, 49, 154, 159, 273; challenges 66, 102–106; creative 40–41, 50–52, 109, 191, 259, 305–306, 310–311; and DEIA 269–272, 275, 295; place-based 81–82, 91–102, 109, 135–137, 226, 276–288, **289**; strategies 57, 67, 107, 109, 256, 289; *see also* creative, class; economy, creative
diffusion theory 7, 236
digital age 216; *see also* consumption, virtual; content creators; music, streaming; social media
diplomacy, cultural 221, 252
displacement *see* gentrification
distributed connectivity 121
districts: arts *25*, 42, 51–52, *51*, 64, *64*, 68, 81–82, 83–84, 106, 107–108, 109, **123**, 136, 174, 220, 281–284, **289**, 291–293, 294; creative 57; creative business 220; cultural *13*, 42, 92, *93*, 94, 102, 106, 107–108, 109, **123**, 134–136, 174, 281–284, **289**, 294; financing 107; overlay zones 284–285, 294
DIY (do-it-yourself) 28, 135
Drescher, Fran 38
Dunlap, Janelle 294

Eames, Charles and Ray 161
Earthen Symphony 171
eBay 70
economics: Coasian bargaining 16; efficiency 13, 19, 22, 31; equity 14–15, 20, 24, 31–32; externalities 16, 22,

28–29, 32, 121, 245; government failure 19–21, 32; information asymmetry 18–19, 22, 29–30, 32; "leaky bucket" 15; market-based solutions 19–22, 24–26, 32; market equilibrium 15, 31; market failure 16, 18–19, 20–26, 31; monopoly 16, 23, 31, 33–34; monopsony 16; perfect market 15–16, 23, 31–32; utility 11–12, 24; *see also* good, public
economy, creative 39–46, 75–76, 305–309; centering artists within 160–163, 188–191, 308; champions of 233–235, 239–241, **242**, 249–252, 263–265; critiques of 255–256, 310; definition of 1, 49–58, 75; as development strategy 40, 43, 72–75; measuring of 73–74, 76, 115–117; occupations within 59–72, 165–167; participants in 122–127, **123**; and placemaking 83–89, 99–102, 106–108; policy tools 106–108; *see also* entrepreneurs
economy, cultural 11, 43–46, 58, 75, 198, 244; values-based approach to 26–27, 33
economy, gig 115, 130, 139–141, 142, 146, 147, 184, 215, 273
economy, knowledge 42, 49, 53, 82–83, 91, 95–96, 157–167, 197, 214–215
Economy, Orange 55
Edinburgh Festival Fringe 221
education 21, 24–26, 42, 61, 65, 68, 188, 218–219, 274; *see also* institutions, higher-education
Eggar, Dave *249*
enterprise, social (SE) 170–171
Enterprise Zones 107
entrepreneurs: art 115, 129–131, 140, 146, 147, 167–174, 180, 190, *206*; civic 96; creative 67, 72–73, 113–115, 128, 155, 180, 208, 220, 221, 240, **242**; policy 127–128, 202–205, 208–209, 217, 227, 234, 238, 259, 261–262; social 106, 155, 170–171, 192
environmental: determinism 92, 94; issues 16, 161–162, 246, 264; science 113, 172–173; sustainability 48, 137–138, 162, 172, 179–180, 227, 250, 256, 275, 284
equilibrium: far from 120; market 15, 31, 119; shift 119
Esch-sur-Alzette (Luxembourg) 83
Etsy 70, 71, 130
European Capital of Culture Competition 83, 255
European Research Council 248
European Union (EU) 253, 255
Exit Art (gallery) 121

Faneuil Hall (Boston) 96–97, *97*
feedback loop 119, 126

Fenty 171
festival marketplace 96–99, *97*, *98*, *99*, 108
film and television industry **123**; Atlanta 244–246; Austin 124; Bollywood 72; California 38, 70, 82; Colorado 56–57, 208; Georgia (US state) 244–246; incentives 4, 40, 124, 198, 208, 218; Miami **118**; Minneapolis 200; New York 39; Nollywood 72; SAF-AFTRA strike 36–38, 142; Seattle 57, *58*
Florence and the Machine *158*
Floyd, George 143
Friedman, Milton 24
Fulbright Program 248
funding, sources of 21, 101, 106–107, 132–133, 221, 244; *see also* crowdfunding; incubators
Fuster, José (artist) *44*

Gadhia, Sameer *180*
Garden City (Idaho) *206*, 249–250, *249*
gastronomy 40–41, 260, 261
gatekeeping 71, 134, 156, 160, 184–185, 188, 190
gentrification 46, 89, 109–110, 223, 255, 272; and artists 105, 223, 249–250, 287, 290–292; prevention and resistance 90–91, 107, 287, 288, 292–294; process of 104–105, 223; transnational 256
Georgia (US state) 244–246, 286
Ghost Ship fire (2016) 28, 277–278, *277*, 288
GI Bill 21
Glaser, Milton 161
Glasgow Music Festival 101
globalization: of audience 10, 28–29, 72, 141; and cities 40, 52, 83, 95, 100, 103, 135, 165, 215, 260; economy 40, 52, 72, 83, 100, 103, 135, 165, 167, 215, 216; environmental concerns 161, 257; exchange of ideas 235–239, 265; *see also* industrial restructuring
Gomez, Autumn Dawn 162, *163*
Gonzalez, Martha *248*
good, public 16–18, 21, 23–24, 32, 33; culture as a *17*, 46–47, 134, 213
grants 21–22, 32, 69, 106, 107, 134, 213–214, 221
Greenpoint Manufacturing and Design Center (Brooklyn) 126
Guggenheim Fellowship 248
Guggenheim Museum Bilbao *257*, 260

Hamburg 91
Hanks, Tom 185
Hatay (Turkey) 260
Havana *44*, 84, *182*
Hollywood 81–82, *158*; *see also* film and television industry; Los Angeles

housing, affordable 124, 187, 189, 210, 220–221, 246, 255–256, 273, 279–281, **289**; Artist Live-Work Program (Boston) 280; community land trusts 107, 285–287, 294, 306; *see also* gentrification
housing, public 94

IGO (intergovernmental organizations) 207, 252–256
incubators 178–181, 220, 227
Indego Africa 171
Independent Publishing Resource Center 182
India 72, 171, 221
indigenous rights *18*, 143, 162, 250, 256, 275–276
industrial restructuring 40, 82, 90, 95, 100, 103, 214–215
influencers *12*, 70, 71, 83, 307
informal arts 48–49, 275
Ingberman, Jeanette 121
Instagram 70, 71
institutions, anchor *13*, 103, 135–137, 147, 172, 175, 186, 191, 218
institutions, higher-education (HEIs) 64, 136–137, 156–157, 172–176, 190–192, 218–219, 249, 303
instrumentalism 46–47, 216–217
interactions, non-linear 121
International Confederation of Societies of Authors and Composers (CISAC) 253
International Federation of Arts Councils and Culture Agencies (IFACCA) 253
"invisible hand" 17
Ivey, Bill 44–45

Jackson, Maria Rosario 8, 47
Jacobs, Jane 163
Jay-Z 171
JR (artist) *182*

Kaji, Ryan 70
Kaltonaka Dance Group *166*
Kansas City 30, **118**, 261–263, *262*
Kapoor, Anish (sculptor) 87, *88*, 89
Kaunas (Lithuania) 83
Kaye, London 290
Kei & Molly Textiles 113–115, *114*, 128, *129*, 143, *145*
Kobra, Eduardo *18*
Kresge Foundation 101

land trust, community 107, 285–287, 294, 306
Lateef, Yusuf 184, 187
liberalism 24, 32
liberal market economies (LSEs) 25–26, 33
libertarianism 14, 23–24, 32
Lin, Maya 162

Lincoln Center (Manhattan) 94, 105
Lithuania 83, 238
Lollapalooza 101
London 161, 171, 287–288
Los Angeles 37–38, 69–70, 82, 91, 124
Luethi, Molly 113–115, 128, 143–145
Luger, Cannupa Hanska 161

MacArthur Foundation's Fellows Program 246–247, *248*, 266
Manhattan Graphic Center 177–178
Mannheim 263
mapping: asset 74–75, 76–77, 275, 295; community 74–75
Mapplethorpe, Robert 44
Marvel Studios 244
Marxism 24–25, 33
McCrea, Laci (mural artist) *62*
Miami **118**
Miami Visual Arts 101
Military Arts Connection (Colorado) 57
military bases: closures of 38–39; as film studios 244–245
Minneapolis 87, **118**, 143, 200, 208; Creative City Road Map 29; and DEIA 143, 270
Minnesota 183, 243; *see also* Minneapolis
Mitchell, Surel 250
Montana Arts Council 53
monuments, Confederate 88
Moses, Robert 94
multiple streams framework (MSF) 201–205, *203*, 225–227
murals *17*, *62*, 84, 87, 162, *163*, *168*, *182*, 186, 212, 282, *282*
music: Africa 72; Austin 211, 223; creative policy and 222–225; Kansas City 261–263; London 287–288; Mannheim 263; Music City designation 200, 223, 261–263; Nashville 223; Seattle 52, 57; streaming 3, 27–28, 29–30, 38, 72, 119, 130; therapy 57
Music Policy Forum 225

Nashville 81, **118**, 223
National Cherry Festival 101
National Endowment for the Arts (NEA) 43–45, 47, 48–49, 63, 101, 178, 204, 213–214, 248
National Park Service 182–183
Natural History Museum 126
Neighborhood Improvement Zones 107
neoliberalism 46, 89, 95, 101, 255
network theory 119
New England Foundation for Arts 56
New Orleans 29, **118**, 179–180, 209, *210*, 244
New York (state) 243
New York City 22, 94, 121, 279; Bronx 121; Brooklyn 39, 81, 126, 290;

Index 315

Chinatown 291, 293; Manhattan 94–95, 293
NFTs (non-fungible tokens) 28, 130
NGO (non-governmental organizations) 207
Nobel Prize 247–248
NOLA Arts Incubator 179–180
Nollywood 72
nonplace 85
nonprofitism 45
Nordstrom 126
Novi Sad (Serbia) 83

O'Keefe, Alex 37
Organization for Economic Cooperation and Development (OECD) 253
organizations: international government (IGO) 207, 252–256; management challenges 167; models of 131–139; non-governmental (NGO) 207
outsourcing *see* contracting out
overlay zone 284–285, 294

Pareto efficiency 13–14, 23, 28, 31
Pareto improvement 13–14, 27–28, 31, 33
Parlá, José *182*
path dependency 120, 121, 199, 211
patronage 29, 133, 136, 159–161, 212
pay 142, 156, 184, 187, 189–190, 241–243; *see also* economy, gig; precarity
peer city 233
Pei, I.M. 161
Percent for Art 22, 87, 106, 200
The Perfect Moment (Robert Mapplethorpe) 44
Perry, Tyler 244
Perth (Australia) 260–261
Philadelphia 53, 82, **118**, 273
Piss Christ (Serrano) 44
Pittsburgh 103
place (geography) 81, 83; and creative economy 3–4, 81–84; sense of 84–91, 109; *see also* place-keeping; placemaking
place-keeping 105–106, 275
placemaking 81, 93, 95, 99–103, 106–110, 164, 216, 272
planning: city 219; cultural 219
Plato 17
Plensa, Jaume *199*
policy: actors 205–209, 227; assessment 49, 204, 310; convergence 236, **237**; creative 197–202, 214–225, 226; creative economy 214–228; cultural 4, 197–202, 212–214, 226, 227; diffusion 236, **237**; learning 236, **237**, 244; obstacles 14, 209–211; place-based interventions 106–108; process 204–209; simulation game 228; transfer 236, **237**; *see also* entrepreneurship, policy; multiple streams framework
Portland (Oregon) 67, 182
precarity 141–142, 147, 184
PR:EPARe 171
printmaking *175*, 177–178
privatization 20, 21, 26, 32, 46
Project for Public Spaces 101
property, intellectual 31, 43, 55–56, 59, 132, 134, 146, 197, 253; protection of 45, 140, 154, 156, 185, 189–190, 217–218, 250, 253
public-private partnerships 42, 101, 108, 109, 136, 207, 218, 220, 223, 310
PUD (planned unit development) 107
Puente, Jr., Tito *139*
Pulitzer Prize 248

Rawls, John 14, 24
redlining 94
Red Titan (superhero) 70
Rhianna 171
Richardson, Rachel 184, 186, 187–188
Rio de Janeiro *18*
Rockefeller Foundation 247
Rodriquez, Aaron 125

Sacramento **118**
SAF-AFTRA strike 36–38, 142
San Antonio **118**, 178–179, 261
San Diego 38–39
San Francisco 222, 241–243, 285–287, *286*
Santa Monica 278
Seattle 52, **118**, *141*, 201, 244, *245*; Office of Arts and Culture 273; Office of Film and Music 57, *58*; Olympic Sculpture Park 126; Pike Place Market *141*, 156, *157, 170*
Seattle Art Museum 126
segregation 94
Serious Games Institute 171
Serra, Richard 88
Serrano, Andres 44
Shanghai 220
Shapeways 70, 71
Simpson, Phillip 186
Smith, Adam 17
social enterprise (SE) 170–171
socialism 24–25, 33
social market economies (SMEs) 25–26, 33
social media 3, 11, *12*, 70, 83, 121, 130, 292
Sound Co-op, The 176–177
South Carolina 181
space (geography) 81
Spotify 72
Standing Rock Sioux Tribe Reservation 161–162

Starbucks 90
suburbanization 95
suburbs 85–86
sustainability, environmental 48, 137–138, 162, 172, 179–180, 227, 250, 256, 275, 284
Swift, Taylor 185
Sydney 279
system behavior 120
systems theory 119

tax 4, 22, 107, 109, 132, 218, 244–245
television *see* film and television industry
Three Sisters Collective 162, *163*
Tilted Arc (Serra) 88
Toledo (Ohio) 97–99, *98*, *99*, 184
tourism 4, 7, 40, 59, 95, 109, 134, 200, 220, 213, 238, 255–6; and arts districts 81–82; cultural 59, 83, 159, 198, 217, 221, 246, 256, 261–263; and sense of place 83, 89, 221; Sustainable Travel Pledge 256
trauma, community 28, 142–144
Traverse City (Michigan) 101
Treefort Music Festival 49, *50*, 101, 138–139, *139*, 189
Tsuzuki, Kei 113–115, 128, *129*, 143–145
Tucson 282–284, *283*
Tumblr 70
Twitch 70, 71

UCCN (UNESCO Creative Cities Network) 122, 208, 221, 253, 256–263, 265–266; critiques of 255–256; selection process 257–258
UNESCO 6, 55, 122–124, **123**, 212, 253, 256–257; *see also* UCCN
United Nations (UN) 55; *see also* UCCN; UNESCO; United Nations Conference on Trade and Development (UNCTAD)
United Nations Conference on Trade and Development (UNCTAD) 55, 72, 116, 252, 254–255
universal basic income (UBI) 243

universities *see* institutions, higher-education
urban: decline 94; development 220–221; renewal 94–95, 100, 108, 109
USM (urban social movement) 91

value-based approach 26–27, 33
Vancouver 274–275
Van Dyke, Randy *131*
Venice (Italy) 84
Visionkit Studio 125
visual arts therapy 46
vouchers 21, 32

Warhol, Andy 171
Washington, DC 16, 54
The WaterShed (Boise) 47–48, *48*
welfare state 5, 12–13, 15, 22–24, 32
Westover, Amy *41*
Wordell, Matthew 125
WordPress 70
Works Progress Administration (WPA) 212
World Intellectual Property Organization (WIPO) 253
World's Columbian Exposition (1893) 92–93, *93*
World Trade Organization (WTO) 253
The Wrinkles of the City (JR/Parlá) *182*
Writers Guild of America (WGA) 37–38, 142
Wyland, Robert 186
Wyoming 54

Xi'an (China) 84

Yerba Buena Center for the Arts 241
Young the Giant *180*
YouTube 70

zoning 39, 108, 109, 210, 219–220, 276–285, **289**, 294, 306; *see also* overlay zone